THE 3 BEST OPTIONS STRATEGIES FOR BEGINNERS

THE ULTIMATE GUIDE TO MAKING EXTRA INCOME ON THE SIDE BY TRADING COVERED CALLS, CREDIT SPREADS & IRON CONDORS

FREEMAN PUBLICATIONS

Disclaimer Notice:

The following work is presented for informational purposes only. None of the information herein constitutes an offer to sell or buy any security or investment vehicle, nor does it constitute an investment recommendation of a legal, tax, accounting or investment recommendation by Freeman Publications, its employees or paid contributors. The information is presented without regard for individual investment preferences or risk parameters and is general, non-tailored, non-specific information.

Freeman Publications, including all employees and paid contributors, agree not to trade in any security they write about for a minimum of three days (72 hours) following publication of a new article, book, report or email. Except for existing orders that were in place before submission (any such orders will also always be disclosed inside the document). This includes equity, options, debt, or other instruments directly related to that security, stock, or company. The author may have indirect positions in some companies mentioned due to holdings in mutual funds, ETFs, Closed End Funds or other similar vehicles, and there is no guarantee that the author is aware of the individual portfolios of any of those funds at any given time. Such indirect holdings will generally not be disclosed.

Warning: There is no magic formula to getting rich, in the financial markets or otherwise. Investing often involves high risks and you can lose a lot of money. Success in investment vehicles with the best prospects for price appreciation can only be achieved through proper and rigorous research and analysis. Please do not invest with money you cannot afford to lose. The opinions in this content are just that, opinions of the authors. We are a publishing company and the opinions, comments, stories, reports, advertisements and articles we publish are for informational and educational purposes only; nothing herein should be considered personalized investment advice. Before you make any investment, check with your investment professional (advisor). We urge our readers to review the financial statements and prospectus of any company they are interested in. We are not responsible for any damages or losses arising from the use of any information herein. Past performance is not a guarantee of future results.

CONTENTS

COVERED CALLS FOR BEGINNERS

CREDIT SPREAD OPTIONS FOR BEGINNERS

IRON CONDOR OPTIONS FOR BEGINNERS

HOW TO GET $182 WORTH OF INVESTMENT RESEARCH FOR FREE

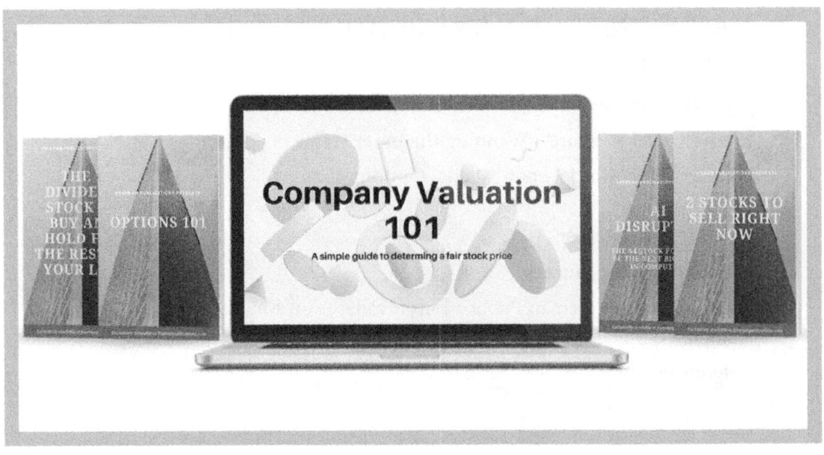

To get your bonuses go to
https://freemanpublications.com/bonus

Free bonus #1: Company Valuation 101 video course ($77 value)

In this 6 part video course you'll discover our process for accurately valuing a company. This will help you determine if a stock is overvalued, correctly valued or a bargain. Giving you an indicator whether to buy or not.

Free bonus #2: Guru Portfolios Analyzed ($37 value)

In these videos we analyze the stock portfolio's of Billionaire investors like Warren Buffett as well as top entrepreneurs like Bill Gates.

Free bonus #3: 2 Stocks to Sell Right Now ($17 value)

These 2 stocks more than any other are in danger of plummeting in the next 12 months. They're both popular with retail investors, and one is even in the top 5 most held stocks on Robinhood. Believe us, you don't want to be holding these going into 2021 and beyond.

Free bonus #4: AI Disruptor - The $4 Stock Poised to be the Next Big Thing in Computing ($17 value)

This under the radar company, which less than 1% of investors have heard of, is at the forefront of a breakthrough technology which will change our lives as we know them. Soon this technology will be in every smartphone, tablet and laptop on the planet.

Free bonus #5: Options 101 ($17 Value)

Options don't have to be risky. In fact, they were invented to *reduce* risk. It's no wonder that smart investors like Warren Buffett regularly use options to supplement their own long-term portfolio. In this quickstart guide we show you how options work, and why they're a tool to be utilized rather than feared.

Free bonus #6: The 1 Dividend Stock to Buy and Hold for the Rest of Your Life ($17 Value)

Dividends are the lifeblood of any income investor, and this stock is a cornerstone of any dividend strategy. A true dividend aristocrat with consistent payouts for over 50 years which you'll want to add to your portfolio for sure.

All of this 100% free, with no strings attached when you subscribe to our free investing emails. You don't need to enter any details except your email address.

To get your bonuses go to
https://freemanpublications.com/bonus

COVERED CALLS FOR BEGINNERS

A RISK-FREE WAY TO COLLECT "RENTAL INCOME" EVERY SINGLE MONTH ON STOCKS YOU ALREADY OWN

2020: A CHAOTIC YEAR - HOW WE GOT TO THIS POINT

Wow. What a year 2020 has been. We went from the stock market hitting record highs to having the largest single week decline since the 2008 Financial Crisis. Then within six months, we were back to the previous highs again.

However, this year was just part of a larger period of unprecedented economic activity. While the stock market saw one of its best decades ever after the lows we experienced after the 2008 financial crisis. Economic recovery has hinged on something that is almost artificial.

Governments initially began printing money in the form Quantative Easing to prevent the entire financial ecosystem from collapsing. They quickly got used to the habit though and now printing money is second nature to them. Another monetary policy they've adhered to is rock-bottom interest rates. The theory behind this being that with interest rates so low, consumers will be less fearful of borrowing cash to fund purchases. This in turn will kickstart the economy.

That's the theory anyway. In practice, results have varied. While American economic activity increased, the likes of Japan never truly recovered. The Japanese economy has grown at a fixed rate of 1.14% (well below other developed nations) since 1986, and interest rates have been at an all time low throughout this time. However, the recent pandemic has wiped out even those meager gains, and the economy has fallen back to the same level it held in 2008.

For an investor, this environment has been a tricky one to navigate. Buying an index fund that tracks the S&P 500 would have been a profitable investment. On the flip side though, we have the specter of increased inflation thanks to relentless money printing.

There is also the fact that rock-bottom interest rates don't provide any safe sources of income. In the past, savings accounts and certificates of deposit provided some degree of investment return that allowed you to stay ahead of inflation.

This isn't the case anymore. Inflation is currently hovering at around one percent but is projected to increase to around two percent (Ferreira, 2019). In 1999, the average return for a 1 year bank CD was 4.85%. Today that same 1 year CD pays just 0.46%, which doesn't even allow you to keep up with inflation.

At this point, savings accounts aren't really savings accounts; they're more like depletion accounts as inflation eats away at the real value of your money.

In such an environment, alternative investments have gained popularity. Gold and silver prices have surged thanks to the steady devaluation that paper money printing has caused. Cryptocurrencies have risen in popularity to the point where they're a bona fide alternative investment class.

Even the likes of hedge fund managers such as Paul Tudor Jones have dedicated portions of their portfolio to invest in cryptocurrencies (Schatzker, 2020). The central idea behind all of these investments is that they're a hedge against the devaluation of paper money.

But as attractive as they may be, none of these alternatives address the real issue - the possibility of utilizing cash flow to overcome inflation.

CAPITAL GAINS AND CASH FLOW

Traditionally, we as investors tend to think of our stock market investments in terms of capital gains. We buy a stock hoping that it will rise in price in the future, which will make us money.

While capital gains are undoubtedly the primary drivers of profit in the market, by solely focusing on capital gains, we ignore another source of investment profits: cash flow.

Cash flow provides us with the opportunity to leverage our investments for free. Consider the way a traditional dividend reinvestment plan works. We get paid to buy more stock or units of whatever is paying them the dividend.

Real estate investors understand the value of cash flow, but stock market investors tend to overlook this. Stock investors rely solely on capital gains and end up focusing on gains that are mostly unrealized. Unrealized meaning that you only receive cash when you sell your investment.

The smart thing to do is to receive cash flow from your investments. If you receive enough cash, you can overcome the relatively low inflation rates that currently exist. Doing this also gives you more options (no pun intended). You can reinvest into the same instrument or you can use the cash to power other investments.

This is the same strategy that Warren Buffett used to power the initial growth of his investment vehicle, Berkshire Hathaway (Schroeder, 2009). Buffett would buy companies that produced huge amounts of free cash flow and use the cash to buy even more cash producing companies.

This is why he has always favored the insurance industry since these companies produce loads of free cash flow thanks to excess premiums, known as *float*. By doing this, Buffett managed to leverage his initial investment across multiple companies. While you, as an individual investor, can't buy entire companies in this way, you can use the same underlying strategy to put extra money into your brokerage account each month.

There's a problem that investors will face, however. The cash flow that you receive in the form of dividends comes at a cost. Every company grows over the long term, at the rate at which its earnings grow. By paying dividends, the company is choosing a lower growth rate. Companies that pay dividends also tend to be mature and well past the growth stage.

So what should an investor do? Do you have to choose between capital gains and cash flow? This is where our solution comes into the picture.

USING COVERED CALLS FOR INCOME

The covered call strategy involves writing or selling options. It is a safe and straightforward way to generate steady cash flow every month. It does not hamper your long-term capital gains in any way, so you get the best of both worlds. More importantly, the covered call is entirely safe if executed correctly, and contains no additional risk than just owning stock.

You might be thinking that since it involves options, it's guaranteed to be tricky to execute. You're not alone in thinking this way. Most long-term investors avoid options like the plague because of their perceived complexity. While it's true that options can be complicated, the fact is that you can choose the degree of complexity you want to implement when using them.

Contrary to popular opinion, options are often used by famous long-term buy and hold investors such as Warren Buffett and Bill Ackman. Ackman's firm Pershing Square Capital Management recently made over two billion dollars with options designed to profit from the fall of the markets following the COVID-19 crisis (Nagarajan, 2020). While Ackman's shorts involved the use of complex derivatives, they were essentially options trades. Buffett has famously written puts (a type of option that you'll learn all about shortly) as a means of generating cash flow to invest in other activities (*Case Study - Warren Buffett Writing Put Options To Obtain A Lower Stock Purchase Price*, 2019).

Covered calls are one of the simplest options strategies you can employ. They require you to understand a few basics about options, but you don't need any special market access or even a margin account to execute them. Most brokers will allow you to write covered calls with a standard cash account.

This means you don't need to worry about maintaining a higher account equity balance or even worry about violating the pattern day trader (PDT) rule. You won't incur higher commissions or trading costs. In short, covered calls are as much of an investment strategy as buying and holding stock.

You do have to start somewhere, though. You need to learn the basics of how options work and how they help you generate steady gains in the market. This book is going to walk you through every single step of the covered call strategy. We've just said that it's simple and easy to understand, but this doesn't mean we're going to cover it cursorily and then leave you to it.

We're going to take you on a deep tour of why covered calls are so powerful and how you can benefit from implementing them. Best of all, you'll be making consistent monthly cash flow with this strategy in addition to accumulating capital gains with your buy and hold investments.

Covered calls should be a part of your portfolio since the cash they generate will allow you to invest in growth-oriented strategies, or you can utilize them for any other purpose. Leveraging your investments without debt is a powerful way of increasing your wealth. Covered calls allow you to do exactly that.

There are no complex technical analysis charts in this book. The few illustrations that are here are simple and easy to understand. You don't need to learn fancy chart patterns or any other geometrical shapes that somehow reveal the market's intentions. Truth be told, most of those techniques don't work as well as they claim.

Instead, you'll learn how you can identify simple cues that make writing covered calls a viable strategy. The best part is that once you implement them, you'll make money even if the market does nothing, which, as we'll explain later in this book, is its default state.

We've made some assumptions when writing this book. We've assumed that you already have investment experience and have an active brokerage account where you hold your investments. If you understand the basics of how the stock market works, this book will pose no challenge to you.

We also hope that you are curious about using options as an alternative asset class to generate cash flow and gains. For this reason, we'll begin this book by first explaining how options work and the terminology associated with them. So without further ado, let's dive into the world of options!

1

OPTIONS 101 – FROM OLIVE PRESSES TO WARREN BUFFETT

What are options, and how do they work? Are they really complicated securities that you should stay away from as a level-headed investor?

Options are an instrument that have been used since ancient times. In fact, their usage predates even the stock market.

The term "options contracts" is a relatively new term when considering how long they've been in use. This name was given to them once the stock market started to gain popularity. However, in a business sense, they've existed in one form or another for thousands of years.

If you're a follower of philosophy, you'll probably recognize the name Thales of Miletus. In case you aren't, Thales was the founder of the Stoic philosophical school of thought, which began in ancient Greece. Thales became famous by standing in a public arena (known as a stoa) and voicing his thoughts and opinions.

Thales was an intelligent man, and one of his passions was the weather and climate around ancient Greece. He reasoned that the climate was a part of the universe, and since man was also a part of the universe, man must take the time to understand the weather.

One of his most notable breakthroughs was in his understanding of solar and lunar cycles. In fact, he is believed to be the first person to predict a solar eclipse successfully. However, because Thales was not a wealthy man, societal elites ridiculed him. Although his ideas were revolutionary, they lacked practical application.

So Thales put his knowledge of the climate to use by predicting future olive harvests. He predicted these and also had "skin in the game" because he used a very similar tool to a modern-day options contract to profit from the harvests.

THALES' OLIVE PRESS CONTRACTS

Thanks to his meteorological bent, Thales managed to figure out that weather patterns indicated favorable conditions for the upcoming olive harvest. The olive harvest was the largest event in Thales' hometown of Miletus. Olive farmers and olive oil traders flocked to the town in the hopes of realizing a profit.

As with any farming endeavor, understanding weather patterns gave a person in these markets an edge. Thales had an edge, but he also had a problem. He was broke. So he needed to find a way to take advantage of his insight without putting up too much money.

He hit upon an ingenious plan. The concept of buying usage rights to the olive presses (which were used to turn olives into olive oil) was common in ancient Greece. The idea was that any person could approach an olive press owner and pay a small amount to obtain first usage rights to the press.

These rights would be valid for a certain period of time as negotiated by the buyer and the press owner. The buyer of the rights would pay the seller a small amount as a token of good faith. This system made sense for the olive press owners since they were guaranteed a payment. The rights holder acted as a salesman and brought olive farmers and traders to them without the press owner having to worry about finding customers.

The rights holder, in turn could then sell these rights to someone else and collect a profit on the amount they paid to acquire said rights. Thales planned to use these rights to turn his meager savings into a fortune. He went around buying the first-use rights to every press in Miletus. There are no official records that mention how much he spent, but one imagines he went all-in on his investment.

His prediction about the weather was right, and there was a bumper olive harvest. Farmers and merchants flocked to Miletus to process their olives and discovered that some guy named Thales owned the usage rights to all the presses in town. Thales sold these rights to merchants and gained far more than what he originally paid for them. After that, he lived out the rest of his days as a now wealthy philosopher.

Lessons Learned

There are certain aspects of Thales' deal that we would like to draw your attention to. First, note that the cost of these rights was far lower than the cost of buying an olive press outright. Thales could have purchased a few presses and competed against other olive press owners. Given the bumper crop, he would have made some money, and it would have been a solid investment.

However, it wasn't the best choice in terms of potential profit. For the same amount of money that would have bought him several presses, he managed to corner the olive press market by purchasing the rights to use all the presses in town. These rights therefore enabled him to leverage his investment massively. His risk was limited to what he invested in the purchase of the rights.

A common problem with utilizing debt-based leverage is that you can lose more than what you invest. This wasn't the case here. Thales put himself in a position to multiply his investment and earn a huge profit without exposing himself to any additional risk above what he had initially invested.

Lastly, note that the press merchant kept the money earned from the usage rights, no matter what. Thales could not ask for a refund. Also, the person who bought the usage rights from Thales still had to pay the press owner money to use the machine. The right only granted them access to it and not the right to use it for free. Thus, the merchants had no risk in the deal, aside from Thales not being able to draw in anyone. This was mitigated by the bumper harvest of course.

Thales' mechanism had all the hallmarks of a modern *call* option contract.

- **The Option:** Thales bought the rights, but not the obligation to use the olive presses
- **The Expiry Date:** These rights expired on a specific date
- **The Ability to Trade the Option**: He could keep these rights for himself, or he could sell them to another buyer
- **The Premium:** Thales paid for his rights upfront, and this amount stayed the same no matter the eventual state of the harvest

Keep these points in mind as you read on. Leaving ancient Greece, we now travel to Holland in the 17th century. This episode will highlight another aspect of options contracts that will be useful for you to understand.

TULIP MANIA

By the 17th century, the industrial revolution had seized control of Europe, and the continent's financial markets were booming. These markets had also acquired the sophistication of modern markets in terms of instruments available to trade. The average Dutch citizen was as aware of the stock market as the average American is today (*History of Options Trading - How Options Came About*, 2017).

This is to say they were aware of the money-making possibilities but were prone to making bad choices due to a lack of investment education. Dutch merchants visited far-flung corners of the globe and brought back all sorts of luxuries with them. One such luxury was the humble tulip.

The Netherlands is famous for its tulips these days, but back then, tulips were an exotic flower. No one in continental Europe had grown them, and the Hapsburgs of Austria were one of the few royal families who even had access to these flowers. They grew primarily in Ottoman-ruled Turkey and this infused them with an even more exotic aura.

As prosperity grew in Dutch society, ownership of tulips became a status symbol. It's hard to equate this fervor with anything in modern times since many things are viewed as desirable these days. Perhaps diamonds come the closest. However, in that time, with very few outlets for distraction and newfound prosperity, the fervor for tulips was probably a thousand times stronger than it is for diamonds these days.

The tulip mania as it's called these days began slowly. First, the prices of tulips began to rise. Dutch farmers noticed this and began growing tulips instead of boring stuff like wheat. These farmers brought their flowers to the market and noticed that tulip prices were significantly higher in cities than in the countryside.

There were simply more wealthy people in the cities, after all. Within cities such as Amsterdam, tulip connoisseurs were springing up every day. The various varieties of tulips were dissected and soon a tulip wasn't just a tulip. Different types were given different levels of status. Similar to how different varieties and vintages of wine can sell for upwards of $10,000 a bottle.

Farmers began flooding the markets with their tulips, and the demand kept increasing as more people became wealthy and wanted access to them. The less prosperous sections of society recognized that tulips seemed to be in favor for some reason. Everyone was buying them, so even those without means dipped into their savings and bought tulips as well. Demand began to grow exponentially, and soon Dutch farmers could not keep up with it. After all, no one can make a tulip grow faster, and people wanted their tulips right away! Which is why importing tulips from Turkey wasn't possible due to the long transit time, because overland routes were still the primary means of transport - combined with the tulips being subject to theft from bandits along the way. As a result, demand outpaced supply and prices rose exponentially. The prices of tulips, which began at the equivalent of a few modern dollars, rose as high as the price of a house!

With euphoria firmly in control, everyone wanted in on the action. The person who had bought one tulip cursed themselves for not having bought two. The person with 100 wanted 200. Soon, the existing owners of tulips spotted an opportunity. Much like how Thales bought the rights to use the olive presses, tulip owners began selling rights to buy or sell their tulips.

These rights traded for high prices thanks to insatiable demand. As the tulip supply remained exactly the same, the prices of these options increased dramatically and became almost equal to that of a tulip itself. People offered their homes as collateral in exchange for the right to buy a tulip. They then sold these rights for even higher prices to someone else and so on.

At some point, sellers of these rights could not find new buyers. The prices were simply too high, and so they began decreasing. As prices began decreasing, people realized that they were trading a pretty ordinary-looking flower. The rich had moved on and found other pleasures since tulips were now a dime a dozen. It was as if everyone woke up at the same time.

Exact records are hard to find, but by all accounts, the prices of the humble tulip fell right back to where they began. People who had pledged their homes as collateral were out on the streets. Almost everyone lost money, and as a result, the Dutch economy collapsed. Some sources argue the Dutch never regained their financial footing thanks to this event and would eventually lose out to the British and French in the race to colonize the world (Mackay, 2014).

Points To Consider

The colonial ramifications of this episode aside, here are a few points you need to understand that relate to present-day options. First, the options traded on tulip ownership were almost exactly the same as modern options that trade on stock ownership. The features that we pointed out in the example of Thales' trade existed here as well.

However, the big difference is that while Thales' bet is an example of intelligent investment, the tulip incident is an example of unintelligent speculation. The option to buy a tulip is just a tool. It wasn't the options' fault that tulips themselves were worthless or that their demand at the time was shaky.

If a speculator risks too much while buying options, they will lose a lot of money. Options in this scenario were used as speculative tools, and this is what created the problem in the first place.

Notice that Thales' bet was based on sound principles. Sure, it was based on the weather, but the man was investing in the probability of there being a good harvest of olives. He tied his investment to something tangible. The people of 17th century Holland were not.

Options are just a tool, not a get-rich-quick scheme. They tend to attract the label of being risky thanks to the way in which people use them. They can be misused just as stock investments can be. This misuse is why options trading was banned in London and Japan at the same time when tulip mania was unfolding. In fact, as the world moved into the 19th century, America was one of the few places where options could be traded.

MODERN OPTIONS CONTRACTS

The boom in options trading in America began in the late 1800s when Russell Sage created an over-the-counter market for them. Sage used the options he sold to take control of entire companies in the railroad industry. He eventually lost his money as the authorities began cracking down on such behavior.

Another famous speculator who used options was Jesse Livermore. Livermore used options unknowingly during his initial days when he would trade in bucket shops. Bucket shops no longer exist but were a fixture of the stock market in the late 19th Century. You can think of them as mini black market stock exchanges, where anyone could buy or sell shares. These establishments would often offer their customers money on margin, often at ridiculous levels like 100:1 (where $1 could be used to trade up to $100 worth of shares). The shops would then "bucket" their customers' orders together and then trade against them, reasoning that most of their customers were wrong about the markets. This is completely illegal today, but stock trading was far less regulated in Livermore's day than it is now.

Once Livermore became wealthy, he would use options to help manipulate the prices of a company's stock. The Securities and Exchange Commission (SEC) was formed partly due to such activities, and Livermore's trading days ended with a whimper.

The advent of the SEC ensured that the securities markets lost their Wild West nature. Laws were put in place and these have evolved to the point where the markets these days are completely transparent. The stock market is intensely regulated, and investors can place their money knowing that the authorities are on the job.

Most options contracts these days are available on stocks. There are options available on forex instruments and even on bonds and interest rate instruments. However, these are usually available only to institutional traders and investors. From a retail investor's perspective, stock options are the most commonly available ones.

A major advantage of options trading is that unlike buy and hold investing, in which you only profit when a stock moves up. Options allow you to profit regardless of if the stock moves up or down, or even if it moves laterally and stays at the same price.

There are two kinds of options that will be available to you. The first is a call option. Call options, or *calls* as they're known, give the buyer the right (but not the obligation) to buy the underlying stock at an agreed price - before a certain date. If you choose to not buy the underlying stock, this is perfectly fine.

Thales' first-use rights were effectively a call option. He was betting on the fact that the desirability of those olive presses would increase. Similarly, buyers of calls bet on the fact that the price of the underlying will increase. Call options buyers make money only when the price of the underlying increases. This is irrespective of whether the underlying is a stock, bond or anything else.

The second kind of option is a *put*. Puts give you the option to sell the underlying. Just as with calls, you have the option but not the obligation to sell the underlying. Note that you still buy a put despite it giving you the power to sell the underlying stock. You're obtaining the option to short a stock without going on margin.

There are many other kinds of options that are available to institutional investors, but these two are more than enough for you to make money with. When used in a smart manner, you can use options to not only provide you with a solid monthly cash flow, you can also use them to *reduce* your risk.

Where They Trade

Like stocks, options have their own exchange. This is the Chicago Board Options Exchange or CBOE. The CBOE was founded in 1973 and brought options trading to the modern world by taking it off the over-the-counter (OTC) markets. OTC markets still exist for options, but the ones you'll see on your broker's software will be traded on the CBOE.

Like stocks, options have a price spread. In case you're unfamiliar with it, the price spread identifies the buying and selling price of a particular instrument. The price at which you buy an instrument is the *ask* or *offer* price. The price at which you can sell it is the *bid*. Options spreads depend on the liquidity available in the market and on the volatility of the stock itself.

The more volatile a stock is, the larger the options price spread will be. The price of an options contract is called a *premium*. This is because options often function as insurance against adverse market moves. This is why some insurance-related terms are connected to them.

Like stocks, calls and puts can be bought or shorted. Shorting an option tends to confuse many first-time investors. After all, if you want to bet on the price of a stock declining, you could simply buy a put. Why would anyone want to short a call? The answer is that options allow you to make non-directional bets.

When you buy a put, you're explicitly stating your opinion that the price of the stock (underlying) is going to fall. You'll profit only if the price falls. If it moves sideways, you won't make money.

However, by selling a call, you're stating your opinion that the stock price will not rise. This is different from saying you're betting on a fall. Saying something will not rise is to say that it might move sideways *or* it might go down. Selling a call gives you the ability to profit no matter what happens. This highlights one of the huge advantages of options. They give you the ability to profit even in sideways markets.

Below are some of the other advantages.

. . .

Superior Cash Flow Opportunities

Options contracts allow you to leverage your investment. They do this in two ways. The first is in the way they're structured. Each options contract covers 100 shares of the underlying stock. Options premiums are usually a fraction of the price of the individual shares so you can control 100 shares by paying a much smaller amount.

For example, to purchase 100 shares of the exercise equipment company Peloton, which currently trades around $80, you would need to pay $8,000. However, if you purchased one $20 call option (with each contract representing 100 shares), your total outlay would be only $2,000 (1 contracts representing 100 shares * $20 market price). Giving you $6,000 to invest elsewhere.

Calculating options contract prices is a separate topic that we'll explain in the next chapter. Briefly, the price of a contract depends on how long it has until it expires and on the current market price. Calculating this isn't essential for your trading, so it isn't as if you need to calculate prices all the time. It's just good information to know.

The second way in which leverage is created is by using options to generate cash flow. As we mentioned in the introduction, covered calls are a strategy that create this kind of situation.

Non-Directional Trading

Where options truly shine is when it comes to implementing non-directional trading strategies. You've seen just one example of this in the previous section where you can take advantage of stock prices that either fall or move sideways with one options position. Options also allow you to take advantage of situations with unpredictable prices movements.

For example, if you have a situation in a stock where prices will either fall or rise massively, options trading strategies can help you set up a trade where you don't care about the direction in which the prices move, just the degree with which they move. These strategies are called *Volatility Trading Strategies.*

In stock trading, volatility refers to the degree and force with which the price of an instrument moves. If a stock jumps around all the time, it's far more volatile than a stock that moves steadily without too many surprises.

Investors in the stock market treat volatility as a known unknown. They may not know in which direction prices will move, but they can say with a degree of certainty that there will be a significant move in one or both directions. It can help them or hurt them, and since they don't have a way of taking advantage of it, they simply hold onto their investments through it.

Options traders, however, can target some obvious scenarios where volatility will be present in the market. For example, an important economic announcement such as an increase or decrease in interest rates will produce massive market volatility. You might not know which way the market will move, but you do know that volatility will increase. Certain options strategies allow you to target the increase or decrease in volatility.

Another major advantage of options trading and investment is that they allow you to define your risk with pinpoint accuracy. Let's say you've bought shares of a company at $100. Theoretically, your maximum risk is realized if the price of the stock falls to zero.

Many investors utilize stop loss orders to cap their risk. They place a stop loss order at $50. This theoretically limits their risk to $50 per share. However, stop loss orders are not infallible due to liquidity and volatility. In extreme market conditions, prices jump stop loss orders and investors receive prices that are far worse than intended.

In our scenario above, if the price spread skips past $50 (like if bid prices move from $51 straight to $40 due to a lack of liquidity) then you will receive a sale price of $40, which increases your risk to $60 per share.

This situation does not exist with options. You can fix a certain price and that price will be honored no matter what. You'll learn how this works in the next chapter when we detail the specifics of an options contract.

While these advantages are very real, it would be a disservice to you if we didn't discuss some disadvantages you ought to be aware of before trading options.

Improper Use of Leverage

Options provide you with the ability to leverage your money, and this can create problems. There is nothing stopping you from risking more money than you can afford.

This feature of options tends to attract a specific type of market participant. This person is often interested in get-rich-quick schemes and tends to overleverage themselves. As a result, they lose money and options receive a reputation of being risky. Options help you fix a maximum risk limit accurately, but you still need to understand how to use them correctly. They aren't, however, a magic bullet that will eliminate losses.

Another temptation with options is to overcomplicate them. We refer to complexity as being something that you don't understand. There are options strategies that involve many moving parts. If you don't understand these parts of the strategy's nuances, you will more than likely end up making a loss.

This is why we believe that beginners should stick to simple options strategies, such as writing covered calls. These strategies have very few things to keep track of, and they don't require much maintenance. In fact, later on in the book we outline 3 simple rule-based strategies for managing your trades without needing to stare at stock charts all day.

FREEMAN COVERED CALL RULE #2

YOU CAN MAKE A STEADY MONTHLY INCOME BY ONLY USING BASIC OPTIONS STRATEGIES

Time Decay

One disadvantage that will hurt you if you ignore it is the phenomenon of time decay. We'll explain this in great detail in the next chapter. Briefly, time decay refers to the event where option premiums (prices) decrease over time. If you're buying an options contract, then time decay means an ill-timed purchase could make capturing gains very difficult.

However, by selling options, which is what you'll be doing with covered calls, you actually use time decay to your advantage.

Now that you have a clearer picture of what the advantages and disadvantages are of trading options, it's time to dive deeper into them and take a look at how these contracts are structured.

2

THE BASICS OF OPTIONS CONTRACTS AND OPTIONS TERMINOLOGY

One of the reasons understanding options can be tricky is that they come with a lot of terms and phrases that scare away ordinary investors. Investing in stocks is pretty straightforward. There's no jargon involved, or at least not so much so that it makes the entire endeavor intimidating.

Options terminology revolves around the way a contract is structured. Once you understand how the structure works, you'll have no problems grasping what the various terms mean. You've already learned that you'll have access to two kinds of options: Calls and puts. Let's look at each of these contracts separately and understand how the terms and conditions associated with them work.

CALL OPTIONS

A call option gives you the right to buy the underlying security at a certain price. Here's how it works. The underlying security is typically a stock. Your broker will provide you with access to various calls that you can buy on this stock. All of these calls will have different strike prices.

An option's strike price is the level at which it will make you money. For example, let's say you decided to buy a call on Amazon stock. Amazon shares are currently trading at $3,100. If you buy a call with a strike price of $3,000, you can immediately use it to make money on the stock. However, this isn't profitable because you have paid a premium for the option contract, which will not offset the gains from the stock itself.

A call with a strike price of $4,000 cannot be used just yet to make money. The price of the underlying stock (Amazon) has to move past the $4,000 mark first. Choosing the right strike price is very important with a call or a put because it determines how far the underlying has to move in order for you to start making money.

For example, let's say Amazon moves past $4,000 to $4,500. In this scenario, you've earned a profit of $500. You can use your call to buy Amazon at the fixed price of $4,000 and then sell it back to the market at the current price of $4,500. This is why investors buy calls when they're bullish about a stock's prospects.

How do you use a call to buy the underlying? This is as simple as clicking a button in your broker's software. The process is called exercising your option. If you have the money required to buy the requisite number of shares of the underlying stock, your broker will buy them for you and debit the cash from your account.

Remember that each call options contract covers 100 shares of the underlying. This means if you exercise a single call options contract of Amazon at $4,000 you'll need to pay $400,000 (4000*100) in cash from your account. Over and above this, you'll also need to pay the premium when you buy the call.

The premium is not recoverable under any circumstances. Whether your trade goes for a profit or a loss, you will lose this money. Therefore, when exercising or selling a call, you need to make sure you earn at least this much back in order to break even. This is why you can't just buy calls for options which are lower than the current stock price and exercise them immediately.

Looking at the example of Amazon, you might be thinking that $400,000 is a pretty steep price to pay. What if you don't have that much cash? Does this mean you can't trade the options of high price stocks? Not quite. The option's premium fluctuates as well depending on how close the underlying market price is to the strike price.

The closer the strike price comes to making you money on the contract, the higher it rises in value. For example, if the underlying price is $100, the call option with a strike price of $101 will be priced higher than the option with a strike price of $105. This is because the 101 call is more likely to make you money since the underlying is closer to it and therefore, will be priced higher.

An option's premium has two portions to it: The intrinsic value and the time value (also known as extrinsic value). In order to understand how these work, you first need to understand expiry dates.

Expiry Dates

All options contracts have an expiry date attached to them. This means that whether you want to exercise or sell the option, you need to do that before the expiry date. Typically options are available with expiration dates in the current month, the next month and the month after that, although many larger stocks now have weekly options as well. There are also special options known as LEAPs, which expire more than six months in the future.

Different stocks have different monthly cycles that govern when their options are available to trade. All you need to do is look at your broker's software and that will display all the options contracts available to trade, as well as the number of days until that particular contract expires.

Let's consider an example. Amazon stock is selling for $3,100. You can buy two calls: one with a strike price of $3,000 and another with a strike price of $2,600. Both of these calls expire in the same month, which is 30 days away. Their premium will differ since clearly, they're not worth the same.

The 2600 call will make you more money. Its price will be a sum of its intrinsic value and its time value. The intrinsic value is a straightforward mathematical calculation. It's simply the difference between the underlying price and the strike price. In the case of the 2600 call, it's calculated as:

Intrinsic value of 2600 AMZN call = $3,100 - $2,600 = $500

In the case of the 3000 call, the intrinsic value will be:

Intrinsic value of 3000 AMZN call = $3,100 - $3,000 = $100

This leaves us with the time value. Unlike the intrinsic value, the time value is not a straightforward mathematical calculation.

Here's how it works. The longer an option has until expiration, the more valuable it is. The reasoning is that there is more time for the underlying to move into a position where the option can make you money.

The closer it is to expiry, the less value it has, since there is less time for the option to make you money. Time value is a constantly changing thing and there is no straightforward method of calculating it. The people who figured out a model to accurately calculate the value of an option by taking time value into account won a Nobel Prize for it. That should give you an idea of the complexity.

But don't let this put you off. The concept of time value is far more important for you to understand than calculating the value itself. Specifically, you need to understand that time value decreases as the option approaches expiry.

This phenomenon is called time decay. Time decay usually accelerates once the option is less than 30 days away from expiry. This means the price of the option will decline faster and will rise less forcefully in this period. This is irrespective of whether the option can make you money or not.

The expiry date can work in one of two ways. Some options can be exercised or sold only on the expiry date, these are called European options. The other type of options, called American options, can be exercised on any day leading up to the expiry date. As the majority of covered calls are written on American options, that is what we'll be focusing on in this book.

In and Out of the Money

In the case of a call option, the investor makes money only when the underlying price is greater than the option's strike price. If an option can make its owner money, it's said to be *in the money* or ITM. When the strike price equals the market price, the option is said to be *at the money* or ATM.

When the call option is *outside the money* or OTM, the strike price is greater than the market price. In this scenario, the option buyer would lose money if they exercised it. Remember how intrinsic value is calculated for a call? The strike price is subtracted from the underlying price.

However in the case of an OTM option, this would result in a negative value. For example, if Amazon is at $3,100 and if you buy a call with a strike price of $4,000, the intrinsic value is -$900. Options cannot have negative values. Therefore OTM options always have zero intrinsic value and have just their time value attached to them.

With OTM options, if the underlying price increases past the strike price turning the option ITM, the option premium value will rise accordingly since it will gain intrinsic value. Its time value will also increase by some amount despite moving closer to expiry since the probability of making money is taken into account in this value. It won't rise as quickly in the final 30 days as it would the rest of the time, but there will be some appreciation.

A Sample Options Trade

Let's say you've spotted a reason for Amazon to increase in value from its current price of $3,100. You think it's going to go past $4,000 over the next two months easily. Buying the stock is going to be expensive, so you decide to pull a Thales and buy calls (the right to buy Amazon) instead. After all, buying 1 options contract (which covers 100 shares) is a much smaller upfront investment than buying 100 shares of the stock.

Since you think a price target of $4,000 is probable, you'd want to pick a call with a strike price that is less than $4,000 but still leaves you with enough room to earn a profit.

You take a look at the calls available and decide that $3,500 is the right strike price. At this level, the option has no intrinsic value since it's OTM. If you choose an expiry date that is 60 days away, you'll give yourself enough room for the time value to increase once the underlying moves past the strike price.

Let's say this call costs you $50. You'll pay $5,000 upfront since every options contract controls 100 shares. Options prices are quoted on a per share basis, so you'll need to multiply their prices by 100 to figure out how much you need to pay. Once this is done, you sit back and wait.

As Amazon increases in price, your calls become more valuable. Eventually, with a week remaining until expiry, the underlying sells for $3,900. This results in a $400 gain in intrinsic value per share. However, your time value is quickly decreasing since there isn't much time left till expiry.

At this point, you have two choices. You could exercise the call and buy 100 shares of Amazon at your $3,500 strike price. Or you could simply sell the call (which is what Thales did) and earn a profit. Let's assume the time value declines to zero. This isn't a problem because the call still has an intrinsic value of $400 per share in it.

Selling the option will result in a credit of $40,000 to your account. You paid $5,000 to buy the call. This leaves you with a profit of $35,000. Pretty good for a couple months' work! However, this is the best-case scenario. If the price moves to, say, $3,501, you'll earn a far lower profit of $100.

The worst-case scenario for you would be the underlying not moving past your strike price of $3,500. What happens then? This condition illustrates why options are so great. Your contract will be worthless since it will be OTM upon expiry. You can simply let it expire and do nothing. All you'll lose is your initial $5,000 investment, which is how much you paid to buy the call.

PUT OPTIONS

Call options give you the right to buy the stock at a particular price, whereas puts give you the right to sell the underlying at a particular price. You can choose to not exercise the put, of course, since you aren't obliged to do so. Puts tend to confuse new investors a bit since you're effectively shorting the underlying stock, which is not something you'd usually do with regular investing.

Going back to our example with Amazon, let's say you felt that it was due to fall from $3,100 to $2,000. You could short the stock, but this requires a margin account and you'll need to take care of maintenance and initial margin requirements.

Put options solve this problem. You don't need a margin account to buy puts as part of a basic strategy. We'll clarify this towards the end of this chapter. For now, let's look at how the sample trade with Amazon can work out.

Shorting Amazon with Options

The terminology associated with puts is the same as it is with calls. It's just that ITM and OTM conditions are flipped. Puts make you money when the underlying value is *less* than the strike price. This is when they're ITM. Puts are OTM when the price of the underlying is higher than the strike price.

For example, if Amazon is selling for $3,100, the 2,100 put is OTM, and the 3,500 put is ITM. In the case of a call, the 2,100 call will be ITM and the 3,500 call will be OTM. Always keep this in mind.

The calculation of intrinsic value is also flipped in the case of a put. A put gains intrinsic value when the underlying moves lower than the strike price. It has no intrinsic value as long as the underlying is greater than the strike price. The time value works in the same way as it does with a call.

Getting back to our example trade, you think the price of Amazon will decline to $2,000. Instead of shorting the stock, you buy puts with a strike price of $2,500. This is far enough away from the current market price to make the options cheap and is far enough away from the target price to give you a decent profit if the trade works out.

If Amazon declines to $2,000, you'll earn a profit of $500 per share or $50,000 per contract. If the put expires OTM you'll lose only the premium you paid for the put. Thus, the trade works pretty much the same way as it did in the case of a call.

We'd like to point out once again that you'll be buying the put, not shorting it. You can short or write a put, but that's not what's going on here. If you wish to benefit from a decline in prices, you buy a put. This is the equivalent to shorting the underlying without the hassle of having to borrow shares to do so.

BUYING AND WRITING OPTIONS

So far we've only dealt with scenarios that involve buying options, but we haven't considered the other side of the coin. Just as you can short stocks, you can sell options. Given the insurance-like function that options play, selling an option is also called writing an option. This is why you'll often see the covered call strategy referred to as "writing covered calls"

When you write an option, you're taking the other side of the trade. The buyer of the option has a choice of exercising it or not. The option writer, however, has no choice. They need to do whatever the buyer wants. If the buyer chooses to exercise the option, the writer/seller has to deliver.

This makes option writing a bit riskier than buying an option. The option buyer knows there is no obligation, but the option writer needs to construct their trade in such a way that they eliminate any risk.

Having said that, it isn't as if this risk cannot be managed. As you'll learn in the next chapter, with good risk management, you'll make *more* money with *less* risk writing options than buying them. In fact, covered calls are essentially risk-free, because writing the option itself doesn't increase your risk profile.

More on that later. For now, let's take a look at some sample scenarios so that you understand how writing an option works.

Writing a Put

This is something Warren Buffett has done in the past with Berkshire Hathaway. He has written puts on both Coca-Cola and the broad stock market index, the S&P 500 (SPX). Given his bullish bent, it makes sense why he'd follow this path. If he was convinced that the market or Coca-Cola's stock was going to rise, he'd take the bullish option.

Why did he write puts, though? Why not buy calls? This highlights an important difference between writing an option and buying one. When you buy an option, you're marrying yourself to the strike price. You need to be able to predict not just the strike price that will make you money but also the time it will take the underlying to move past that strike.

Most of us can't predict the next few minutes, let alone what will happen to a stock over the next few months. Writing a put allowed Buffett to divorce himself from the stock having to move past a particular strike price. Let's say Coca-Cola was selling at $40 and Buffett wrote puts at $20.

He's effectively saying that he believes the stock price will not fall below $20 over the expiry period of those puts. This is very different from saying the price will definitely rise past $50 (which is the case if he bought a call.) With a put option, even if Coca-Cola moves sideways and remains at $40, he makes money.

How does he make money? Remember that when you buy an option, you pay a premium. This premium is being paid to the option writer. Thus, if you write an option, you receive money from the option buyer, and you get to keep this cash no matter what. The put premium represents the maximum profit you will earn in the trade. The trade ends once the option expires.

When you write an option, the money is deposited into your account immediately. Therefore, writing an option is all about generating cash flow for yourself and keeping an eye out for the possibility of the option being exercised.

Therefore it is in your best interest for the option to expire worthless since you'll get to keep your premium.

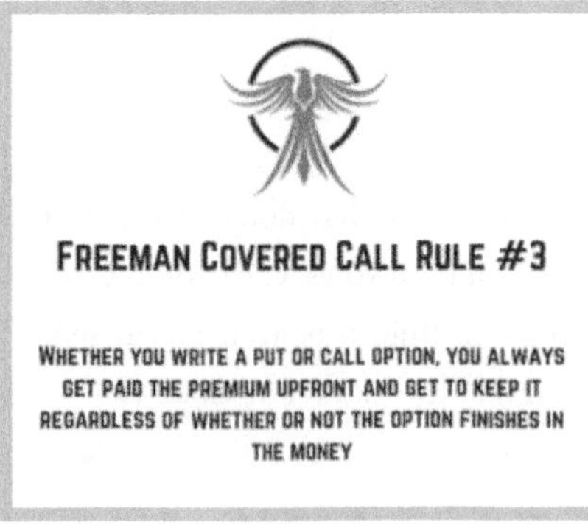

But what happens if the option moves ITM and you're hit with an exercise from the option buyer? This process is called an assignment. If you're assigned an option, it means the buyer has exercised the option and you need to deliver. In the case of a put, the buyer is seeking to sell the stock. This means you'll have to buy the underlying at the strike price of the put. You'll have to hold onto these shares or sell it immediately for a loss; it's up to you.

For example, let's say the underlying price moves to $50 and you wrote a put for $55. Since his put is ITM, you are assigned it. You need to buy the stock for $55, which will be used by the put buyer to short the stock at that price.

You've just bought stock selling for $50 at $55. You can either hang onto the stock and hope for the market price to rise or you can sell immediately for a loss of five dollars per share and move on. Theoretically, writing a put exposes you to a small upside and a huge downside.

The price of a stock can go all the way to zero. This means your maximum risk on the trade is equal to the strike price of the put (strike price minus zero.) Your broker will require you to have a certain amount of cash in your account and you will also need to have a Level 3 options trading margin account. We'll explain these levels shortly.

Writing a put is therefore not something anyone can do. Generally speaking, writing puts is not a consistent way of making money and it isn't something you want to do if your aim is to earn steady cash flow.

Writing a Call

If writing a put is risky, writing calls is one of the riskiest things you can do. This is because the price of a stock can rise till infinity. In order to write a call, your broker will require you to have a Level 4 options trading margin account and will need to see proof of substantial experience. Even then, they might decline you these privileges.

But wait, isn't this entire book about writing calls? Why would we discuss a strategy which is so risky? Well the risk all has to do with the type of calls we are writing.

For now, let's look at what happens when you're assigned a call. Assuming you've convinced your broker to let you write a call, you'll earn the call premium upfront. You're now betting on the stock either declining or moving sideways. If you've been assigned the call, the worst has happened and the price has risen.

You'll now need to buy the underlying at the market price and sell it to the option buyer at the call's strike price. If the market price is $105 and the strike price is $90, you'll realize a loss of $15 per share. The risk in writing a call is that the price could rise to $200, $500 or even $1,000 before the buyer chooses to exercise it.

However, there is an easy way to eliminate the risk of writing a call. It's by already holding the stock you are writing calls against. This way, you profit both from the upside movement of the stock, and from the premium you received by writing the option. It's a win-win scenario and why the covered call is such a great options strategy.

TYPES OF OPTIONS TRADING ACCOUNTS

Different brokers have different ways of dealing with opening an options trading account. Most brokers classify options account types based on the type of strategies you can employ. There are four levels. The first level, Level 1, allows you to implement strategies where the maximum risk is defined. In order to trade covered calls, you need a Level 1 account. This is a pretty easy account to qualify for. Now, with many online brokers it's as simple as ticking a box when you open your stock trading account stating you would like the ability to trade options.

Your broker may also ask you if you need margin to trade. If you indicate that you do, you'll have to qualify for opening a margin account. Brokers usually require you to have a higher minimum balance to qualify for this. Covered calls don't require you to trade on margin, so you don't need this. Other strategies you can execute with a level 1 account are *cash secured puts,* which is writing an OTM put and having enough cash on hand to cover the assignment.

Level 2 accounts allow you to buy options. You can execute the strategies of the previous level, and you can buy puts and calls. This level's strategies don't require margin, but there is the possibility of loss that is undefined. This is why brokers consider these Level 2 strategies.

Level 3 and 4 accounts are reserved for complex strategies that require you to borrow on margin. Some brokers even have a Level 5 that is reserved for the riskiest strategies (from the broker's perspective, not necessarily from an execution perspective.)

The most important thing to know at this stage is that you can execute covered calls from a level 1 account, which is the easiest to get and will be available to any investor.

OPTION CHAINS

Another item you'll need to become familiar with is the option chain. While it may look complicated at first glance, it's quite simple once you get the hang of it. The option chain is just a visual representation of which options are available for you to buy or write at a particular time. Typically, the strike prices are listed in a column in the middle of the page. The call options are displayed to the left of the strike price, with the puts on the right.

	Calls							Puts					
Exp. Date	Last	Change	Bid	Ask	Volume	Open Int.	Strike	Last	Change	Bid	Ask	Volume	Open Int.
November 20, 2020													
Nov 20	103.00	[illegible]	100.10	104.05	385	6018	400.00	53.00	[illegible]	59.10	62.40	233	6662
Nov 20	--	--	98.20	103.15	--	--	405.00	62.10		61.60	65.05	11	--
Nov 20	100.84	[illegible]	96.05	99.25	116	2071	410.00	66.85	[illegible]	64.45	67.55	21	521
Nov 20	96.75	[illegible]	95.00	97.90	1	5	415.00	75.90	--	67.15	70.45	--	4
Nov 20	94.28	[illegible]	92.00	96.00	164	2772	420.00	71.35	[illegible]	70.70	72.00	110	1296
Nov 20	96.40	[illegible]	86.80	93.80	23	56	425.00	76.23	[illegible]	72.90	76.20	3	157
Nov 20	90.00	[illegible]	89.05	91.95	255	684	430.00	74.66	[illegible]	75.65	79.10	64	373
Nov 20	90.40	[illegible]	85.25	89.75	35	74	435.00	75.54	[illegible]	78.60	81.90	44	1
Nov 20	85.70	[illegible]	84.75	87.45	521	6620	440.00	82.45	[illegible]	81.65	84.95	157	9168
Nov 20	85.21	[illegible]	81.35	85.15	177	37	445.00	85.65	[illegible]	84.60	88.05	42	2
Nov 20	82.19	[illegible]	80.45	82.05	754	7308	450.00	87.55	[illegible]	89.00	91.35	56	1656
Nov 20	82.20	[illegible]	77.60	81.45	21	28	455.00	91.85	[illegible]	90.60	94.45	1	5
Nov 20	75.98	[illegible]	75.20	79.70	162	2969	460.00	93.42	[illegible]	93.05	97.70	9	211
Nov 20	77.70	[illegible]	74.05	77.95	22	5	465.00	--	--	97.20	100.85	--	--
Nov 20	77.00	[illegible]	72.85	76.05	43	2452	470.00	109.68	[illegible]	100.50	104.15	4	253
Nov 20	73.40	[illegible]	70.70	74.55	41	31	475.00	--	--	103.75	107.45	--	--
Nov 20	72.71	[illegible]	70.00	73.10	106	2110	480.00	105.50	[illegible]	107.15	111.10	6	962
Nov 20	71.60	[illegible]	67.30	71.40	12	11	485.00	--	--	110.50	114.10	--	--

LAST TRADE: $442.15 (AS OF SEP 18, 2020)

Figure 1: The options chain for Tesla stock (source: Nasdaq.com)

Brokers use color codes to indicate which options are ITM and which ones aren't. In figure 1, the shaded columns are ITM, and the white columns are OTM. Notice that the ITM call options are below the stock's current market price, whereas the ITM put options are above the current market price.

There will be a dropdown box on top that will indicate the expiry date of the options in the chain. In this case, the expiration date of the options (November 20th 2020) is listed on the left hand side.

The page will also list the bid and ask prices of each option at the different strike prices.

In addition to this, your brokerage platform may display other data, such as implied volatility, volumes and open interest. Volume is the same thing as with stocks, which is to say they indicate the number of contracts being traded. For example, in Figure 1, at the time the screenshot was taken, there were 177 call options contracts available at the 445 strike price. Remember, each contract represents 100 shares of stock.

On top of this, a typical option chain will display Implied volatility (not shown in figure 1) and open interest, which are option-specific terms.

Implied volatility or implied vol is denoted by the Greek letter sigma (Σ). It is expressed as a percentage or in terms of a standard deviation number and indicates how much the stock is likely to move in the near future. A higher implied volatility value indicates that the stock is going to be more volatile. You should also note that volatility is not directional, so higher volatility does not mean a stock will definitely move up or down. It is a measure of the amount it could move in *either* direction.

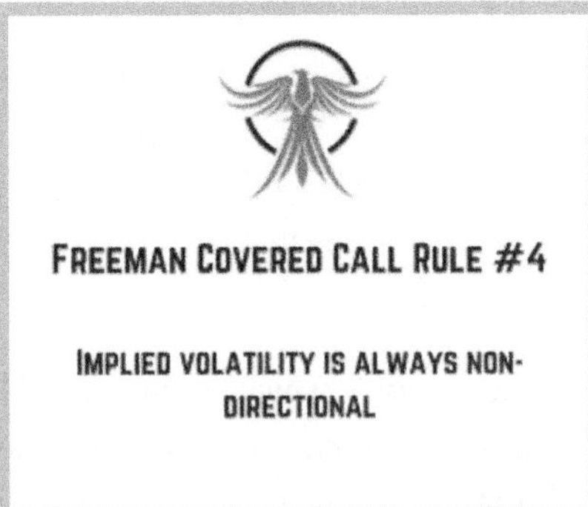

Implied volatility should not be confused with historical volatility or beta. Beta indicates how volatile the stock has been in the past. Implied volatility is concerned with the near future. Also note the implied volatility can be divorced from the overall market volatility. The market's volatility is captured by the volatility index or VIX. Unless you are writing calls on indexes rather than stocks, your focus should be on implied volatility of that particular stock, rather than the VIX.

This brings to a close our look at how options contracts work and the terminology associated with them. As you can see, there are a lot of similarities present with options and stocks. For example, writing an option is the same as initiating a short position in it. It's just that the words used are different.

Now that you understand the terms, it's time to address the elephant in the room. Why have options acquired the reputation of being risky, and what are the things you should be aware of to mitigate these risks?

But before we get to that, as we've covered A LOT of ground in the past two chapters, here is a quick summary of everything we've learned so far:

- **Options** give the buyer the right, but not the obligation, to buy an asset at a specific price
- They have been around in one form or another for thousands of years and even predate the stock market
- You can use options if you think the price of an asset with rise, fall or stay the same
- A **call option** gives you the **right to buy** an asset at a fixed price
- A **put option** gives you the **right to sell** an asset at a fixed price
- The price you pay for an options contract is called the **premium**
- You pay the premium regardless of the outcome of the contract
- The price of the option premium is made up of two factors
- **Intrinsic value** - the difference between the price of the underlying and the how far the option is **in the money**
- If the option is **out of the money**, then the premium has no intrinsic value
- **Time value (or extrinsic value)** - the amount of time left in the options contract
- All options are fixed time contracts, which have a specific **expiry date**

- When you use your options contract to buy the asset at the agreed price, this is known as **exercising** the contract
- You must exercise the contract before the expiry date
- 1 options contract covers 100 shares of the underlying asset
- You can also **sell (or write)** options
- When you sell an options contract, you receive the premium upfront and get to keep it no matter what
- The **covered call** is a strategy which involves **selling call options on a stock you already own**
- You get paid the premium upfront, as well as benefitting if the price of your stock rises

And now, some questions to check that you've understood everything so far. Use the options chain in figure 1 for data. The answers are on the next page.

1. Using the bid price, how much would it cost you to buy 1 call options contract for Tesla at the 455 strike?

----

2. Using the ask price, how much would you receive if you sold 1 call options contract for Tesla at the 460 strike?

----

3. The options in figure 1 have 60 days to expiry. All other things being equal, would the price of these options be higher or lower in 30 days time?

----

4. Tesla traded at $442.50 when figure 1 was printed. The price of the call option at the 420 strike is $92. How much of this $92 is intrinsic value, and how much is time value?

ANSWERS FOR THE PREVIOUS QUESTIONS

1. At a bid price of $77.60, the price for 1 call option at the 455 strike would be $7,660. Remember, each options contract represents 100 shares of the underlying. So you need to multiply the bid price by 100 to find the price you will pay.
2. At the ask price of $79.70, if you sold 1 call option at the 460 strike you would receive a credit of $7,970 into your account. Selling options works the same way as buying them, in that each contract represents 100 shares of the underlying.
3. All other things being equal, we would expect option prices to **decline** in 30 days because options are an asset that decreases in value over time.
4. If Tesla is trading at $442.50, and the price of the 420 call option is $92. This $92 consists of $22.50 of intrinsic value, which is the difference between the price of the underlying and the strike price (442.50 – 420). The remaining $69.50 is therefore time value.

Remember, only ITM options have intrinsic value, because intrinsic value cannot be negative. OTM options only consist of time value.

3

MISUNDERSTANDINGS REGARDING OPTIONS

Options are misunderstood instruments in that they are often mischaracterized as being risky even by the most experienced investors. This depiction harms many investors because they incur massive opportunity costs by choosing to stay on the sidelines when it comes to options.

We're not suggesting you start trading options full time. What we recommend you do instead is use options as a part of your overall investment strategy. You can use options, particularly covered calls, to generate a safe return for yourself without exposing your account to additional risk.

As we mentioned earlier, many investors rely solely on capital gains from their investments. This is a mistake. It's a bit like buying a piece of property and letting it sit there in the hope that it'll increase in value over time. Smart property investors monetize their investment immediately by renting it. This gives them cash flow every month and they earn money from both the cash flow as well as capital gains. It's quite obvious for real estate investors to do this. However, many stock market investors don't follow this basic principle.

Instead of looking to generate cash flow, they seek more complicated ways of hedging their investments by investing in gold and silver. Some even stray into alternative assets like cryptocurrency. These may bring you capital gains, but they do nothing to provide additional cash flow.

Before we dive deeper into options as an investment tool, we must examine the difference between investment and speculation. Examining the differences will help you understand why options trading is a good move for your portfolio and why so many traders mischaracterize these instruments.

INVESTMENT AND SPECULATION

Benjamin Graham was one of the first people to tackle the question of investment versus speculation in his book *The Intelligent Investor* (Graham, 1949). Graham famously suffered through the Great Depression, resulting in him adopting an extremely conservative view of the market. This is not to say that conservative views are wrong. If anything, Graham's views were necessary at the time since almost everyone viewed the markets as a casino.

He defined investment as an operation that was carried out based on sound principles and had a high probability of success. The high probability of success resulted from the use of sound principles. This makes the principles an investor follows the central driver of profits. The stronger your principles, the higher your overall likelihood of long term profits.

Speculation, according to Graham, was the exact opposite of this. It was carried out using unsound principles and was implemented to earn unrealistic results. It's crucial to recognize that Graham did not include the names of any instruments when defining these terms. He merely characterized them.

In his own career, Graham used all kinds of instruments for investment purposes. He passed this habit onto his greatest student, Warren Buffett. Buffett used all kinds of weird instruments when he started out working in Graham's investment firm. One of his more famous investments was exchanging shares of stock (that traded for $34) for cocoa beans certificates (valued at $36) and reselling the beans on the market for a $2 profit per share (Wathen, 2013).

This isn't an example of options trading, but it shows that the instrument used in investment isn't all that important as long as the principles are sound. If

Buffett was simply betting on the value of cocoa bean futures to increase, he would have been speculating. Instead, he took advantage of an extraordinary situation where he purchased an asset worth $36 for $34.

Buffett would graduate to using far more complex instruments in his deals as his abilities grew. One of his more famous bets was negotiating a convertible preferred share deal with Goldman Sachs that netted him over a billion in profits for a very low investment.

There are other examples of investors using seemingly "risky" instruments to profit. Carl Icahn famously used call options to assume control of Herbalife during his feud with Bill Ackman (Belvedere, 2019). Icahn used options to leverage his investment and despite his bullish sentiments on the company, he clearly didn't want to risk a significant amount of capital on the bet. Options gave him the ability to profit if Herbalife went up and they also restricted his downside to an acceptable limit in case things went pear-shaped. Icahn seemingly entered the investment to spite Ackman, with whom he's had a long running feud, yet there's no doubt that his bullish sentiment on the company was founded on sound principles. At the end of the day, Icahn was right on the company (even though Ackman wasn't necessarily wrong).

OPTIONS AS INVESTMENT

The point of these stories is that you need to reassess the idea of a particular instrument being risky simply because of its structure. Options can get extremely complicated, but this depends on the person using them. Someone who has traded options for over a decade will not find the advanced options strategies too complex.

Another investor who doesn't understand how calls or puts work is going to fail almost certainly at executing these strategies. The key is to match your abilities with appropriate strategies. It goes back to Buffett's warning about investors needing to stick to what they know, or their circle of competence, as he puts it.

If you're still on the sidelines, here's an example. When you read anything about the credit crisis that occurred between 2007 to 2009, you will come across the term Collateralized Debt Obligation or CDO. These were highly leveraged instruments that ultimately caused the meltdown. By all accounts, CDOs were the villain of the crisis. However, there were hedge funds that used CDOs to earn a profit (Baird, 2007). Like options, CDOs can represent many different assets. The key isn't to look at what the instrument is but what your investment thesis is. Anyone can misuse a tool and cause damage, this isn't the tool's fault.

MISUSING OPTIONS

The usual manner in which options are used is to implement them as a part of speculative strategies. Traders make short-term bets using options because they provide a lower cost of entry into the market. Instead of placing a directional bet, they use options to try to profit from the volatility spike that they foresee.

While there are trading strategies that use intelligent principles, there's no guarantee that traders use them in such a manner. A survey conducted by the brokerage firm FXCM revealed that 90% of their traders blow their account within a year (Russel, 2009). There are no statistics available publicly for stock traders, but anecdotal evidence suggests that the number may be even higher due to the larger number of people taking part in the stock market.

With such high failure rates, it stands to reason that options end up being viewed as risky. In fact, the stock market is viewed as being risky thanks to the prevalence of such statistics. As we highlighted in the previous section, it isn't the market or the instrument's fault. It's simply the phenomenon of the majority of people misusing market instruments.

If speculation is the opposite of investing, it stands to reason that an intelligent investor stands to gain by doing the exact opposite of what the average speculator does.

The most common manner in which most speculators trade options is to use them as tools to bet on price movements. If they think the price of a stock is about to rise, they buy call options. If they think it's about to fall, they buy puts. It's safe to say none of these directional trades work well consistently.

The thing for a smart investor to do is to take the opposite side of these trades. If there was a way to short these traders' activities, you'd stand to make a lot of money. In fact, many hedge funds do this already by designing ETFs that take advantage of common trader mistakes.

However, there is an easier way for the individual investor, and that's where options come in. Since most traders look to buy options, the thing for you as an intelligent investor to do is to write options to them. Most options trades fail because they end up expiring outside the money. If this is the case, it makes sense to align yourself with the best odds.

This is the core thesis behind writing covered calls: By writing options, you're placing yourself in a position of maximum success since the odds are in your favor right from the start.

HOW MANY OPTIONS EXPIRE WORTHLESS?

We must point out that there is a myth in this regard. The myth states that 85% of all options expire worthless. This is not true. In fact it's the result of a miscalculation by uninformed sources. This number is often quoted because the average researcher doesn't take into account the fact that a lot of options trades are closed out before expiry (Smith, 2019).

This doesn't mean you don't stand to gain an advantage by being a net seller of options. However, don't make the mistake of wildly exaggerating this advantage in your mind. You will read sources mentioning that you can align the odds in your favor much like a casino does and that you can expect win rates of above 85%. This is not true at all. Believing such false tales is to indulge in speculative behavior.

Another statistic that is often quoted is that only 10% of options contracts are ever exercised. This is used as evidence that only 10% of options finish ITM. However, that's a false leap of logic. Options can be sold prior to expiry if the buyer wishes to capture the increase in premium.

Often, options investors don't have the cash on hand to exercise the option. Recall our previous example about Amazon calls. You could have exercised the ITM call, bought stock and sold. It's far easier to simply sell the call itself and earn a profit. Close to 60% of options are closed out prior to expiry. This is done by both buyers and writers.

A writer might be looking to close out their position by covering their investment (by buying back the option) and capturing the decline in premium. Not every option writer allows their option to expire worthless. Sometimes, short-term volatility drives prices extremely low and they close it out in order to avoid a bounce up in prices prior to expiry.

Buyers close out their positions for reasons mentioned previously. The point is that the true number of options contracts that expire worthless is closer to 35% or so. This is still a significant number and places the odds in favor of option writers.

Our objective is to educate you with realistic numbers and statistics. While the strategy we're presenting requires you to sell options, we're not going to claim that this is foolproof or will make you a million dollars overnight. We're also going to resist making claims that cite the incorrect numbers we've highlighted. It's best to begin your options journey using sound investment principles, and this is what we'll be presenting to you throughout the remainder of the book.

Win Rates and Average Wins

Most speculators don't fully understand the role that win rates and average win amounts play in determining the profitability of a trading system. The average person chases a 100% win rate since this is how all of us have been conditioned since our childhood.

In our school days we were told to get as many answers right on our exams so that we could pass to the next level. We carry this behavior over to our workplace and live our lives chasing the right answers. In the markets this principle doesn't quite hold up, however. Having the right answers in the market is no guarantee of making money.

As an example, there are many traders who can correctly predict the short-term direction of the market. They still lose money. Why is this? It's because the markets are chaotic. They can go up, but before they do, they're perfectly capable of hitting your stop loss by declining and then rising.

The true way to make money in the markets is to ensure that you lose very little when you do lose and win a lot when you win. If you've ever traded before, you'll have heard the adage "cut your losses and let your winners run." This applies to pretty much any endeavor in the market. You need to remain invested for the right reasons, irrespective of what the price does. When the reasons change, you need to exit your position even if it's continuing to rise. Traders are more concerned with the price, and this is why they exit the trade if it goes against them.

On the other hand, investors aren't concerned (or shouldn't be) when the price moves up or down in the short term. Their thesis is the most important thing, so entry and exit depends on that entirely.

When it comes to writing options, the odds of being right and the option expiring outside the money are high. This means you'll win more often than not. However, the money that you'll make on these winners will be less, on average, than what an option buyer will make.

An option writer's challenge is to stick to their rules and not get carried away by their regular stream of wins. This is easier said than done. It's great to make money. It's easy to start thinking of yourself as the best investor ever when this happens. The key is to keep executing your strategy over and over.

Some investors sabotage themselves by demanding excitement. When everything is said and done, the covered call is a pretty boring strategy. It's not exciting and the money you receive will start becoming monotonous, even if such a state of affairs seems unrealistic to you right now.

As you read the rest of this book, keep these points in mind. You might get carried away at the thought of winning most of your positions, but recognize that the win amounts will be low. However, by repeatedly executing your strategy, you'll ensure that you have a safe and steady return.

FREEMAN COVERED CALL RULE #5

THE BEAUTY OF THE COVERED CALL IS NOT THAT YOU WIN BIG. IT'S THAT YOU WIN SMALL, AND OFTEN. MAKING IT A RELIABLE AND REPEATABLE INCOME SOURCE

4

AN OVERVIEW OF COVERED CALLS

Now that you have a good foundation on options basics, it's time to explore the covered call strategy in more depth. The covered call is an entry-level strategy within options trading or investing. It's a safe strategy that limits your downside risk thanks to the way in which it's structured.

As described in the previous chapter, the covered call has a higher success rate because of the large number of options that expire worthless. Like many options trades, the strategy has two legs to it. Unlike regular stock investments, most options strategies will require you to open two separate positions. This sounds complicated, but it's quite straightforward when it comes to the covered call.

The reason is that one of your trade legs will already be open, so there's nothing additional you need to do. The two legs of the covered call strategy are:

1. A long stock leg
2. A short call option leg

LEGS OF THE TRADE

The long stock leg in the covered call is the regular investment you hold in your account. For example, if you hold Disney (DIS) stock, then you'll receive capital gains and dividends over time. While dividends do provide cash flow, they yield around two to three percent at best. Covered calls can generate a far higher rate of cash flow, as you'll shortly see.

We must mention that the long stock leg is implemented using your usual investment principles. You don't need to think of the covered call when buying the stock. The main point of the covered call is to monetize your existing investments for cash flow. Think of it as owning a car and using that car to make some extra cash every month. You wouldn't buy the car for the sole purpose of earning a few extra bucks.

Most investors hold their long stock legs in an individual retirement account (IRA). We advise against writing covered calls on investments held in a retirement account. This strategy is relatively straightforward, but there is a chance of you having to sell your long stock leg. If you do this from an IRA and withdraw the money, you'll end up paying a 10% penalty plus taxes. Note, that your stock being called away is not a taxable event in itself. However as the point of an IRA is to maximize your after-tax profits, using it to generate cash flow is not advisable.

For this reason, use a normal stock holding account with your broker when implementing the covered call. Something else to keep in mind is that you must own at least 100 shares of stock if you wish to use a covered call strategy. This is because each option contract covers 100 shares and you'll need this amount in stock holding to be able to execute a covered call. This is why you can execute covered calls with a Level 1 options trading account.

The second leg of the trade is a short or written call. We previously mentioned that writing a call is perhaps the riskiest thing a market participant can do. We must clarify that statement. Writing a *naked* call is the riskiest thing to do. Naked in this context doesn't refer to your clothes but to the nature of the call.

A naked call is something that isn't backed by equity or cash. Let's say you write a call on Amazon with a strike price of $4,000. You don't have any equity in your account (in the form of Amazon stock) or cash to cover the cost of assignment should the underlying rise enough to move the call into the money.

Remember that if you're assigned a call, you need to sell stock to the option buyer. If AMZN is selling at $4,500 when you're assigned the option, you'll need to buy it for this price and sell it to the option buyer for $4,000 (the strike price) for an instant loss of $500 per share. Every contract covers 100 shares, so that's a loss of $50,000.

This isn't even the worst-case scenario. The price of Amazon can theoretically rise till infinity. If it rose to $6,000 or more you'd probably bankrupt yourself. This is why selling a naked call is a risky thing. Most brokers will not allow you to do this even if you have a Level 4 or 5 options trading account.

However, they will allow you to do this with a Level 1 account if you cover your risk. How is this done?

COVERING YOUR CALL

As long as you own the underlying stock on which you're writing the call, your position is covered, hence the name covered call. In this scenario, if the option is assigned to you, you'll be able to deliver the stock to the buyer since you already own it. Your broker will automatically sell your stock holding to the buyer at the option's strike price.

This means you have zero risk of not being able to come up with the money to cover assignments. Your downside risk is always defined, and you won't even come close to losing too much money. The only scenario in which you'll lose money is when you buy the stock and then are immediately assigned the option. In this case your long stock leg won't have enough time to appreciate and you'll be stuck with a loss. However, this is an infrequent scenario and not something you'll likely ever encounter, even in a multi-year span of writing options.

IMPLEMENTING THE COVERED CALL

Here are the steps you need to take to implement the covered call:

1. Buy the stock (at least 100 shares to cover one options contract. If you plan on writing more contracts, you'll need to buy shares in multiples of 100)
2. Write calls.
3. Monitor your trade.

That's all there is to it. The only thing you need to take into account is the strike price of the calls.

For a quick video of how to write covered calls in your brokerage account, we have one on our YouTube channel, which you can find at

https://freemanpublications.com/youtube

Since you're writing calls, you're expressing an opinion that the price of the underlying stock won't rise beyond a certain point for as long as the trade is active.

Some investors get confused at this point. Buying the stock means you're bullish about it, so why would you sell calls against it? This is where the investment horizon of your strategy comes into play. Remember that the long stock leg is bought with the intention of holding onto it for a long time.

You might be bullish over the long term, but if you think the stock isn't going to do much over the short term, say the next month or so, then you can use covered calls to generate cash flow for yourself. Do this often enough and you'll manage to generate enough cash to significantly reduce the cost basis of your investment.

Cash comes in from writing the call. Recall that when you write a call, you receive the premium that the buyer pays. You'll get to keep this premium no matter what happens. If the option expires outside the money, you don't need to pay anything. If you're assigned the stock, your broker will sell the long stock leg at the strike price to the buyer of the option.

Choosing the strike price for your call is critical. You want to pick a price that is far enough away so as to reasonably expire OTM, but you also want it to be close enough to the underlying price so that the option premium is high.

Since you'll be writing OTM calls, they will have no intrinsic value. So the entire value of the option comes from the time value attached to them. Time value decays as the option you've written enters the last 30 days of expiry, therefore you want to choose options that expire beyond this term. Ideally, volatility will also be decreasing when you write the option, but this is something we'll address later.

A SAMPLE COVERED CALL TRADE

Let's look at an example of a covered call trade on Disney to see how it can make you money. For the purposes of this example, we'll assume that you own 100 shares of Disney stock that you bought for $80 per share. The current market value is $128 per share. This means your original investment was $8,000. This purchase was made with the intention of holding onto Disney for the long term since you like the company's prospects.

Since you're sitting on a decent amount of gains, you'd now like to generate some cash flow from this position. The covered call should ideally be implemented when you've already captured unrealized gains from your stock position. This way, even if you do get assigned the stock, you'll make money since you bought it at a lower price.

You take a look at Disney's chart and determine that $140 seems to be a level that it won't breach over the next month or so. We'll get into methods to reasonably determine this later in the book. For now our focus is on writing calls at the $140 level. We take a look at Disney's option chain and see that the 140 call, which will expire in 30 days, is selling for a premium of $0.59.

You'll need to multiply the price as stated by 100 to get the full contract's price since it's stated on a per share basis. This means if you write the 140 OTM call you'll receive $59 ($0.59*100) as cash, which will be deposited into your brokerage account immediately after you execute the trade. Now that both of your trade legs have been set up, here are the three scenarios that could play out.

Scenario One

The first scenario is if the option expires outside the money. This is your best-case scenario since you get to hold onto both the long stock leg, and also get to realize the full premium. Since the stock is OTM, it will expire worthless. As time progresses, you will see its value decreasing. Here is what the numbers look like in this scenario:

Long stock purchase price = $80
Long stock leg investment cost = $8,000 (80*100)
Premium received upon writing 140 call = $59
Return on investment = (59/8,000) = 0.73%
Annualized return before compounding = return on investment*12 = 8.85%
New cost basis of investment = (8,000 – 59) = $7,941
New effective purchase price of your stock = (7,941/100) = $79.41

We've used an annualized return, because this trade plays out over a period of just 30 days. Therefore it is completely possible to repeat the same trade 12 times over the course of a year.

This 8.85% annualized return is far higher than a dividend yield that you will realize by investing in most stocks. Even REITs don't pay such high yields. Besides, the annualized return doesn't take compounding into consideration.

You can reinvest your proceeds from the covered call to buy either more stock or invest it into something else that can further grow your portfolio.

There is another bonus to covered calls here, notice that your effective investment purchase price reduces. You've received cash and this increases the profit you've realized from the trade. Over time, you can reduce your cost basis significantly by writing calls. Assuming you earn this same amount of money for a year, you'll have made $708 as cash flow. This translates to a reduction of $7.08 per share in terms of the effective purchase price. So not only have you profited from selling calls, you've also increased your unrealized capital gains by lowering the cost basis of your stock position.

FREEMAN COVERED CALL RULE #6

COVERED CALLS ARE NOT JUST A GREAT INCOME TOOL. THEY ALSO LOWER YOUR COST BASIS ON YOUR LONG STOCK HOLDINGS

Scenario Two

The second scenario is if the option finishes in the money. If you happen to be wrong about the movement of Disney stock and if it exceeds $140 before expiry, you'll be assigned the option. What happens next? Your broker will sell the stock you hold at the call's strike price. You will get to keep the option premium that you earned when you wrote the call. Here's what the numbers look like:

Cost of stock investment = $8,000
Purchase price = $80
Sale price = $140
Premium received from writing calls = $59
Total profit = (140 - 80)*100 + 59 = $6,059
Rate of return = 75%

The only difference between this scenario and the previous one is that you will lose your long stock position. This results in a much higher realized gain since you'll have to sell your stock holding. However, if the stock is rising you'd ideally like to participate in its rise. What if Disney rose to $170 over the next year? You won't be able to take full advantage of this rise.

Having said that, since you bought the stock for $80, you won't lose money even if you're assigned the option. In theory you could even buy the stock at the market currently for $128 and realize a profit of $12 per share if the option finishes ITM.

However, it's inadvisable to do this. What if the option finishes OTM? In that case you'll have to hold onto the stock and wait for it to pass the price for which you bought it. If it declines for years on end, then your capital losses will outweigh whatever cash flow you earn. This is why we recommend initiating covered calls on positions that already have enough of a profit cushion built into them.

Scenario Three

The third scenario that can occur is if the underlying finishes ATM on expiry. In this case you'll be assigned the option and the numbers are exactly the same as in the previous scenario. The price to which it rises is of no consequence to you since your selling price is fixed by the strike price of the call.

In determining these numbers we haven't taken commissions into account. Your broker may also charge an assignment and exercise fee and this is why many options trades look to avoid it. This is why most traders close their positions before expiry if they're in a profit. Assignment fees aren't significant, but over time they will eat into your gains. Your best scenario is for the option to finish OTM. That way you can continue to hold onto your long stock leg and keep writing calls to earn cash on that investment.

WRITING COVERED CALLS VERSUS WRITING PUTS

Once you start running the numbers on different options strategies, you soon find out that writing a covered call has the same risk-reward profile as writing a put does. Which is why there is much discussion in options trading circles about whether it is better to write a put in some cases, since it's a single leg trade as opposed to the covered call, which has two legs.

There's just one problem with this line of thought. Brokers will not allow beginner options traders to write naked puts. Even if you did have the cash required to cover the risk of a naked put, take a moment to think about what each strategy implies.

Writing a covered call implies you're betting on the stock to not rise beyond a certain point. Writing a naked put implies you're bullish on a stock above a certain point. A lot of traders look at the risk to reward profiles of these strategies using the same strike prices. However, it makes no sense to look at it this way. If a stock is trading at $100, you'll write an OTM call above this price and an OTM put below it. Writing an option that is in the money is an extremely risky strategy since you don't know when it'll be assigned to you.

The traders who do things this way bet on the chance that their options won't get assigned or that the underlying will quickly move out of the money and they'll be off the hook. This way, they capture the intrinsic value in the premium for as long as the option is ITM. Couple this with time decay and you have a recipe for huge profits.

However, this is not a repeatable strategy in any way. If the stock doesn't move away from the money, you will almost certainly be assigned the option and lose money on the trade.

The bottom line is that you need to stay away from writing puts. Any arguments that push their efficacy over writing covered calls ignores the fact that you're an investor, not a speculator looking to make a quick buck.

PROFIT AND LOSS NUMBERS FOR THE COVERED CALL

Let's quickly run through the maximum profit and loss numbers for the covered call strategy.

Maximum Profit

The maximum profit you'll receive is calculated as follows:

Maximum profit = (Strike price - stock purchase price) + premium received

This scenario occurs if you're assigned the stock. Don't get confused and think this is all you can earn. One of the things to remember about the covered call is that the long stock position makes it tough to quantify exact maximum profit and loss numbers. For example, the option could finish OTM and earn the premium in full.

This means you'll hold onto the long stock position, which can theoretically rise for as long as possible. It could also decline to a value of zero. This makes calculating an exact number tough. To make the maximum profit quantifiable, we've assumed that you'll be assigned the option. However, this isn't the best-case scenario as we've explained previously.

Maximum Loss

Like with the maximum profit number, we've had to make some assumptions to quantify it. In order to do so we've assumed the worst-case scenario for everything. We've assumed that the option will finish OTM but the long stock position will decline all the way to zero. The probability of this happening is low, but it is a valid scenario nonetheless.

However, we must mention that this trade has the same risk profile as holding the long stock. Writing the covered call doesn't add any additional risk. This means the maximum loss can be calculated as:

Maximum loss = Stock purchase amount - premium received

The break-even point of your trade will be the purchase price minus the premium received. The premium you'll receive will lower your cost basis as explained. We'd like to reiterate that the maximum profit and loss scenarios here do not necessarily reflect the best and worst-case scenarios. The presence of the long stock leg complicates calculations.

You should always look to have your call finish OTM and hang onto your long stock leg. The best-case scenario is for you to partake in the capital gains from your investment and keep earning steady cash flow on it using covered calls.

Something else to keep in mind is that since you'll be owning the stock, all dividends that will be paid during this time will accrue to you. These dividends will also increase your profit and reduce your loss. If you happen to have been an owner of the stock as of the ex-dividend date, losing the stock position will not affect receipt of the dividends. You'll still receive them, and this will reduce your cost basis even further.

5

THE TWO BEST REASONS TO WRITE COVERED CALLS

There are many advantages to writing covered calls, but two stand out above everything else. There are some investors who believe covered calls are risky and loath to place their long stock position at risk of being called away. This is understandable. However, if you're looking to generate income from your investments, simply sitting on your position is also not a smart move.

Recall the previous comparison we made to real estate investment, where investors regularly generate cash flow from their properties. You won't lose cash due to sitting on your investment, but you will incur opportunity costs. The best way to illustrate this is with an example.

From the previous chapter, we saw that writing covered calls on Disney stock produced an annual return of around eight percent. This is a pretty significant return. Coupled with the stock market's average performance of 10% per year, this will yield a significant gain for you over time. The best part is that this eight percent return can be reinvested into other opportunities.

Let's say you have $5,000 invested in Disney and are receiving eight percent in cash every year. Let's assume that Disney performs at the market average and returns a steady 10% per year for 20 years. This means you'll have $5,500 at the end of the first year. If you were to simply hang onto this principal without looking to generate cash against it, you'd do very well over a 20-year span. After the end of the 20-year period, you would end up with $30,580.

Now, what happens if you generate eight percent per year from covered call writing and reinvest it back into the stock? By doing this, not only are you compounding your original principal, you're also compounding the eight percent you're generating as cash. At the end of the 20-year mark, you'll have $116,072 in your account. That's a 279% increase in capital. This scenario assumes you won't be making any contributions to the account over the 20-year period.

So what happens if you were to contribute an additional sum of $1,000 every month for a $12,000 annual contribution? In the first scenario, where you hang onto your investment solely for capital gains, you'll have $644,488 in your account, which is a handsome sum.

However, in the covered call case, you'll have $1,597,034 in your account. You'll more than double your money in the same time frame by following this strategy.

Aside from the numbers highlighting the stark differences, we must also consider where covered calls really shine using the phenomenon of asymmetric returns.

ASYMMETRIC RETURNS AND SYNTHETIC DIVIDENDS

Let's tackle asymmetric returns first. In the previous example, we outlined that the stock market returns around 10% per year. Over the long term this is the case, however, it doesn't return a flat 10% per year on autopilot. The market moves up and down and even loses you money in some years. Many investors don't have the stomach to hang onto their investments during the tough times and end up selling precisely when they should be buying.

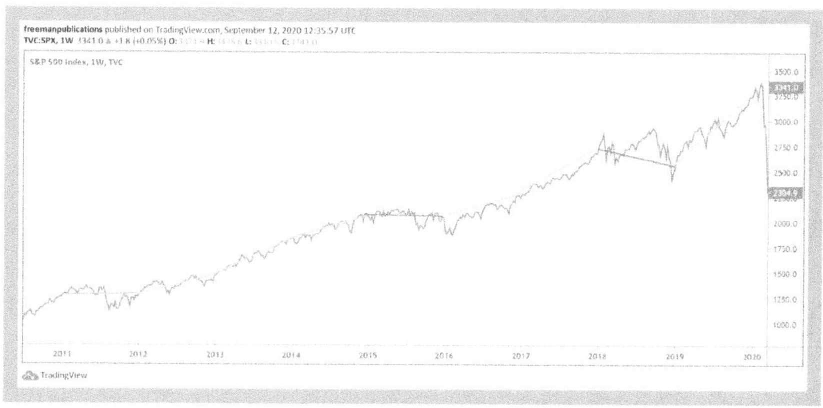

Figure 2: The annual returns of the S&P 500 index between 2011 and 2019. In the past nine years, there were six bullish years, one flat year and two years (2015 and 2018) where the index declined

Figure 2 illustrates the annual returns of the S&P 500, over the past nine years. While the overall trend has been upwards, with an average gain of 11.7% per year over this 9 year period. There are many periods where the market has either remained flat or dipped and wiped out its previous gains. We'd also like to remind you that this run you're seeing in Figure 2 happens to represent the longest bull market run that American markets have ever witnessed.

Even in such record-breaking markets, you can see that the market has had years where it has been unfriendly towards investors. The fact is that investors need all the help they can get when it comes to managing their emotions. These kinds of gyrations where the market gains 20% one year and then declines by 50% the next tend to make investors very nervous.

The average investor follows the financial news media quite closely and is likely to buy into the hype or hysteria, depending on what the media is selling at that moment. If you're looking at holding on for the long term and rely on just capital gains, you'll need to possess high levels of emotional strength.

Assuming you have this, there is another problem. Inflation continually eats away at your gains. With the current money printing policies in place, it's a given that inflation will increase at some point down the road. If you're like the average investor, you're looking at holding onto your position for at least a decade. This means you're seeing your gains being eaten into even when they rise and especially when they fall.

What would make your life easier? Inflation and taxes aren't going to go away anytime soon, so you might as well not hope for that scenario.

Earning a dividend is an attractive proposition. If you could earn cash flow while you held onto your investments, that would be great. The issue with dividends is that they come directly from the bottom-line profits of the companies that pay them.

We explained this previously in the book. A company's stock price rises in line with its earnings over the long term. Any payment from these profits potentially detracts from capital gains increases. Besides, companies that pay dividends have usually left their high growth days behind them. You're placing your money in these companies to preserve capital and increase cash flow as a best-case scenario.

Capital gains are present, but these stable dividend payers aren't the kinds of companies that will make you wealthy. For example, companies such as Amazon don't pay dividends and probably never will thanks to the enormous cash flow requirements they have. Investing in dividends for the cash flow gives you a yield of two to three percent at best.

There are companies that pay higher yields, of course, but these are a bit unsafe. There isn't any company out there paying 20% of its earnings and yielding eight percent. Such a combination is preposterous and will probably not last for very long. Either the company will go bust or the market will adjust the price for which the shares sell.

REIT dividends tend to pay high yields, but once again you'll not be earning much in the way of capital gains. These companies grow at the average rate at which their real estate appreciates and this isn't all that much. In essence, they behave like companies that are present in the Dividend Aristocrats Index.

The solution to this is to generate a *synthetic dividend*. Synthetic here refers to an external source that behaves as an asset that produces cash flow. The asset in this case is the covered call that you will write. If you're earning eight percent yields per year on your investment, then you won't mind hanging onto your investment through tough times will you?

It's a bit like buying a property and then seeing its price drop. If your tenants are paying you enough to realize an eight percent yield, you're probably not going to sell the place anytime soon. Consistent cash flow puts your mind at ease and helps you remain calm. You'll be able to ignore the constant shouting in the media. This is where the entire concept of earning "rental income" on your stocks comes from.

The great thing about covered calls is that they work very well over the course of a year. You'll initiate them in 30-45 day intervals, which removes the need for you to predict what the stock price will look like in a year. All you need to do is look at the reasonable level to which prices might rise over a month, and that's it.

For the most part, stocks act the same as the market average. They don't just trend slowly upwards throughout the year. They experience perhaps one of two good trending moves in a year, but the rest of time, move sideways. We've illustrated this in Figure 3 below.

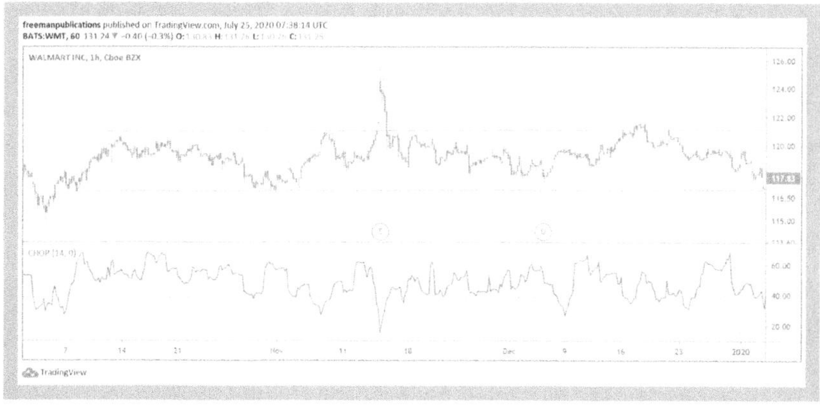

Figure 3: The hourly chart for Wal-Mart (WMT) between October 7th 2019 and January 3rd 2020.

Except for a couple of quickly corrected after-hours moves, Wal-Mart stock traded between \$116 and \$121 for 90 days straight. This would have been a perfect opportunity for Wal-Mart stockholders to earn additional income with some covered calls. Note the numbers on the Choppiness index on the bottom of the image; we'll be discussing how important those are later.

This chart indicates that for the vast majority of the year, your investment isn't making you money. It's just sitting there doing nothing. Forcing it to earn you a synthetic dividend by writing covered calls will boost your investment returns immensely, as you've already seen. These sideways periods are perfect for you to earn some additional cash.

In fact, in such markets, you can get away with writing calls that are closer to the underlying price. The sideways movement ensures that the probability of prices rising is remote. You'll earn greater premiums on the calls you write as a result.

REDUCING COST BASIS

The second advantage of generating synthetic dividends is the reduction they provide to your cost basis. A reduction in cost basis also helps you hang onto your investment for longer since you can withstand more significant capital losses.

From the previous example of Disney, we can see that the covered call premiums amount to around eight percent per year. This means your cost basis is reduced by this amount every year. If you bought Disney for $80, within three years your effective purchase price will be $58. If the stock were to decline to $70 during this period, it wouldn't cause you any problems since your effective purchase price is so much lower than that.

This effect is present in regular dividends as well, especially in REITs. However, the way the IRS handles REIT taxation means you won't get as many benefits from it as you would with covered call options. A portion of REIT dividends are considered return of capital and this reduces your cost basis.

However, the IRS taxes your capital gains from that reduced cost basis when you sell. This means you'll pay capital gains taxes on it no matter what. If you receive enough dividends, then your tax bill will be high despite paying them at the reduced long-term capital gains tax rate.

This isn't the case with option writing. Your premiums will be treated as income and you'll pay the marginal tax rate. However, you'll not be charged capital gains taxes from the effective cost basis. This means should you choose to sell your stock for the price of $70, the IRS views this as a capital loss. However, in reality, you've earned a gain of $12.

You can use this capital loss to offset other gains and reduce your tax bill. While this isn't a direct effect of covered call writing, it is an added bonus. A reducing cost basis means your capital gains are increasing by the premium earned every time you write covered calls.

This is a great thing to have going for you. Combine this with the compounding effect, and your investment value will skyrocket. Admittedly, both of these benefits are connected to one another, so it isn't as if you'll realize gains from them separately. However, the underlying cash flow that you'll generate is what powers these two benefits.

Once you begin to prioritize generating cash flow from your investments, you'll manage to increase the rate at which your money compounds. You'll also be able to hold onto your positions despite the hysteria that surrounds the markets.

6

DEBUNKING 4 COMMON MYTHS

There are a few myths floating around about covered calls. Some of these arise from legitimate concerns around covered calls, while some are just flat-out nonsensical. In this chapter we're going to clarify these situations and help you better understand how you can go about executing covered calls.

MYTH ONE - COVERED CALLS CAN ONLY BE WRITTEN AGAINST STOCKS

This is a pretty big myth and causes a lot of damage to investors. It results from a lack of knowledge of how options work and how they differ from stocks. As a stock investor you've probably realized that you cannot buy an index. Indices are not tradable instruments. They're simply a snapshot of a certain group of securities.

If you're like most intelligent investors, you probably follow an indexing strategy to some extent with adequate diversification. This is an indirect way of taking advantage of stock indices. They're designed to increase in value over the long term thanks to keeping up with inflation and screening in the best companies automatically.

It isn't guaranteed that the index funds and ETFs that track them will be able to capture all of their gains. Most of them lag to a certain extent thanks to incurring trading costs and having to constantly maintain their portfolio weights. Stocks therefore, don't offer you a direct method of profiting from index movements, even though index funds are a very good option.

This is not the case when it comes to options contracts. You can buy calls and puts on indices directly. This allows you to benefit from the underlying moves. There are options available on the S&P 500, the Dow Jones Industrial Index and so on. As a result you can run the covered call strategy on index options.

It might seem a bit confusing at first. The covered call strategy assumes that you will hold a long position in the underlying. However, you can't buy an index. Different brokers handle this differently. Some of them are fine, with you holding a collection of stocks that are on the index. Some brokers insist on the investor holding a representative piece of the index in their portfolios. You'll need to check with your broker about this.

Other details to watch out for when executing covered calls (or any options strategy against index options) is that they're European or they're cash-settled. Let's tackle the European bit first.

European options, if you recall from earlier in the book, can only be exercised on the day of expiry. They cannot be exercised at any other times. Certain exceptions exist, but these are low in number. For the most part, if you're in a long strategy (buying an option) you'll have a rough time of it. However, for the writer of an option, European options are great. The probability of an asset finishing at exactly the strike price or above it for one single day is lower as opposed to it moving into the money over a longer period of time.

This means European option premiums are lower since the writer has the upper hand in the deal. However, the writer has a greater probability of gaining the premium without having to worry about assignment. This makes the covered call strategy on index options a very reliable one. Your cash yield will be low, but if safe cash flow is your priority, then owning a basket of the major index stocks and writing index options against it could be worth your while.

Cash settlement is the other feature of index options you need to be aware of. Since there is no underlying instrument, if you happen to be assigned the option, your broker will settle the trade in terms of the cash difference an exercise would have cost you.

For example, if option exercise would have resulted in you buying the underlying for $100 and selling it for $90 per share, your loss would have been $10 per share. Your broker will simply debit this amount instead of you having to physically close your positions. Thus, you'll manage to hang onto your basket of index-related stocks even if you happen to be assigned the option.

Index options have different volatility characteristics and they tend to adhere to the standards of the VIX. However, some of the smaller indices might have their own whims. You should take the time to study these indices before deciding to write calls against them.

Another option you can use to take advantage of market indices is to write options against index funds and ETFs that track them. All of the major index funds have options on them and this can be a great way for you to benefit. Keep in mind that you'll be indirectly betting on the movement of the index. In essence, you'll be using a derivative to bet on the movement of a derivative of the index.

However, these options are American in nature and their premiums are higher. As a result you stand to earn more income than with regular index options.

MYTH TWO: COVERED CALLS CANNOT BE WRITTEN IN AN IRA

We've mentioned the scenario where you could write covered calls in an IRA. There is a belief that this isn't possible for some reason thanks to the tax-advantaged nature of an IRA. This is not the case at all. While an IRA does have contribution limits, there are no limits on the kind of assets you can hold within them.

The Roth IRA does not allow you to hold real estate properties within it, but there are no restrictions on holding financial market instruments. If you end up making a ton of money writing calls against your IRA holdings, then these will be tax-free until you withdraw them. This gives you greater scope to compound your holdings.

That's the good news anyway. The bad news is that if your strategy doesn't work or if you don't choose the right strike prices to write your call at, you stand to lose your long position. If you sell the holdings in an IRA, you can leave it as cash in the account, but you can't withdraw it. This will attract a penalty of 10% plus any taxes you owe on the gains.

There are investors who write covered calls in their IRAs and 401(k)s. The latter especially provides immense benefits thanks to employers matching your contributions. This free cash can cause some people to become reckless and start employing strategies that promise to make them a lot of money in a short period.

We don't mean to say that you should never write covered calls in a retirement account or that it's an unsuccessful strategy. It's just that the point of a retirement account is to stash your cash away passively into an investment and not worry about losing it. Employing an active strategy in such an account doesn't always make sense.

Covered calls are a step above passive investing strategies because you need to return to them every month and also monitor your investment every day to make sure you're not in danger of assignment. This can get stressful if you have a particularly large long investment position.

The only situation in which you should write covered calls in a retirement account is when you have enough of a long position that you can dedicate a very small portion of it to writing covered calls. For example, if you hold 500 shares of a stock, then you can dedicate 100 shares and write a single contract.

The tax-free nature of your investments coupled with the increased compounding in a retirement account means you can rely on it to beat inflation pretty easily. This isn't the case in a regular investment account, which is why writing covered calls in investment accounts makes sense.

If you still wish to write covered calls in a retirement account, then make sure you have a backup plan to invest the cash you'll have left over if you're forced to sell your long position. Also make sure you've amassed enough of an unrealized capital gain before choosing to write covered calls.

Something to note is that you can write options only on self-directed IRA accounts. If your account is being managed by another investment firm, you can't implement the covered call strategy. But you can convert your managed IRA to a self-directed one pretty easily. You can notify the firm in charge of your IRA and request to convert it. You'll have to notify your broker as well if this isn't done automatically by the management firm. Once this is done, you're free to write options in the account.

A potentially lucrative investment option is to combine dividend investing with covered call writing. Your money will compound at the highest rate possible since you won't be charged any taxes. Take care to write calls at sensible levels, though. Don't get carried away by the high premiums of options that are close to the money. You'll only find yourself having to reallocate cash and then having to wait as your unrealized capital gains build up.

It's far better to focus on holding onto the long stock position since this will ensure you'll be writing calls at sensible levels and will not be chasing high yields on your investment just for the sake of them.

MYTH THREE: YOU WILL NOT RECEIVE DIVIDENDS ON STOCKS YOU WRITE CALLS AGAINST

The origin of this myth is a bit of a head-scratcher, but it exists nonetheless. Some investors believe that writing calls is akin to taking a short position, and therefore you will not receive dividends. It's made worse by the fact that many brokers allow you to enter a covered call trade via a buy-write order.

A buy-write order is one where you simultaneously enter a long stock position and write a call against that stock position. Needless to say, this is a speculative position to take since you don't have enough capital gains built up or indeed any built into your long stock position.

The combination of these two orders makes it seem as if they're joined at the hip. Investors feel that one cancels the other and therefore, you won't be entitled to receive dividends. As far as the company whose stock you hold is concerned, they don't particularly care that you've written a call against your position.

You're still a shareholder on their records and are entitled to receive all the benefits that are due to such a position. Take care to note the ex-dividend date. As long as the option's expiration date is after this, you'll receive a dividend even if you're assigned the option.

A bigger problem is the psychological discomfort some investors feel when they write calls against the stocks they own. The feeling is that they've been rooting for the stock to rise and now are somehow wanting it to remain in place. This feels like a betrayal of sorts for them.

For starters, investing in anything for emotional reasons is not intelligent investing. Suppose you find yourself becoming emotionally attached to your investments to the point where you start thinking of them fondly or use your account balance to make yourself feel better. In that case, you need to take a step back and review why you invested your money in the first place.

You're not rooting for anything. It's just a means of making money, and you should not be getting emotional about it. Focus your energies on doing the intelligent thing and take care of the basics of the strategy. This will ensure that you do the right thing and won't get emotionally carried away.

Some traders try to time writing covered calls with dividend announcement dates. During such times the stock price of the company in question rises in anticipation of the dividend. This ensures a small capital gain. Add to this the dividend as well as the covered call premium and you have the recipe of a strategy that can make you a lot of money on an annualized basis.

Should you follow such a strategy? This isn't an investment strategy and is based entirely on the public perception of a stock. The dividend announcement can go the other way as well. If the company announces a dividend cut, then the price will crash, leaving you with a capital loss. The call premium and the reduced dividend won't make up for it.

Such strategies have a whiff of "get rich quick" about them. This doesn't mean the strategy won't work. It's just that the amount of time you'll spend implementing and monitoring it is better spent elsewhere. Spend an additional hour or so at your regular job and earn overtime or spend that time creating another source of income.

MYTH FOUR: COVERED CALL WRITING WORKS BEST BEFORE SPECIAL EVENTS

This myth is closely connected to the previous one, and it comes from the way in which many options strategies are structured. As we mentioned earlier, options allow you to bet directly on the volatility prospects of a stock. You can short volatility or go long on it, depending on the conditions as you evaluate them.

Volatility is primarily created due to special announcements. These can be earnings announcements, certain company event-related press releases such as restructuring, dividend cuts, the result of a lawsuit, a merger, an acquisition etc. There are also macroeconomic announcements such as the release of interest rate announcements, the release of notes from the Federal Reserve Bank's monthly meetings, press conferences that announce new monetary policies and so on.

All of these events cause unpredictable price movements, and in many cases, create unpredictable volatility as well. Options allow you to profit no matter what happens. For example, a common volatility-based strategy is the straddle. In this trade, an options trader profits no matter which direction the stock's price moves.

It makes sense for a straddle trader to look at special events and time their trades accordingly. It doesn't quite make sense for a covered call trader because this is a directional strategy. Covered calls require prices to be under the strike price for the trader to earn a profit. This is not the case with non-directional strategies that don't depend on the direction of the price move.

By trying to time your covered call execution with a special announcement, you're explicitly expressing the view that you believe this announcement will not be great for the company's short-term prospects.

Of course, if the trade works out in your favor and if the announcement is bad for the company, then you'll get to keep the option premium and might even be able to buy more of the company's stock at a lower price. However, it's still speculation. You don't know what the effect of a news release will be. More often than not, the market has already accounted for the news impact in the stock price.

The stock markets are governed by strict insider trading rules and prevent institutions from gaining an unfair advantage. Everyone is privy to the same information, and the SEC does a very good job of enforcing these rules.

However, this doesn't mean informational advantages don't exist. Most institutions operate in the bond markets, which are much larger than the stock market. Unlike the stock markets, bond markets don't have insider trading rules. Everyone's an institutional player, and the SEC figures that everyone knows what they're doing. Bond prices often affect stock price movements, and many stock traders keep an eye on bond price movements.

Bonds are affected by a company's prospects just as much as stocks are. While it's tough to correlate stock and bond price movements exactly, a relationship does exist. Therefore, many institutional traders have orders locked and ready to go prior to the announcement. The average retail trader/investor is simply hoping that they're on the right side of the announcement.

Writing a covered call based on your prediction of an announcement with all of these factors in place is madness. Instead, it's far better to be conservative and to assume a defensive position by writing covered calls every month. This way, you can focus on generating steady cash flow for yourself without having to worry about what kind of price moves you'll have to account for.

We must stress that you still need to take news announcements into account. It's not as if you can simply ignore what's going on with your stock investment. Our point is you shouldn't try to time your strategy on the basis of special events. Instead, stick to your regular monthly schedule of writing covered calls and factor special events into your choice of strike prices.

This brings to a close our look at some of the myths that surround covered calls. It takes some time to understand why they're invalid, and we would suggest going back and revisiting these myths from time to time.

7

COVERED CALL "RISKS"

Although covered calls themselves do not cause additional risk to your stock position (hence the term "risk-free" in the title of this book), no investing strategy exists without risks.

In order to figure out whether writing covered calls suits you or not, you need to fully understand what you're getting into. There are three areas in particular that you should be aware of. All of these can be mitigated by adhering to a simple rule.

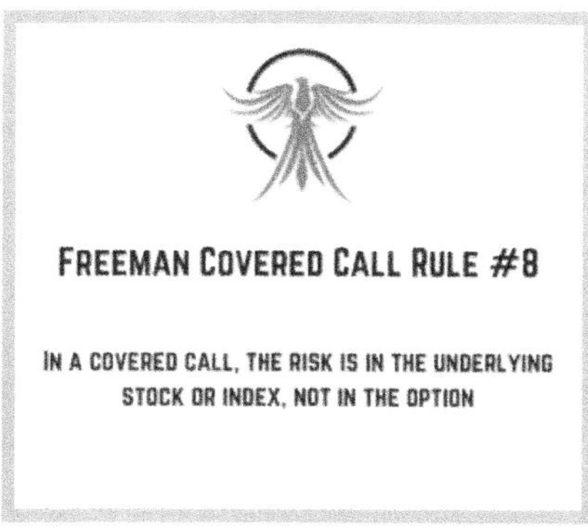

RISK ONE - STOCK PRICE APPRECIATION

This sounds like an odd thing to identify as a risk. After all, the covered call guarantees a profit if the stock price appreciates. The call is written at a higher level and if the option moves into the money, we'll end up selling the long stock leg for a higher price. So where's the risk in this?

The problem with the stock appreciating is that you'll incur a significant opportunity cost. Your reward is always capped at the level at which you'll write the call. This leaves you with the opportunity for a small profit, but you won't be able to participate in any further price appreciation.

Let's look at an example. Let's assume you initiated a covered call position on Disney when it was at $100 and wrote the call at $110. Let's say that at expiry, the price has moved all the way up to $190. In this scenario, your maximum profit is limited to the premium you earn by writing the call plus the difference between the strike price and the stock's purchase price. This equates to a little over $10 per share.

However, if you had simply bought the stock and left it at that, you would have earned a profit of $90 per share. You've given up $80 in profit per share in exchange for a smaller premium that you received in exchange for writing the call. It doesn't take a genius to figure out that this is not a very good trade. It's a bit like someone offering you the choice of $2 in profit or $80 in profit and you choose the former option.

There's no predicting how prices will behave in advance, so it's not a fully relevant comparison. However, over the long run, if you use covered calls to speculate, you will run into such scenarios. If you write calls at incorrect strike prices despite wanting to hold onto your stock for investment purposes, you'll still run this risk.

On the surface of it, this risk is best avoided if you choose the right strike prices. However, the real trick to avoiding this risk is to make a mental shift and to look at covered calls as a little boost to your gains instead of being a primary driver of them. The real driver of gains is the long stock leg of the trade.

This is what makes you the large capital gains which make people wealthy. You need to prioritize holding onto the stock at all costs. Of course, your initial investment decision needs to be based on how good of an investment the stock is, as we mentioned previously. If you're buying stocks to benefit from the short-term price rise and to write covered calls on them, there are easier strategies to make money.

In such cases, it's easier to simply buy calls on the stock instead of writing a covered call. Why would you implement a two legged trade when a simple one legged trade will do the same job? You'll also encounter lower commissions with a one legged trade. Buying just the stock to speculate in short-term price rises requires significant capital.

However, buying the calls doesn't require as much capital and you can leverage your position safely. If the price declines or if your long call doesn't move into the money, you can simply let it expire. The covered call is meant for investors who already hold long positions with a decent level of capital gains built up in them already.

This puts them in a win-win situation, no matter what happens. If the stock price rises from the date of initiating the trade but doesn't move the option ITM, they earn the premium. If the option moves ITM, then they make significant capital gains plus the premium. If it declines, they earn the premium and still have a cushion of unrealized gains.

Make this mindset shift, and you'll avoid incurring this cost. In case you're still not convinced, here's a chart that ought to convince you.

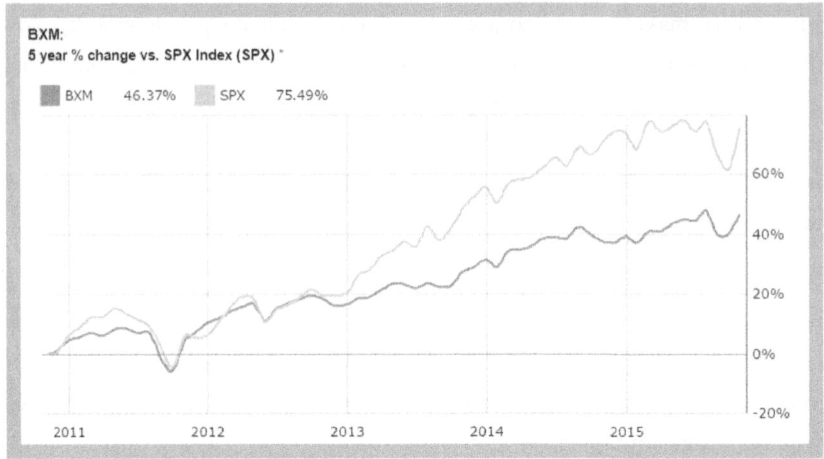

Figure 4: A graph showing a buy and hold strategy of the S&P 500 vs. a strategy which sold covered calls on the same index every month

Figure 4 shows the difference in gains between a strategy that simply bought the SPX versus a strategy that bought covered calls on the index every month and moved ITM. Notice how the covered call strategy makes money but its performance is far inferior to that of the SPX. Simply buying and holding would have been the better choice.

This does not mean that the covered call is a poor strategy. This scenario illustrates the importance of executing it for the right purposes. You should strive to write calls at levels that are unlikely to be hit, and write them at times when the market is flat rather than trending. You'll earn lower premiums, but this will be worth it because you'll supplement your capital gains and can reinvest your premiums into the stock purchase. That is what truly boosts gains and creates free leverage.

RISK TWO - STOCK PRICE DECLINES

This is the worst-case scenario for the covered call. What if the stock price declines and creates a capital loss. You'll then be faced with a decision to sell the stock or hold onto it in the hopes that its price rebounds. The option premium you'll receive will be scant relief in such situations.

There's no easy way to help you navigate the situation since so much depends on why you entered the long stock leg in the first place. If you're using the covered call for short-term profits, then the wise thing to do would be to follow sound trading principles and cut your losses.

You might be tempted to hold onto the stock, but this is not in line with what trading calls for. The worst thing a short-term trader can do is turn themselves into a long-term investor with a position.

If you bought the stock for long-term investment purposes and if the original investment thesis is still valid, then you ought to be delighted that the stock price has declined. You've earned income, and you get to buy the same asset for an even lower price. The trick is to evaluate the asset properly, of course.

Assuming you did that, this could very well be the best possible scenario for you. Your losses are still unrealized, and the lower stock prices will ensure that your cost basis will decrease even more. If the stock price keeps decreasing, you can write even more covered calls against your position and keep earning income on it.

So carefully evaluate your reason for entering the long stock leg. If your original investment reasoning is no longer valid, then it's best to take the loss and move on.

RISK THREE - MISMANAGEMENT

This is a small risk, but if you've become accustomed to monitoring just one leg in your investments, then the covered call adds a little complexity in that you now have two trade legs to monitor.

If you spot the market rising and moving your call closer to the money, and if you wish to hold onto your long stock leg for long-term investment purposes (as we recommend), it's best for you to cover your option position and take a small loss on the trade. You'll be compensated by the unrealized capital gains you'll earn from the appreciation of the stock leg.

Some investors prefer to remain completely passive with regard to their investments. If this applies to you, then initiating a covered call might not be the best choice. You will need to be aware of the price at which you wrote your call, as well as the stock's behavior. You might feel too much like a speculator and might suffer from additional anxiety thanks to market movements.

If you're not able to stop thinking about your short call's strike price, then you're better off avoiding this strategy. Exchanging a small profit for increased anxiety is not a recipe for success. The aim is to make money safely and sleep well at night.

8

THE RIGHT MARKET CONDITIONS FOR INITIATING COVERED CALLS

Covered calls might be a great way to generate a synthetic dividend, but to get the best out of them, you'll need to select the right market environment in which to initiate them.

Many covered call investors turn into traders and look to profit off the short-term moves of a stock. This is perfectly fine as long as your entry decisions are based on sound principles. If you've been an investor, then making short-term entry decisions might not be something you're familiar with. Short-term trading decisions require you to take technical analysis into account since these methods offer better insight into how the market behaves over the short term.

Many investors stay away from technical analysis because it looks like voodoo to them. We'll admit that certain technical analysis methods do nothing more than draw strange shapes on charts and pick and choose conditions that perfectly suit the chosen method. However, not all technical analysis methods are bogus.

In this chapter, we're going to share some of the best indicators and methods you can use to determine ideal conditions for the covered call. These methods apply irrespective of whether you're looking to hold onto your stock position for the long term or whether you're looking for a short-term profit by buying the stock and having it increase past the call's strike price.

TECHNICAL ANALYSIS IN 20 MINUTES

Before getting into the specific technical indicators you can use to determine ideal conditions for covered call writing, we'll have a brief overview of technical analysis. Newer investors often misunderstand technical analysis, and it's easy to be overwhelmed. Fortunately, there are only a few indicators you need to know to be profitable in terms of covered call writing. Before we cover these indicators, we'll briefly touch on what technical analysis truly aims to measure.

Fundamental analysis, which many long-term investors use, is primarily concerned with a business's economic prospects. On the other hand, technical analysis aims to measure the short-term drivers of a stock's price. Which is to say, it's aim is to try to spot the emotional direction of the market. This seems like a hopeless task at first glance. How well can you predict the emotions of someone you're close to and know very well? You could probably approximate their reactions by asking certain questions and reading their body language, but this wouldn't give you the whole picture.

So how can technical analysis help to predict the emotions of a million anonymous traders? The answer is quite simple. Technical analysis aims to identify the direction of the underlying order flow. This is the number of active buy or sell orders for a stock, which moves the price up or down.

Every indicator, at least the ones that work, captures this in one form or another. There are different types of indicators, but all of them fall into one of the following categories:

- Trend-based
- Oscillators
- Mathematical
- Geometric

Of all of these, the first two types are the ones that do the best job of capturing underlying order flow. All of them are derived from prior price behavior and present us with a picture of what is most probable. Something to note here is that there are no indicators that can predict the future. All of them are lagging by nature and not leading. The point of this discussion is to show you that even something that is largely speculative can have elements of logic to it.

We'll begin with trend-based indicators, which aim to capture the existing force with which price moves in a given direction. All of them capture the strength of a price move, whether it's up or down.

Many people misuse trend indicators because they rely on them to predict the direction in which prices might move. This is not what these indicators are for. In order to predict price direction, it's often best to look at the chart directly. Since we won't be concerning ourselves with predicting the possible direction of price, there's no reason to spend time understanding this.

Oscillators measure short-term momentum in price moves. They're usually bound between two extremes, typically 0 and 100. They also have zones on their charts which indicate levels where the stock is oversold and overbought. Typically, the oversold zones are at the bottom and the overbought ones are at the top. The idea is that if the stock lingers in the oversold zone for too long, it's due for a bounce and vice versa.

However, most oscillators don't work in a trending environment. When prices move strongly in a certain direction these indicators can print extreme values for a long time and this is also a trap that many traders fall into.

Mathematical indicators are our entry point into the voodoo territory of technical analysis. The most famous of these indicators are the Fibonacci projections. The Fibonacci series is a series of numbers where a number is the sum of the two that preceded it. For example 0,1,1,2,3,5,8 and so on is a Fibonacci sequence.

As it applies to technical analysis, Fibonacci levels are measured as a proportion of the pullback in a trend. Some of the most relevant Fibonacci levels are 100%, 61.8%, 50% and 33%. The idea is that once a price begins to pull back downwards from an uptrend, or upwards from a downtrend, prices always react at these levels. In the case of an uptrend, traders measure the length of the upswing and then mark the 33% level from the top of the push upwards.

They lay in wait at this level to watch for signs of prices being supported and being pushed back upwards. The same is done in the case of a downtrend. There is no earthly reason these levels ought to work. The markets don't care about random mathematical levels.

However, as with everything to do with emotions, the markets work in weird ways. Thanks to the Fibonacci levels' immense popularity, markets *do* react at these proportions of their up or downswings. This is because almost every trader out there believes in these levels and therefore, they become valid. Much like the phenomenon where if you hear something repeated to you over time, you begin believing it whether it's a fact or not. In this respect, Fibonacci levels work.

Lastly, we have geometric patterns, which people often think of when they hear the phrase "technical analysis." These are the most subjective of all technical analysis indicators.

You may have heard of some of these terms like *cup and handle, head and shoulders, double top* and *double bottom*. These are all just names for specific shapes you can draw onto a stock's price chart, and then use these shapes to determine which direction the stock is expected to go. That's the theory anyway.

Entire 1000 page books have been written just on geometric indicators. However, in practice, most geometric technical analysis "experts" are merely people looking to sell expensive courses or chatroom subscriptions, not those who use these geometric patterns to make money. You can think of it like the 19th Century gold rush, where the people who made the most money were the ones selling shovels, rather than people digging for gold.

A few geometric indicators are useful, such as understanding support and resistance lines and basic reversal/continuation patterns. However, beyond these, there isn't much use for geometric patterns in covered call writing.

Now we've had a high level look at technical analysis; we'll now be discussing a few technical indicators that will help you understand how to predict the short-term flow of markets.

Choppiness Index

The Choppiness Index is an indicator used to identify whether the price of an asset is trending in a direction or moving sideways. It aims to measure the degree to which a market is trending.

The Choppiness Index is an oscillator and is bound by values between a range of zero to 100. The closer the value is to 100, the higher the sideways movement of the stock or asset. Values that are close to zero indicate a trending market. The indicator doesn't give you any measurements with regard to the direction of the trend. A strong uptrend will print the same values as a strong downtrend.

The common threshold values that indicate extreme values are the Fibonacci retracements levels of 61.8 for the higher threshold and 38.2 for the lower threshold. Again, the Fibonacci levels are used here because many traders consider them to be valid. There's no order flow-based reasoning to this particular aspect of the indicator. Our recommendation is to study the stock for a while to determine extreme levels. Use the Fibonacci levels as a starting point and then refine it after a while. Rest assured that the exact demarcation of these extreme levels doesn't influence the indicator's effectiveness.

This is because the Choppiness Index derives itself from the order flow. Its values are calculated from the recent history of price moves. If prices are clustered together, this means they're moving in a tight range, and the index prints a high value. The farther apart they are, the lower the value is.

If the index line crosses the upper extreme from below, it is an indication that the market is most probably moving sideways. Typically this can be verified by simply looking at the chart. Again, the exact definition of this extreme level is not important. Every stock will have its own threshold, and you should spend some time studying the way it moves to figure out this location. If the line dives below the lower extreme, the market is likely to be a trending one. Once again, remember that the indicator doesn't provide directional guidance. It simply measures the trendiness or the degree of the sideways movement in the market. Figure 5 illustrates the Choppiness Index in Disney stock.

Figure 5: An example of a sideways market in Disney

As you can see in Disney's daily chart in Figure 5, when the Choppiness Index crossed the higher 61.8 threshold, it traded in a range (sideways movement) for 29 trading sessions or 42 days. This would have been a great time for Disney shareholders to earn extra income by selling covered calls to collect more premiums by selling strikes equal to recent highs.

In Figure 3, we highlighted the sideways movement in Wal-Mart stock, which is also an example of how the choppiness indicator can be used to determine the trending versus ranging state of the market. In these charts we've used the Fibonacci levels for ease of illustration.

So now, we've learned how the Choppiness Index is an oscillator that you can use to identify a sideways move. Let's look at an example of using a trend indicator to do the same.

Average Directional Index

The average directional index, or ADX, is one of those evergreen indicators we mentioned earlier. It's a pretty simple yet powerful indicator to use. The premise is simple. Anytime the indicator prints a value greater than 25, a trend is on. Anything below this value indicates a range or sideways movement in the stock price.

Trend traders use the ADX to determine the relative strength of a trend. They usually look for values greater than 50 to enter a trend. This makes the ADX a very useful indicator for you, just as the choppiness oscillator is. Lower values of the choppiness indicator print when a trend is present. When the ADX prints values higher than 25 or even 50, you can figure out how strong the trend is.

Figure 6 illustrates how the ADX is represented on a chart.

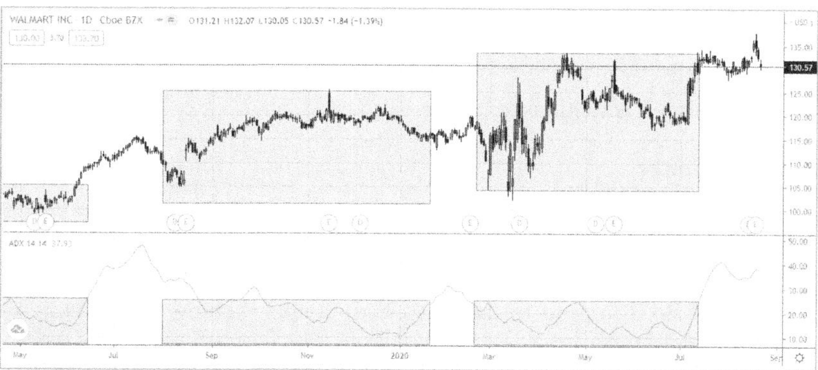

Figure 6: The ADX on Wal-Mart

Notice the areas colored by the boxes in Figure 6. This is where the indicator was below 25. Note the respective boxes on the price chart. The movement is invariably sideways. Like the choppiness indicator, the ADX doesn't provide any directional guidance. The only exception is the third box where we see initially choppy movement and then WMT makes a higher high despite the ADX remaining under 25.

This illustrates how no indicator is perfect and that you should take adequate precautions with all of your trades. In this scenario, notice how the range of each price bar widens. This shows that there is a possibility that volatility is increasing. As a result, strikes further OTM would have made more sense. In fact, that third box presents a great opportunity for covered call traders. Not only is the price movement largely sideways, volatility increases at first and then decreases. This would have meant that the OTM calls would have increased in value and then would have rapidly decreased.

Buyers would have paid you overpriced amounts for the calls, and you would have earned higher premiums despite being further OTM. However, as you can see from the price chart, volatility can be tricky to get right. This is why we urge you to use covered calls as a means of earning additional income on your long stock holdings. Volatility might change and you might find yourself choosing incorrect strike prices.

Between the choppiness index and ADX, you have all you need from a technical analysis standpoint to determine whether a market is trending or sideways. The biggest thing to remember is when you do not have a strong trending market; you have the ideal conditions for writing a covered call.

Bollinger Bands

Bollinger bands are a fantastic indicator because they can be used to measure the degree of volatility in a stock's price. They're plotted over price bars, and this removes the need for you to take a look at another window when trying to interpret them. The bands themselves are constructed using prior price action.

Figure 7: Bollinger Bands on Wal-Mart

There are three curves that constitute the Bollinger Bands. In the middle of the envelope is the 20 days Exponential Moving Average (EMA) of the price. This is the average of the prior 20 values that Wal-Mart stock closed at. The curves above and below the EMA are two standard deviations away from it.

The idea is that a price move that is more than two standard deviations away from the average price movement is an extraordinary one. A move to such extremes will almost always result in a pullback towards the mean. This is because 2 standard deviations represent a 95% chance of prices being between the bands rather than outside them. From the chart, you can see how Wal-Mart pulls back towards the center every time it hits one of the outer envelopes. The only exception is when it enters a strong trend. In that case prices stick to the envelopes for a lot longer.

While this is a great trading strategy by itself, it isn't the one we're interested in. Since our objective is to write options on Wal-Mart, what we're concerned with is volatility. The Bollinger Bands give us a great way to measure this visually. Notice that the bands contract and expand as price moves from left to right.

A contraction of the band represents a narrower range that prices are trading in. In the area indicated by the ellipse on the left of Figure 7, you will notice how the bands expanded when Wal-Mart moved into a decent uptrend. Also notice how the bands visually squeezed before moving apart.

The squeeze is something that many traders use to time moves in the markets. Once the bands move close to one another, traders anticipate a strong move in some direction to occur eventually. The bands don't provide directional guidance, but they do alert the trader that a strong move might arrive shortly. Notice the portion of the chart represented by the rectangle. Here the bands are close to one another. You would have immediately known that Wal-Mart is moving in a small range.

Also notice how the bands keep coming close to one another. Like a coiled spring that is released, the stock then jumps up massively before declining to erase close to three quarters of the gains. The objective here isn't to predict this up and down movement. As a trader, when you see the bands continuously squeeze, you can be sure that an explosion is coming.

Therefore, write your calls at a farther distance than usual. If you see bands that are wide, you'll know that a trend is on and you'll write your calls far away by default. Bollinger Bands prevent you from falling into the trap that many new traders walk right into. They see a tight sideways move and try to capture the high premiums on the calls that are closer to the money.

The result is that they get taken out by the market's upward swing and lose their long position as a result. This is not a bad thing if you're a short-term trader. In such cases you can actively target band squeezes and write calls close to the money. This way you'll increase your chances of capturing gains on the stock leg as well as on the option leg.

Parabolic SAR

SAR stands for *stop and reverse,* and it's a pretty apt description of this indicator. The SAR is plotted on the price chart itself as a series of dots. When the dots are plotted above price, it's a short indication. When they're below price, it's time to go long.

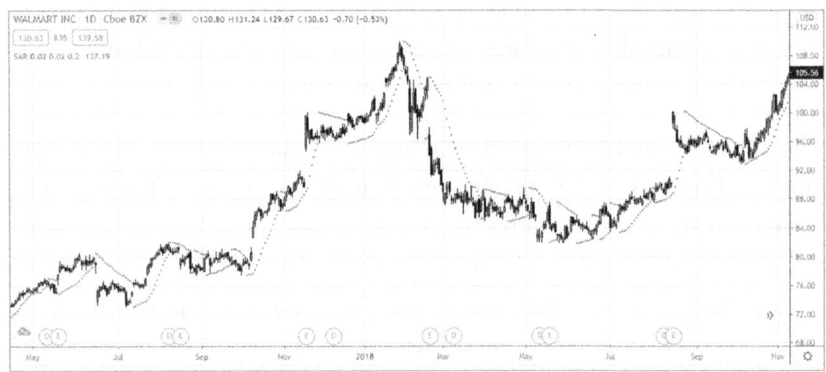

Figure 8: Parabolic SAR on Wal-Mart

In this chart you can see Wal-Mart on a strong uptrend followed by a strong downtrend, which then reverses into an uptrend once again. In short, this sort of a chart is a nightmare for most traders to profit from. It's extremely volatile and predicting short-term directions is tough.

The SAR makes your life a lot easier when it comes to this. It doesn't work very well in sideways markets as you can see towards the left of the chart. The dots alternate very quickly and it isn't enough time for you to predict the direction.

However, as a covered call writer, you can easily ride out such moves because you have at least a month's holding time.

If you spot a dots pattern that alternate in quick succession, you can risk a closer call. However, if you see dots constantly printing on one side of price, especially at the bottom, you'll need to push your calls out further. The great thing about the SAR is that you don't need to evaluate any numbers. It's as simple as looking at the dots and making a decision.

You can combine this with the Bollinger Bands for greater effectiveness. However, it's best to keep your system as simple as possible. Explore one indicator and notice how it moves. Add layers on top of it once you're comfortable making money on it.

This covers our quick introduction to technical analysis, in the next chapter, we will build upon this with stock charts and demonstrate how easy it is to find great stocks for covered call writing.

Note: If you do want to dive deeper into the world of technical analysis, there are three additional books we recommend.

The first is *Technical Analysis Explained* by Martin Pring, which is often referred to as the "Bible" of technical analysis. The second, which focuses more on candlestick patterns, is *Japanese Candlestick Charting Techniques* by Steve Nison.

If you want a shorter read, which goes beyond just using technical analysis for covered calls, but is more in line with our own views, then the aptly named *Technical Analysis is Mostly Bullsh*t* by Tim Morris is worth a look as well.

9

A SIMPLE METHOD FOR SELECTING THE RIGHT STOCKS TO WRITE COVERED CALLS ON

How should you go about selecting the right stocks to write covered calls on? Once again, the answer to this question depends on the reasons you wish to enter the long stock leg of the trade.

As we've mentioned before, the best scenario would be for you to enter the long stock leg for investment purposes. Discussing the correct process of long term stock investing is something we've covered in our other books, particularly *The 8 Step Beginner's Guide to Value Investing*. If you're interested in learning all about the correct method of investing in stocks, we highly recommend you read that book in addition to this one. You'll learn the ins and outs of the Freeman investment approach and will learn the right principles to successfully invest your money.

In this chapter we're going to deal with the scenario where you're looking for stocks to earn a short-term profit using covered calls.

STABILITY

Stability is an important quality you must look for when writing covered calls. You don't want to be writing covered calls against penny stocks that can increase by 1,000% and decline by the same amount. Other stocks to avoid are hot stocks that are being discussed in the media or are present in sectors that attract many speculators.

Some examples include stocks such as Tesla and Apple in mid 2020 or marijuana companies in late 2017 to early 2018. Everyone piles into these stocks, making their volatility extremely high. This makes covered call writing less than profitable because it limits the upside of your long stock holding by nature.

Therefore the ideal covered call writing candidate is a boring stock that you would be thrilled to own for the long term.

Ideally, it pays a dividend, so your profits will be boosted by the income you earn from the call premiums. These stocks should not be sexy or high-growth in any way. An excellent example of this is Coca-Cola. Everyone knows what to expect from this company. It'll earn money, it'll earn enough to reinvest into keeping its business running, and it will earn enough to pay a steady dividend. Its stock price reflects this and rarely does anything out of the ordinary. Here are some other criteria for you to screen for.

Gently Rising Profits and Revenues

When choosing covered call candidates, you want to choose companies that have a good record of profitability but not those that are expected to increase exponentially anytime soon. This is why it's best to start off choosing large or mega-cap companies. Amazon and other tech companies are an exception to this rule since no one knows how large tech will become at this point. Amazon is a mega-cap company but is still arguably growing.

You want to choose well established businesses that have simple business structures. We highlighted Coca-Cola as an example. Ford is another example. This company has never sought a bailout, unlike its rivals, and isn't ever talked about in the hot stock news like Tesla and other electric car companies. Ford can release a fully electric line of cars should they choose to, so it isn't as if the company is behind the curve. AT&T is another example of a stock that has historically been a solid covered call candidate.

These companies are predictable and their stock prices aren't going to shoot in one particular direction. On top of this, even if their prices decline, you'll be more than happy to own them for the long term.

Low Debt

The objective of covered call writing is to generate free leverage for yourself. Leverage is something that boosts your gains immensely. The problem is that debt-based leverage can cause as much harm as the good it creates. When it comes to company finances, a leveraged balance sheet will cause the equity value to jump around.

This translates to excessive volatility in the stock price, and this is a bad thing for covered call writing. You'll never know when the price will rise. Even worse, it could fall dramatically and leave you holding onto a stock that is too unpredictable. Look for companies with very low debt to equity ratios and note the trend of this ratio. The optimal ratio varies from industry to industry, but in general, you want to look for companies with a debt to equity ratio of less than 2. Equally as important, we want the trend to be declining, meaning the company has less debt on its books year after year.

Sector and Age

It's best to stick to companies that are at least five years old and are operating in sectors that aren't prone to exogenous shocks. This means cyclical sectors such as travel, real estate, basic materials, and airlines are out. For this reason, we also stay away from writing covered calls on commodities and commodity ETFs.

Sticking to older companies also assures you that the management is well-versed in dealing with shocks to their industry. FedEx and UPS might be considered boring companies, but they're run by stable management teams that have handled multiple issues in their sector. Look for companies that largely promote from within and don't bring outside CEOs on board.

This hints at a stable corporate culture that rewards commitment to the business. As a result, the management knows the business inside and out and you'll be more than safe holding onto their stock.

. . .

Trading Volumes

Stick to companies that trade an average of over a million shares daily. This ensures no one can corner the stock in the short term and manipulate the markets. Market manipulation typically happens with penny stocks where large promoters buy the stock and pump prices up to squeeze shorts.

Dividend Yields and Payouts

It isn't necessary for you to insist on companies that pay dividends, but you can still consider them. Dividend-paying companies have a history of stability and you'll know for sure that the company is stable and in a predictable business. A company such as AT&T is a fantastic candidate to write covered calls against because the stock's current dividend yield is around 7%, which drives your potential gains even higher.

One thing to note is how long a company has been paying dividends because this can act as a proxy for stability. In fact, there are publicly traded companies that have *increased* their dividend payouts every year for the past 50 years. To find a list of these companies, you can search online for Dividend Kings, which have increased dividends every year for the past 50 years, or Dividend Aristocrats (companies who have increased dividends every year for the past 25 years).

You could choose companies that pay high dividend yields (the percentage a company pays out in dividends relative to its stock price), but don't chase yields just for the sake of them. These companies are typically in a declining business and their previous payouts are high compared to their currently depressed stock price. Thus, the high yield is artificial. Also stay away from companies that have a high payout ratio. Stick to large companies that are paying out less than 40% of their net profits on average over the past decade.

Implied Volatility

Look for stocks that are trading at implied volatility levels between 30 and 70. We'll explain implied volatility in more detail shortly. For now, just keep these numbers in mind.

. . .

No Upcoming Special Events

The stock in question must not have any major events taking place anytime soon. The most notable of these for any company is an earnings announcement. Earnings announcements tend to increase volatility in a stock and make them unpredictable. This is especially the case if there's an earnings announcement close to the option expiry date. The option's price will be inflated, which makes it likely that the stock might start jumping around too much for your comfort.

When writing index options or on ETFs that track indices, stay away from writing them during times when events that could cause a lot of volatility in the markets occur. For example, don't write calls during the month of the presidential elections or significant world events which have the power to sway an entire index one way or another.

FINDING QUALITY COVERED CALLS STOCKS FOR FREE USING SCREENING SOFTWARE

Using stock screeners is a great way to save time finding stocks that qualify according to this criteria. You might think that most screeners are expensive, but the fact is that many free screeners are more than capable of doing the job. One particular screener that we recommend using is Finviz, because the free version has everything you need to screen for covered call candidates.

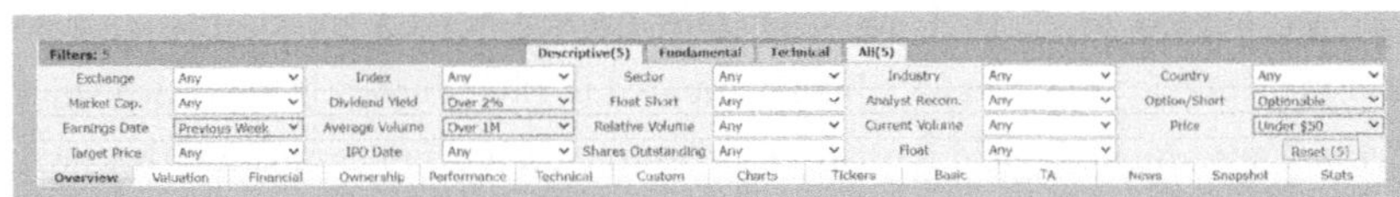

Figure 9: The basic Finviz.com screener using the free version of Finviz

Here are the screening criteria you need to input into the software to find suitable candidate:

- Optionable (this just means you can buy/sell options on the stock)
- Dividend Yield over two percent (to act as a proxy for company

stability, and to earn extra premium if we're holding the stock when it goes ex-dividend)

- Over one million shares traded daily (to satisfy our volume requirements)
- Earnings reported in the previous week (so there is no earnings season to deal with - on the paid version of Finviz you can customize this field and use larger time frames such as the previous 30 days)
- Price under $50 (not a necessity, but this assumes you have a small account to begin with - remember that you need to purchase a minimum of 100 shares to write a covered call)

There are many stocks that will be thrown up from this screen. Often more than 50, which fit all of these criteria. Once this is done, you can proceed to analyze their charts to determine whether they're good candidates to implement a covered call strategy.

Note: If you want to see a video of how to set this up on the Finviz website, then we have an entire series of "Covered Call Basics" for free on our YouTube channel, which you can find by going to

https://freemanpublications.com/youtube

The most important thing to remember is that you want to avoid stocks that look like they might decline in price. This is the case only when you're looking to enter for a short period of time. It doesn't apply to situations where you're looking to hold onto the stock for a long period, as we explained at the start of this chapter. When you look at charts to determine covered call candidates, look for the ones that are headed into a potential uptrend.

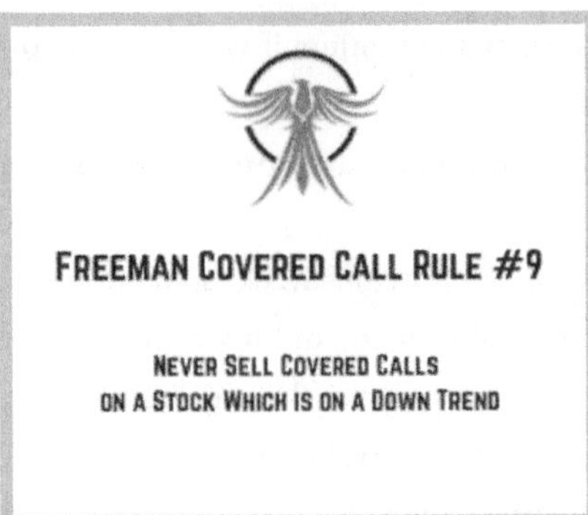

A way you can use the technical analysis capabilities of Finviz to help you with this is to go to the "Technical" tab and select stocks that are trading above their 50-day moving average. This will give you those stocks that are more bullish than neutral, and will increase your chances of being profitable.

We'll now present four candidates to analyze for covered call suitability. Our screen was run in August 2020 and all information is given as of that month. We will present the following trade ideas:

- Two companies that could be good covered call writing candidates
- One trade idea where you can possibly make money through call option premiums, but the call option you wrote has a high likelihood of being assigned. So you would have to sell 100 shares of that particular stock
- Two companies which would be unsuitable for covered call writing
- One trade idea where you will receive call option premiums, but with the probability that the call options received will not cover the possible losses of the 100 shares of stock with declining prices

Solid Candidate 1: Morgan Stanley (NYSE:MS)

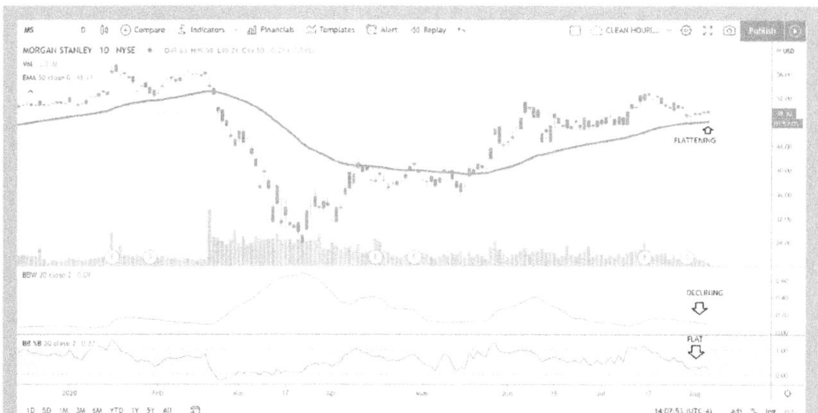

Figure 10: The daily price chart of Morgan Stanley

This chart shows the price action of Morgan Stanley (MS). The thick red line represents the 50-day Exponential Moving Average (50EMA) indicator we used in the screening section to look for stocks on a more bullish trend. Because the current price of MS is above the 50EMA, and the 50EMA is currently flattening, after rising since May 2020, this indicates that the current price of MS will probably trade within the USD44-54 range like it has been since June

Right below the main price chart is the Bollinger Band Width and the Bollinger Band %B indicators. These two indicators are derived from the Bollinger Band indicator, which indicates the probability that a stock would enter either a trending or a consolidation (sideways) phase.

As we mentioned before, Bollinger Bands move like a rubber band. If the stock trends (up or down), the bands stretch, with the Bollinger Band Width and %B increasing in value. If the stock begins flattening, then the Bollinger Band Width and %B declines in value, indicating a shift in stock price action, from trending to a consolidation phase.

In Figure 8, the Bollinger Band Width is below .20 and it is currently declining, which gives us the probability that MS will stay in the USD44-54 range. The

Bollinger Band %B is currently flat, which also gives us the probability that MS will stay in the USD44-54 range.

As far as the covered call goes, the best strike price which fits our analysis is the September 18, 2020 $52.50 call option, which had 42 days left to expiry at the time of writing. This strike price has only a 26.91% chance of being in the money, and for one contract, you could receive premiums of USD111.00 (minus commissions).

Solid Candidate 2: Pfizer (NYSE:PFE)

Figure 11: The daily price chart for Pfizer

This chart shows the price action of Pfizer (PFE). The current price of PFE is above the 50EMA, with the 50EMA currently flattening, after rising since July 2020. This gives us the probability that the current price of PFE will be trading within the USD36-40 range.

Like the previous chart with Morgan Stanley, the Bollinger Band Width is below .20, and it is currently declining, which gives us the probability that PFE will stay in the USD36-40 range. The Bollinger Band %B is currently declining, which also gives us the probability that PFE will stay in the USD36-40 range.

There is a September 18, 2020 $40 call option which has a strike price with only a 29.74% chance of being in the money. For contract, you could receive premiums of USD70.00 (less commissions).

Poor Candidate 1: Bank of America (NYSE:BAC)

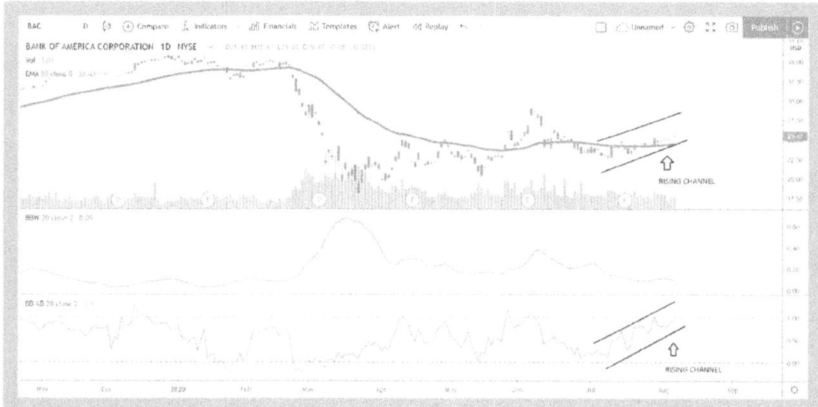

Figure 12: The daily price chart of Bank of America

Figure 12 and the next chart are examples of stocks that are not good candidates for writing covered calls. Figure 12 shows the price action of Bank of America (BAC). The current price of BAC is above the 50EMA, and the 50EMA currently flat. However, the price of BAC is currently inside a rising channel, signifying an uptrend is in progress.

The Bollinger Band Width is below .20, and it is currently flat. The Bollinger Band %B, however, is currently in a rising channel, which gives us the probability that BAC will have higher prices in the next 30-45 days.

BAC is not a good covered call writing candidate at this time, since the price of BAC will increase in the next 30-45 days, which presents the probability that the call option we wrote will be assigned, forcing us to sell the 100 shares of BAC.

Poor Candidate 2: Western Union (NYSE:WU)

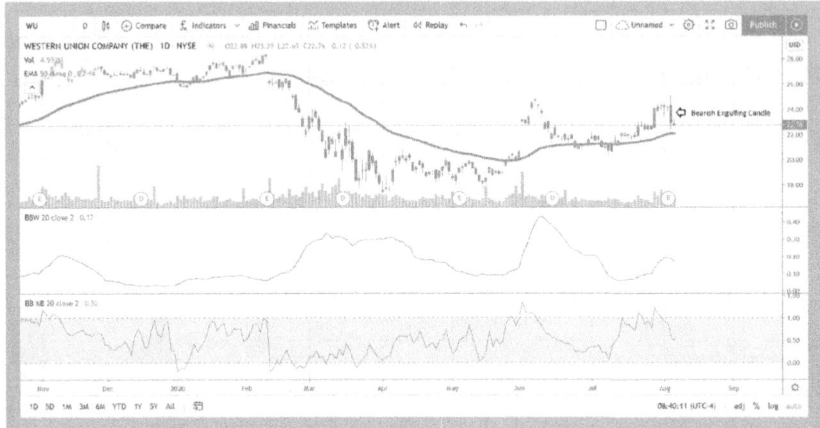

Figure 13: The daily price chart for Western Union

This chart shows the price action of Western Union (WU). The current price of WU is above the 50EMA, with the 50EMA currently rising.

However, WU's price is expected to decline, as the chart of $WU showed a big, bearish, engulfing pattern when its earnings report was released August 4, 2020.

This shows that WU is not a good covered call writing candidate at this time, since we expect the price of WU to decline in the next 30-45 days. This gives us the probability that the call options premium collected will be less than the losses to be incurred in the 100 shares of stock, making this particular covered call option idea futile.

10

THE ROLE OF IMPLIED VOLATILITY IN COVERED CALLS

When trading options, there are three types of volatility you need to take into account. The first is the overall market volatility. This is measured by the volatility index, or VIX. The VIX is an index maintained by the CBOE and lists the current volatility in the market. This is particularly useful if you're looking to trade index options.

When it comes to individual stocks, though, the VIX isn't of much use. This is because every stock has its own volatility characteristics, and the overall market doesn't affect it too much. Each stock has its own following amongst traders and in the short term, this causes stock behavior to diverge from the market's overall behavior.

When it comes to an individual stock, there are two types of volatility to take into account. The first is historical volatility or beta. Beta is a measure of how much the stock moved around in the past compared to the index. Which aisn't all that important when it comes to determining the viability of writing a covered call. As covered call writers, what's far more important to us is the implied volatility of the stock we're writing the call against. Let's look at this in more detail.

IMPLIED VOLATILITY

A stock's implied volatility is a forward projection of how much the market expects the stock to move, given all of the future events and considerations that are known at this point. For example, if the market recognizes that an upcoming earnings announcement might create volatility in the stock price, the implied volatility on its options will be high.

The closer an option is to expiry, the lower its implied volatility will be. This is because the underlying price moves have less chance of impacting the price of the option. Much like the time value of an option, the implied volatility will decrease as an option moves closer to expiry. However, this isn't always the case.

If the market expects a piece of news to create significant volatility, and if this event occurs before expiry, then the option's implied volatility will not decrease as much. Implied volatility is a key component of the Black-Scholes model which is the formula that is used to calculate the fair price of an option. It plays a significant role in the final value that is determined by this formula.

The first thought that most covered call writers have is that they ought to target options with low implied volatility. This makes sense since you want stocks that are in moderately bullish conditions or those that are moving sideways. However, do note that implied volatility doesn't indicate direction. It only indicates how forcefully you can expect the stock to move.

Secondly, a low implied volatility reduces the price of the option. This means the premium you earn on writing it will be low and this reduces your returns. Over a long-enough time period you'll end up making less money by targeting these options.

Figure 14 illustrates the impact that implied volatility has on the option premium.

$120 calls for Disney (3 strikes OTM) trading at $116.18

Expiry Date	DTE	IV	Option Premium	CC Yield	News
8/8/2020	9	43.53%	1.78	1.53%	Earnings (Aug 4)
8/15/2020	16	39.06%	2.36	2.03%	
8/22/2020	23	36.77%	2.65	2.28%	
8/29/2020	30	35.51%	3.15	2.71%	
9/5/2020	37	34.83%	3.50	3.01%	
9/19/2020	51	32.29%	4.03	3.47%	
10/16/2020	79	33.14%	5.35	4.60%	
1/15/2021	170	33.25%	8.55	7.36%	Earnings (Nov 5)

$13 calls for American Airlines (3 strikes OTM), trading at $11.77

Expiry Date	DTE	IV	Option Premium	CC Yield	News
8/8/2020	9	87.89%	0.26	2.2%	
8/15/2020	16	84.57%	0.29	2.5%	
8/22/2020	23	87.80%	0.6	5.1%	
8/29/2020	30	92.38%	0.73	6.2%	
9/5/2020	37	83.40%	0.92	7.8%	
9/19/2020	51	88.57%	1.12	9.5%	
10/16/2020	79	102.34%	1.58	13.4%	Earnings (Oct 22)
1/15/2021	170	97.46%	2.67	22.7%	

Figure 14: The relationship between IV and covered call yield (option premium divided by the price of underlying)

As you can see, there is a higher yield for the higher IV options on American Airlines, but this comes with additional risk. You don't know which way volatility might push prices. It could go up or down. Notice that in the case of Disney, the January options have a high IV. This month's options contracts have both a large time value as well as implied volatility built into them. This is what results in the high contract price. However, if the earnings announcement goes pear-shaped for Disney, covered call writers will be left owning a stock position that has large capital losses.

When looking at implied volatility, choose options that are between 30 to 70%. Contracts that are below 30 won't give you enough premium, and those above 70 will be far too volatile and might go the other way, leaving you with a large capital loss.

It is even possible for stocks to have an implied volatility greater than 100%. This generally happens for two reasons. The first is with deep ITM and deep OTM strikes close to expiration where only an extreme event could result in an unexpected outcome. The second is for cases where the company share price hinges solely on one key piece of news, such as the result of a drug trial for a biotech company. Avoid stocks where this is the case, because covered calls limit your upside by design. If you're writing calls on stocks with an IV over 100, you're exposing yourself to higher risk without being able to capture the higher reward.

FREEMAN COVERED CALL RULE #10

STICK TO WRITING COVERED CALLS ON STOCKS WITH AN IMPLIED VOLATILITY OF BETWEEN 30 AND 70

11

A RELIABLE METHOD FOR SELECTING THE CORRECT STRIKE PRICES

How should you go about selecting the right strike prices? In order to understand the answer to this question better, we need to first begin with the reason an investor enters the long stock leg of the trade. Investors can enter either for long-term investment purposes or for short-term profits.

If you are entering for the long term, you want to choose strikes that are far enough away so that the option finishes OTM, and your long stock position doesn't get called away. You also want the option at that strike price to have enough of a premium so that you earn a decent level of cash flow income on your investment.

If you have a short-term bias, on the other hand, you'll looking for your call to finish in the money. Your objective is to be able to capture both the capital gains in the stock as well as earn a decent option premium. When executed well, the returns on this strategy are enormous.

Central to both strategies' success is choosing the right strike price. In order to understand how to choose the right strike price, we need to dive into the world of the Greeks.

The Greeks are five variables that measure different aspects of an options contract. You don't need to learn about all of them, and in fact, there are just two (delta and theta), which are most relevant to covered call writing. So providing you have a basic understanding of what these two Greeks represent, then you'll have more than enough knowledge to make profitable trades consistently.

DELTA

When it comes to covered call writing, the most important Greek to understand is delta. Delta (Δ) is the ratio that measures the change in the price of an asset to the corresponding change in the option connected to the asset. When writing covered calls, we use delta to help us choose optimal strike prices.

An option with a delta value of 0.5 will increase by $0.50 for every dollar's increase in the share price, assuming there are no special events to account for. These values can be positive or negative and this depends on the option type. Call deltas are always positive and range from 0 to 1. This is because as prices increase, the value of a call option increases. Put deltas are negative and range from 0 to -1 since the value of a put option increases as the stock's value decreases.

Delta values are designed to be read as percentages, and in some instances you will see them represented as such. For example, if you see a delta of 30% this is equivalent to a delta of 0.3. It indicates that the option will increase in a value equivalent to 30% of the overall increase in the stock's price. In the case of a put, a decrease in stock price will produce the equivalent percentage change.

Like implied volatility, delta is a key input to the Black-Scholes model. You don't need to understand how it works, as long as you know that delta helps us understand how option prices ought to vary depending on the price of the stock. Delta is particularly useful since it is extremely predictable and is often used by professional options portfolio managers.

A call option's delta depends on where the underlying price is relative to the strike price. Options that are ITM are usually pretty close to 1, while OTM options are closer to 0. The closer an option is ITM, the higher the delta values are. An ATM option usually has a delta of around 0.5.

The interesting thing about delta is that it is used as a proxy to determine how likely an option is to finish ITM. There isn't a direct correlation between the price change of an option and its probability of finishing ITM, all things remaining the same, but traders have observed that delta is a pretty good substitute for this. This is where the key to picking correct strike prices lies.

PICKING STRIKE PRICES

Option Chains

AUG 07 '20 12 DAYS | AUG 14 '20 19 DAYS | **AUG 21 '20 26 DAYS** | AUG 28 '20 33 DAYS | MORE

CALLS

BID x ASK	VOLUME	OPTN OPN I...	DELTA	GAMMA	VEGA	THETA	STRIKE
• 4.55 x 4.70 •	8		0.961	0.029	0.007	-0.005	25
• 4.05 x 4.25 •			0.950	0.037	0.009	-0.006	25.5
• 3.60 x 3.75 •			0.936	0.048	0.010	-0.007	26
• 3.10 x 3.30 •			0.919	0.063	0.013	-0.007	26.5
• 2.67 x 2.76 •	3		0.889	0.083	0.016	-0.009	27
• 2.23 x 2.31 •	2		0.848	0.108	0.020	-0.010	27.5
• 1.83 x 1.89 •	153		0.794	0.137	0.024	-0.012	28
• 1.40 x 1.49 •	17		0.722	0.168	0.028	-0.013	28.5
• 1.10 x 1.15 •	76		0.633	0.194	0.030	-0.014	29
• 0.79 x 0.84 •	187		0.532	0.211	0.032	-0.015	29.5
• 0.58 x 0.60 •	2.36K		0.426	0.211	0.031	-0.014	30
• 0.37 x 0.43 •	282		0.326	0.195	0.029	-0.013	30.5
• 0.26 x 0.30 •	1.12K		0.239	0.168	0.026	-0.011	31
• 0.16 x 0.18 •	267		0.168	0.135	0.022	-0.009	31.5
• 0.12 x 0.13 •	13.5K		0.122	0.105	0.018	-0.007	32
• 0.06 x 0.10 •	39		0.086	0.079	0.015	-0.006	32.5
• 0.06 x 0.07 •	344		0.065	0.061	0.011	-0.005	33
• 0.03 x 0.06 •	103		0.046	0.045	0.008	-0.004	33.5
• 0.03 x 0.04 •	69		0.035	0.035	0.006	-0.003	34
• 0.02 x 0.04 •	25		0.025	0.025	0.006	-0.002	34.5

Figure 15: The call side options prices for AT&T with 26 days left to expiry (Source: Interactive Brokers)

Figure 15 shows the option chain for AT&T, which was trading at $29.57 at the time of this writing. The strike prices are listed in the extreme right-hand column, while delta is listed with the other Greeks in the columns to its left.

Notice that the 25 strike price has a delta of 0.961. Which means for every $1, the stock price increases, the price of the 25 call option will increase by $0.961. This makes sense since it is deep in the money. Based on what we said above about delta being a proxy for the probability this particular strike will finish ITM, you can interpret this situation as the 25 strike AT&T call has a 96.1% chance of finishing in the money.

At this point, many traders will run away and start writing ITM options since these have a good probability of finishing in the money. However, this isn't a good idea for two reasons.

The first is that deep ITM options have barely any extrinsic value to them. This means the entire value of the option is intrinsic, and thus you are barely receiving a premium as the writer. The second is that your option will nearly always be exercised, and you'll have to sell the stock at much lower than the market price, which means you don't benefit from any upside price movement.

Writing ATM options isn't intelligent either since you'll be relying on just the option premium income. This doesn't suit the long-term investor's needs either, so for covered call writing, writing ATM or ITM options isn't a very smart thing to do.

The point here isn't to pick the strike with the highest delta. It's to pick the strike that is OTM and has a reasonable chance of finishing ITM. That's what makes you a ton of money, because you can collect the premium from writing the strike *and* benefit from the capital gains if the stock price increases.

Using the option chain in the table above for AT&T, let's say we choose to write the option with a strike price of $30. This is quite close to the current price of $29.57 and the delta reflects this. Remember, an ITM option has a delta of greater than 0.5. The delta for the 30 strike is currently .426. This means it has a 42.6% chance of finishing ITM.

Once this happens, you have a decent chance of the underlying being called away, and this leaves you with a profit of 43 cents per share. You'll also earn the option premium which is $0.60 per share. Here is how the numbers work on this trade:

Cost of entry = Cost of buying 100 shares of AT&T at current market price = $2,957
Premium earned on writing 30 strike call = $60
If option finishes ITM, profit = Profit on stock sale + Premium earned = ($43 + $49) = $92
Percent return = 3.1%

Remember that this is the return you'll receive for a trade which lasts just 26 days. Because you'll be writing options that will expire 45 days away at most, if you could replicate this return over the course of a year, you'll earn an annualized return of 37.3%. That is a massive return for a stable stock which isn't appreciating much.

You'll have to take commissions into account, of course, but these days many brokers don't charge traders any commissions on options trading. Some don't even charge commissions on assignment or exercise. Assuming this is the case, short-term capital gains taxes are your only expense. These come out of your profits, so it's not as if it's a massive hit.

In the case of the long-term investor who wishes to hang onto their stock investment, choosing a strike with a delta that is as close to zero as possible is the smart thing to do. Referring to the table in Figure 15, we can choose the 34.50 call, which has a delta of 0.025. This is effectively telling us that this option has a 2.5% chance of finishing in the money, assuming all things remain the same and that no volatility shock occurs.

The premium you'll earn from writing this option is 0.04 per share. This is $4 per contract. This is a yield of 0.13% on the current market price, which isn't much. However, it's a monthly yield. Multiply this by 12 and you'll realize a 1.6% yield by writing these OTM options.

Remember that if you're going to be a long-term investor, you'll be earning dividends on your stock ownership as well. AT&T's dividend currently yields around 7%. This means you're guaranteeing a return of over 8% percent every year (the stock dividend + the deep OTM call yields), whether the market goes up or down or does nothing. This is before any long-term capital gains that the stock gives you.

Then there's also the fact that you can reinvest these gains into the stock to have them compound at the average capital gains rate. We've already highlighted the benefits of doing this and have shown how you can double your money compared to relying solely on capital gains.

As a rule of thumb, if you're looking for extra income from your covered calls, you want to be picking deltas that are as close to 40% as possible. In the AT&T

example, we have two deltas that are at 43% and 32%. Picking the 43% delta makes more sense since this is more likely to finish ITM. Long-term investors can pick the lowest delta that still gives you a satisfactory return on your money.

FREEMAN COVERED CALL RULE #11

IF YOU WANT TO CAPTURE A GOOD PREMIUM, AND RETAIN YOUR LONG STOCK HOLDINGS, PICK THE STRIKE PRICE WITH A DELTA AS CLOSE TO 0.4 (40%) AS POSSIBLE

Conservative investors can choose the delta that is as low as possible almost to guarantee a return on their money. Remember that the delta percentage is not a 100% guarantee. There could be volatility shocks to the market that will cause everything to be thrown out of order. This is just one of the risks of investing.

12

THE SIMPLE SOLUTION FOR CHOOSING EXPIRY DATES

Like with strike prices, choosing the correct expiry dates for your options is critical. Choose the wrong expiry date, and you could be leaving money on the table. This happens because of the way time decay works. We've already explained how a significant portion of an option's premium is its time value.

The time value inherent in an option's price is a measure of the option's likelihood of moving into the money. The more time there is until option expiry, the higher the likelihood of the option moving into the money. This increases the time value in the price of the option.

Here is the golden rule, as an option seller, time decay is your friend. You want the option to expire worthless if you're a long-term investor who wishes to hang onto your long stock position. For short-term traders, the decline in the time value needs to be balanced with the fact that you also want to ensure your option finishes in the money so that you can collect your profit plus the premium.

For short-term traders, choosing the expiry date is a tricky proposition. On one hand the longer term options give you maximum time value, but you also need to make sure that your option has a good chance of being assigned to you. This means you want it to finish deep in the money or at the money upon expiry, at the very least. Some covered call traders bank on early exercise, but this is a mistake.

There is no guarantee your option will be exercised early. In fact, the majority of options are not exercised early. The final week prior to expiry is when most options are exercised since there's very little time value left in them, and most buyers have nothing to gain by hanging onto them.

One important thing to note is that time decay is not linear. Time decay (also known as *theta decay* using Greek terminology) accelerates once the option moves within 30 days of expiry. This means the best time frame for you to target when it comes to expiry dates for covered calls is the 30-45 day window. This will give you enough of a window where you can reasonably predict price movements, and you'll earn a good return as well, thanks to the in-built time value in the premium.

WHEN SHOULD YOU CHOOSE LONGER-TERM OPTIONS?

Some traders might prefer choosing longer-term options since this suits their psyche better. A lot of long-term investors adopt this set and forget approach. While a covered call cannot guarantee that you can forget about your trade, the degree to which you must monitor your trade doesn't change or depend on the expiry date.

If anything, you'll be monitoring your trade to the same degree as you usually would. The only time when a longer expiry date makes sense is if the time premium results in a prorated gain that is far higher than what a monthly option would provide you with. For example, if the premium on a call that is expiring in 30 days gives you a 1.5% yield and one that is expiring two months from now gives you a 3% yield, it doesn't make sense to write the longer term option.

On a monthly basis, both yields are the same. If the longer-term option gives you a greater yield, then opt for it. Take the deltas into account as well. Typically, the longer-term options will have a higher delta than the shorter-term ones. Longer-term options also give you greater opportunities to capture higher capital gains in your investment since the stock has a greater opportunity to rise to higher levels.

Those who wish to hold onto the stock leg for investment purposes should not choose long expiry terms. This is because the yield you will earn on longer-term options will be lower than writing short-term ones. Besides, having a long-term option position will only increase the risk of your stock being called away.

What if you want to get rid of your stock, but don't want to write an ITM option? In such cases you need first to ask yourself why you wish to let go of your stock position.

Sometimes, you realize that there are no significant capital gains on your stock investments and you decide to start collecting income. If the stock you're holding isn't going to be heading upwards anytime soon, and if you wish to invest your money in something else, your best move is to let that investment go instead of trying to squeeze a few yield points from it.

You could write a call that is close to the money in the hopes of it being called away. However, the risk here is that if the stock is indeed going to run into turbulent times, and if your original reason for investing in it isn't valid anymore, you'll face the possibility of far greater capital gains or losses than whatever income you manage to earn. This is something a lot of covered call writers forget.

As great as the additional points of yield are, they pale in comparison to capital gains. Imagine that you buy a stock worth $100. A $1 rise in prices gives you a one percent gain. This isn't such an outlandish rise. However, with covered calls, you'll need to write calls all year to earn around four to five percent if you're being conservative.

A stock can cover a 4-5% rise in a few days, let alone weeks. The only disadvantage with capital gains is that they're unrealized and this is why generating cash flow is so valuable. However, don't make the mistake of minimizing the importance of strong capital gains in your investment. That's what makes you money at the end of the day.

So take this into account if you're a long-term investor. If there's even the slightest chance of your capital gains reducing, sell your stock position as quickly as you can. If the stock is merely going to move sideways, then you can afford to collect some additional cash on the position. Write calls close to the money and maximize your yield on exit.

WATCH OUT FOR EVENTS IN YOUR OPTION HOLDING PERIOD

When selecting an expiry date, make sure there are no significant events such as earnings announcements or political events coming up as mentioned previously. These affect the volatility and make it tough for you to predict where the underlying will end. This is why we used the "earnings in the previous week" filter on Finviz, because earnings announcements are the most frequent event that significantly affects a company's stock price.

FREEMAN COVERED CALL RULE #12

ENSURE THERE ARE NO MAJOR EVENTS WHICH COULD AFFECT THE PRICE OF THE STOCK DURING THE PERIOD YOU HOLD YOUR OPTIONS CONTRACT

13

CALCULATING RETURN ON YOUR INVESTMENT

As with any investment, you need to track the returns you're earning. This will help you measure the strategy's effectiveness and, more importantly, it'll help you avoid incurring opportunity costs. Most investors don't take this into account and end up sticking to tired old strategies that don't make them any money. In this situation, you can invest your money in other strategies that could make you more money. The gains that you forego are the opportunity costs.

Calculating the returns from your covered call position is pretty straightforward. However, the ROI can have some variations based on where the stock or the underlying asset closes on expiration.

STOCK EXPIRES AT OR SLIGHTLY BELOW THE STRIKE PRICE

To calculate the return of your covered call positions, you simply have to divide the net premium received by the cost of your shares and then convert that figure into an annualized number.

For example, you purchased 100 shares of Disney at $125 for the total investment of $12,500 and sold the $128 OTM call option expiring in one month (30 days). In return, you received $3.75 as premium and at the time of expiry the stock expires at or slightly below the strike price of $128.

In the above scenario, your total ROI on the covered call position is:

= ($375/$12,500)*100 = 3%

Afterwards, to convert this figure into an annualized return, you just simply have to take that 3% and multiply it by 365, divided by the number of days left for expiration from the date of entry.

Annualized Rate of Return:

= Rate of return on the existing covered call position * 365/ Number of days left
for expiration
= 3*365/30
= 36.50%

STOCK EXPIRES ABOVE THE STRIKE PRICE

The above example was quite straightforward because your income was restricted only to the premium received from selling the call options. However, in certain scenarios, stock prices expire above the strike price. In such a case, calculating ROI is quite different.

Continuing with the above example, let's assume the stock price expires at $130 (above the strike price) at the time of expiration.

In such a scenario, your return from the premium received will remain the same at 36.5%. But, the stock will be called away. Meaning, you are now obligated to sell the stock at $128 for $300 [($128 - $125)*100] in realized capital gains.

In the above scenario, your total ROI on the covered calls position is:

($375 + $300)/12,500 = 5.4%

Annualized Rate of Return:

= Rate of return on the existing covered call position * 365/ Number of days left
for expiration
= 5.4*365/30
= 65.70%

STOCK EXPIRES SIGNIFICANTLY BELOW THE STRIKE PRICE

Losses are a part of trading. Learning to book these losses and keep tracking them regularly is also equally important. In case of covered calls, the risk lies in the underlying stock and not with the options. A small bearish move won't affect your overall position because you still end up making the premium amount. However, if the stock moves down significantly, it will result in a significant capital loss.

In the above example, let's say Disney gapped down the next day because of some unexpected bad news and it fell to $110. Under such circumstances, it is advisable to close the trade by selling the underlying stock and close the short call position and book the loss. If you don't close the short call position along with the underlying stock, you would end up with a naked call position.

In the above scenario, your total ROI on the covered calls position is:

(*$11,000 + $375 - $12,000)/12,500 = -9%

**$11,000 is the net proceeds from selling the underlying stock at $110.*

We must mention that if you wish to hold onto the stock position for the long term, then a falling stock price should not be of concern to you. The above advice only applies to short-term traders. Keep in mind the differences in mindset between a long-term investor and a trader.

14

COVERED CALL EXIT STRATEGIES - TAKING PROFITS VS. LETTING YOUR OPTIONS EXPIRE

We've previously mentioned that a significant number of options contracts expire worthless, which is why we prefer to be on the writing side when it comes to options trading. A crucial part of using options successfully is making adjustments as the trade evolves. Often, trades don't automatically go your way. You'll need to decide whether you want to close the trade or adjust it to put yourself in a better position. There's a classic saying in the investing world "nobody ever went broke taking profits."

However, this doesn't mean you should take every little profit that comes your way. Doing this will result in you potentially leaving money on the table. By improving your understanding of options a little more, you can set yourself up to know exactly when to take profits and when to keep your trades open.

The first thing to do when entering any trade is to calculate the break-even price. In the case of the covered call, this is the price of your underlying stock minus the premium you received for writing the call. For example, let's say you buy AT&T at $30, and you sell a covered call with a strike at $32 with 45 days to expiry for a $1 premium. Your cost basis and break-even price for the trade is:

($30 - $1) = $29

So as long as the underlying stock price stays above $29, you are making money on the trade.

Now let's look at a few ways this trade can play out.

EXIT SCENARIO 1: STOCK MOVES UP

The first scenario is that we see a bullish move in the stock price. Let's say it's trading at $31.50, and there are four days left to expiry. If you want to realize maximum profits, you can wait and hope the option expires above $32, at which point your stock will be called away at $32 and your profit will be ($32 + $1 - $30)*100 = $300.

If you'd prefer to hold the stock long-term and don't want it to get called away if the option expires ITM above $32, you can lock in your profits by buying your call option back. This will cost you money since you'll need to pay whatever the premium is at that point. This is also called covering your short option position (the same term that's used in stock trading.)

Remember, when buying back the option, you want the option's price to be lower than the price you received upon writing it. It's a simple sell high, buy low process, and is the same as shorting a stock.

However, unlike stocks, you're almost always guaranteed a lower price as the option moves closer to expiry. This is because of the role of your friend time decay, which as we discussed earlier, is always on your side as an option seller.

Back to our example, you have just four days to expiry, and time decay has worked its magic. The price to buy back your $32 call is now just $0.10. Meaning you can pay $10 ($0.10*100) to buy back the option, locking in a profit of $90 on the option itself ($100-$10). Since you've now covered the option position, your stock will not be called away, even if the price is above $32 at expiry.

On top of this $90 realized profit, you also have unrealized gains of $150 on your 100 shares stock after the bullish move from $30 to $31.50.

EXIT SCENARIO 2: STOCK MOVES DOWNWARDS

The second scenario is if the price of the underlying has decreased after you wrote the option. Let's say the stock price is now trading at $27, and you have seven days until expiry. As you own 100 shares, your current unrealized loss is $2 per share, which is your cost basis ($29) minus the current price ($27).

Your two choices here are to either hope for a large price reversal in the next seven days or to close out the trade, then enter a new trade to further lower your cost basis. This is how many options traders adjust their trades once they discover that the position has moved against them.

Because we're closer to expiry, the price of the option has decreased due to time decay. In this case, we can buy back our $32 call option for just $0.02 because it is now far OTM. This means we've made a realized gain of $98 ($100 - $2) on that trade.

This also increases our break-even point for the stock. Remember, our original break-even point was $29. But since we bought back our option for $0.02, our new break-even point is $29.02 ($29 + the price we paid to buy back our option).

We're still holding the long stock leg of the trade, so we have an unrealized loss of $202 on it. One option we have is to continuously lower the break-even point for this leg by writing more calls and earning more premiums. This can be done by writing calls at lower strike prices.

So let's say we write a new call $30 call with 40 days to expiry for $0.60. This gives us a new cost basis of $28.42 ($29.02 - $0.60).

Now with our new lowered cost basis, if our stock rises above $28.42, the long stock position will be profitable once again.

If this new trade works in our favor and the stock finishes above $30 at expiry, we'll make $300 on the trade after the underlying is called away ($30 - $27). In addition to this, we also collected $60 in premiums from writing the second call option. Our net position is now $360 minus the $202 unrealized loss we started with. As a result, our net profits from this second trade are $158.

To summarize the P&L from both trades:

- Net premium received after buying back our call in trade 1: $98
- Unrealized capital loss after trade 1: -$202
- Premium received from entering trade 2: $60
- Realized capital gains after trade 2 ends ITM and our stock is called away: $300
- Total realized net gain after trades 1 and 2: (+$98 - $202 + $60 + $300) = $256

SCENARIO 3: STOCK DOESN'T MOVE

The final scenario is that the price doesn't change at all. Let's assume we're now five days away from expiry with the price at $30. Your first choice here is to let the option ride and wait for expiry, hoping the call option finishes OTM. This will help you keep your premium for a $100 profit.

The second choice is that you can buy back your call and lock in your profits. Thanks to time decay, the option premiums will have gotten much cheaper as we move closer to expiry. Therefore we can buy back our call for just $0.05. By doing this, we no longer have any open options contracts and are left with a profit on the trade of ($1 - $0.05)*100 or $95.

If we wanted to, we could further reduce our cost basis by then selling another call a further 42 days out at the same strike price ($32). This is called rolling out or rolling forward. You do this by writing another option that is further out in expiry. Please note that rolling out an option works differently from rolling forward other derivatives contracts. You cannot substitute an options contract for one that expires later. You need to exit the first contract and then physically enter another one.

In this case, implied volatility is slightly higher, so we collect a $1.20 premium. Remember, this further reduces our cost basis to $27.80 ($29 - $1.20).

As you can see here, writing covered calls is a fantastic way to reduce your cost basis on stocks that you plan to hold onto for the long term.

THE ROLE OF TIME DECAY IN COVERED CALL MANAGEMENT

We've mentioned time decay a few times in this chapter, so it's time to address it in depth regarding the management of your covered calls. Time decay (or *theta* Θ) is another Greek variable that appears complex on the surface but is very simple to understand once you grasp a few key concepts. It is the measure of how an option's premium is affected by time. Remember, all other factors being equal, options lose value the closer they get to expiry.

The numerical value of time decay is the measure of how much the option will lose value each day it moves closer to expiry. As the covered call is a strategy that sells options, time decay is always working in our favor. This is why our strategies involving buying back the written covered call close to expiry work since time decay makes the option premium cheaper than what it was when we first wrote it.

FREEMAN COVERED CALL RULE #13

TIME DECAY IS OUR BEST FRIEND WHEN SELLING OPTIONS, BECAUSE WE'RE SELLING AN ASSET WHICH, WITH ALL OTHER FACTORS BEING CONSTANT, WILL ONLY DEPRECIATE OVER TIME.

In terms of managing your covered calls, theta most affects strikes which are either ATM or very near the money. The further the price moves away from the strike in either direction, the lower the value of theta.

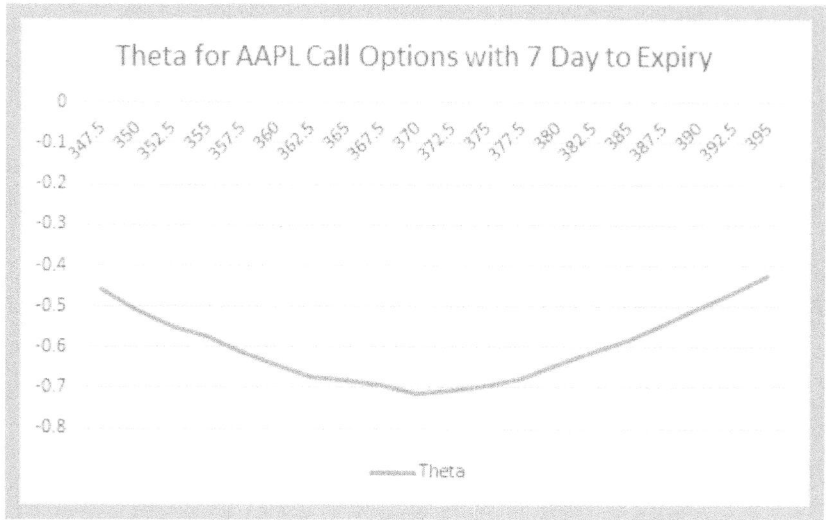

Figure 16: Theta for Apple Options with Seven Days to Expiry, Apple was trading at $370.71 at the time (Source: Interactive Brokers)

In Figure 16, the ATM strikes ($370 and $372) have the highest time decay, with theta declining as we move further away from the money. The value of theta is always negative since it represents a reduction in option premium.

Deep ITM strikes and deep OTM strikes are less affected by time decay because they have a lower likelihood of a different outcome at expiry (the OTM strike finishing ITM and vice versa).

In this way, you can think of time value as a measure of uncertainty. An analogy for this is how a football game tied at 28-28 has a more uncertain outcome with 2 minutes to go (because both teams have a good chance of winning) than a game where one team is winning 28-7 with the same time remaining.

Now that you have a better grasp of how time decay works, we can develop a practical method for using it to manage our trades. To see how we can use theta to better manage our trades, it's important to understand our options' intrinsic and extrinsic value.

Let's say we own Las Vegas Sands (LVS) currently priced at $45.00.

If we buy a $40 call for $6.50, then we have $5 of intrinsic value (because the stock is worth $5 more than the option we bought), and $1.50 of extrinsic value (the price of the option minus the intrinsic value.)

If we buy a $50 call for $1, then we have $0 of intrinsic value because the option is OTM. However, since we could resell the option for $1, it still has $1 of extrinsic value.

Because theta affects deep ITM and deep OTM strikes less, the most optimal management strategy is to roll your short calls when they are deep ITM or OTM, because you will not get a much better price by waiting to sell them closer to expiry. We'll add to this with 3 rules based exit strategies for managing your trades.

THREE RULE-BASED EXIT STRATEGIES

The One Percent Rule

A good rule to use with respect to theta decay is if the value of your call ever loses its extrinsic value to where that extrinsic value represents less than one percent of the underlying price, then roll the option over. This means buying back your existing call and selling the next month's option. A few options platforms such as *thinkorswim,* have a special "roll" functionality which will conduct both of these trades simultaneously. On other platforms, you'll need to do this manually.

If the stock moves sideways, the call option's value will decrease over time. Once the value of the call's extrinsic value is less than one percent of the stock's price, roll the call option to a new strike and expiration.

If the stock moves down, the value of the call option will drop. Once its value is less than one percent of the stock price, roll the option to a new strike and expiration.

In the Las Vegas Sands example, if the underlying price stays at $45, you should roll the option if the option price drops below $0.45, because this is now less than one percent of the underlying.

The Two and Twenty (2 & 20) Rule

We've already discussed how theta decay accelerates as your contract moves closer to the expiry date. However, what if contract prices decrease sharply during the beginning of the contract? Do you keep holding onto it in hopes of greater profit, or should you lock in your profits?

A good rule to use in such a scenario is the 2 & 20 rule. This rule states that if the price of buying back your option is less than 20% of the price you paid, within the first two weeks of you entering the contract, go ahead and buy back the option. So if you were paid a $1 premium for the contract and if it costs less than $0.20 to buy it back within the first 2 weeks, then pull the trigger and buy it back.

By doing this, you should lock in a solid profit on the contract, and you no longer have to be concerned with your stock being called away. You are giving up 20% of your potential profit by doing this, but because you've bought it back within 2 weeks of entering it, this then allows you to have the flexibility to enter into another contract if you want to do so. In essence, you're using time to your advantage by giving yourself more opportunities to enter profitable trades.

Code Red

When you spend enough time in the markets, you'll eventually enter a trade which goes pear-shaped right from the start. With covered calls, there isn't too much which can go wrong in the options leg of the trade, but there are always risks with the underlying stock.

So if you're ever in a scenario where you feel the stock itself could take a large hit in price, exit the trade at any cost and sell the underlying stock. This could be if there are allegations of fraud or if the company is under fire for its business practices.

A recent example of this would be the Muddy Waters Research report, which uncovered massive fraud at Chinese coffee company Luckin Coffee. At the time the report, which alleged that Luckin had fabricated its sales numbers, was released, the stock was trading at $32. Within 3 months the stock had fallen almost 95% and was trading below $3 and was removed from the Nasdaq as a result. However, if you had sold your stock within one month of the report being released, you would have kept the vast majority of your capital gains.

Another thing to bear in mind is not to keep holding onto the stock with the hope of making a greater profit on your options trade, because it's extremely rare that your options yields will offset the loss you made in the underlying stock.

It's an unwelcome scenario to be in, but it's best to be proactive and just get out with your capital intact and then re-enter another trade with a new stock.

This is one of the most difficult decisions for new investors and traders to make because it goes against a fundamental human desire: the need to be right. However, once you can separate your emotions from your trading, you will be ahead of the curve and position yourself to make more money than 90% of traders out there.

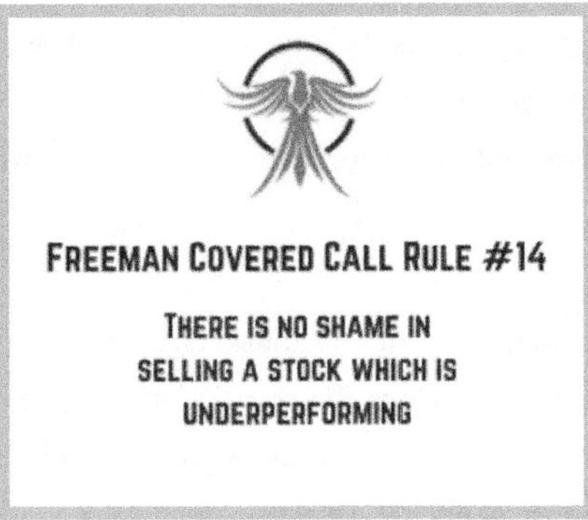

15

THE POOR MAN'S COVERED CALL

As great as the covered call is, there are downsides to it. The biggest barrier to implementing it is that you need to have capital in your account to do so. For instance, if you wished to write a covered call on the SPY, which is the ETF tracking the S&P 500, you'll need at least $30,000 in your account since the ETF is selling north of $300 at the moment.

Understandably, not everyone has this kind of money lying around. What if you have just $5,000 in your account and wish to start earning some money on this? Can you still execute a covered call? The good news is that you can. Remember earlier, we discussed how options can be used to enter a position for a lower cost than simply buying stock? Well now we'll show you how to use this to execute covered calls for a lower cost than you would with a stock position. This strategy is often referred to as executing a poor man's covered call.

LONG DIAGONAL SPREADS WITH CALLS

To understand this trade better, we need to take some time to introduce some more options trading terminology. You'll often read of the word "spread" in relation to options trading. There are three kinds of spreads a trader can create. The first is a vertical spread. These spreads involve options expiring in the same month but with different strike prices.

Next is the horizontal spread, which are two options that have the same strike price but expire in different months. Usually, a horizontal spread involves one option expiring in the near month and the other expiring 30 days after that. Lastly, we have diagonal spreads that are created with calls and puts.

Diagonal spreads can be vertical or horizontal in nature. You could create a diagonal with a call and a put expiring in the same month or in different months. You can even create diagonals with calls exclusively or with puts exclusively but have them in opposite directions. We mean to say that you could have one call leg as a long position and the other as a short position.

Don't worry too much about the complexities of the diagonal spread and its structure. Of the utmost importance is that you understand why it works.

When it comes to creating a poor man's covered call, the setup is quite simple. There are two legs to a long call diagonal:

1. An ITM long call option leg with expiry out in the future, preferably a LEAP
2. An OTM short call option leg expiring within 30-45 days

LEAP stands for **L**ong-term **E**quity **A**ntici**P**ation. These are options that expire well out into the future, usually over a year or more. The great news is that they're fully accessible to retail traders. By buying a call LEAP that expires more than a year from the current date, and one that is ITM, you've established a synthetic long position in the stock.

You can simply keep holding onto this position for a year or more and then either exit the LEAP position or exercise it to establish a long stock position. Like with regular options, each LEAP contract covers 100 shares of the underlying.

Most brokers will allow you to write covered calls against an ITM LEAP. It's still prudent to check with your broker if this is the case. These securities are available with Level 1 options accounts, the same as regular covered calls, so it shouldn't be an issue.

LEAP Substitution

The LEAP substitution strategy works best in mature bull markets. They aren't rising exponentially, and the stock you're interested in is moving slightly upwards or is moving sideways. It's best to choose a LEAP that is a year or two away in expiry. This is a big holding period, but consider that your long stock investment leg is usually held for a while as well, especially if you're using it for investment purposes.

Short-term traders can use LEAPs as well since you could always exit the position by selling the LEAP to the market. If the underlying rises in price then you'll earn a small profit from the price appreciation as you would if you had owned the stock. The risk with this strategy is the same as it is with the regular covered call.

If the underlying stock decreases in price, then the LEAP premium will decrease and you'll be faced with a loss that the premium received from writing the short-term call will not compensate. As a result, our previous guidance with regards to managing this applies here as well.

Here's an example of how this strategy would work on the SPY, which is currently trading at $326.

Buy 1 deep ITM $288 call option on SPY expiring 6/30/2021 (334 days to expiry) for $46

Sell 1 slightly OTM $331 call option on SPY expiring 9/02/2020 (33 days to expiry) for $3.94

Difference between strikes = $43

Our upfront costs are ($43 + $3.94) - $46

Therefore our upfront premium is ($47.94 - $46) = $1.94 or $194

This means we need the cost to buy back our $331 call to drop below $0.94 for us to profit on the trade.

In terms of cash requirements, our single call options contract only costs us $4,600 to buy, as opposed to the $32,600 it would cost to buy 100 shares of SPY.

Volatility Advantages

The LEAP substitution offers an advantage in terms of handling volatility. This involves the way in which another Greek variable, Vega, affects the prices of LEAPs. Vega measures how an option's premium changes given a change in implied volatility.

LEAPs have their expiry dates far out into the future. Any increase in volatility produces a far greater rise in intrinsic value than it does in short-dated options. This means if the underlying starts rising, you'll realize a larger gain in the LEAP premium than you would by holding onto the stock itself. This works when the stock declines in price as well.

Since the LEAP is dated far out into the future, you could simply hold onto the position without fear of having to sell. Your LEAP won't lose too much of its premium since it still has immense time value present, even if it moves OTM. Of course, this won't help if the stock falls to zero, but if you follow the guidelines previously mentioned, this won't be a problem.

In terms of strike prices, you want your LEAP to finish ITM as much as possible, so look to buy options that have a delta greater than 0.75. The previous advice regarding deltas closest to 0.4 applies to the short call.

Worst-Case Scenario

Let's say your trade isn't working out and the short-term option is moving ITM. In such a scenario, you need to cover your position and take the loss on it immediately. This is because if your option happens to get assigned to you, you'll need to have the cash on hand to be able to buy the stock.

You'll need to exercise the LEAP and deliver the stock to the short option's buyer. The primary reason for following this strategy is that you don't have the necessary cash to execute a traditional covered call. Therefore, it's unlikely you'll have the cash on hand to buy the underlying.

If you do choose to execute this strategy, our point is that be very vigilant of the short call moving ITM. If you're assigned the stock, it's far more disastrous for you than in the case of the traditional covered call. It might be worth it to write options even further OTM to prevent any chance of this scenario occurring.

Your broker may even automatically exercise your LEAP for you. If you don't have the cash on hand, you'll be hit with a margin call, and this is a scenario you want to avoid at all costs. This makes trade management even more important while your position is active.

16

THE TAX IMPLICATIONS OF THIS STRATEGY

Taxes are something that no investor can avoid. When it comes to covered calls, taxation can get a bit complex. We must mention at this point that we're not tax professionals. It's best for you to consult one if you're looking to figure your taxes out. The information in this chapter comes entirely from the Options Industry Council, which publishes tax information on the CBOE's website. Options taxation regulations keep changing, so it's best to consult with a tax professional at all times.

According to the Options Industry Council, profits from covered calls are treated as capital gains, with a few exceptions. We'll get to these exceptions shortly. The premium you earn by writing a call is a short-term capital gain and is taxed accordingly. Short-term capital gains are taxed at the same rates as ordinary income.

Gains and losses can be realized from the sale of the stock, from the call or from any combination of the two. If the stock is sold at a higher price than what it was bought for, this is a capital gain. Your holding period will determine whether this is a long-term or short-term capital gain. If you've been investing for a while now, you'll know that long-term capital gains result in lower tax rates.

In case the call is sold, a gain is realized when you cover your position (buy it back for a lower price than the premium you received on writing it). A capital loss is realized when you buy it back for a higher price than the premium you received. In the case that the call is assigned, the net profit or loss is taken into account and is taxed accordingly.

The dividends you earn while holding the stock might also be affected. This can get complicated, so it's best to consult with a tax professional who can walk you through the different scenarios affecting dividends.

As far as the IRS is concerned, the money you receive from selling a covered call is not included in your income upon writing. Instead, it is recognized when the call is closed. The call can close either by expiring worthless or by closing the position by buying it back. Being assigned is also a case where the call is considered closed.

Something to note is that the cash received at the time of the sale is a short-term capital gain irrespective of how long the short position was open. This is something investors miss. Even if you hold onto the short option for more than a year, the IRS will treat it as a short-term gain and tax you accordingly.

In the case of assignation, the strike price plus premium received equals the sale price of the stock when determining the gain or loss (*What Are The Tax Implications of Covered Calls?*, 2020). If the stock was held for a period greater than a year, the gain is treated as a long-term capital gain. The same applies for a loss.

Qualified Covered Calls

A covered call is considered qualified if it has more than 30 days to expiry when written and has a strike price that is not deep in the money. The exact quantification of deep in the money is subjective. The stock price is taken into account, as is the time left until expiry. The IRS is very subjective when it comes to this, so do consult a tax professional to understand the implications of this.

What does a covered call "qualify" for anyway? To understand this we need to look at how straddles are taxed. A straddle is a trade setup which we previously discussed. The nature of the trade makes its tax treatment complex and the IRS is concerned with investors using the losses from the strategy to offset capital gains before the latter have been recognized.

The good news is that as long as you write OTM calls, you don't need to worry about tax straddle rules. If you write ITM calls, you'll need to consult with a professional to determine your liability.

Qualified covered calls also impact the holding period of the underlying stock. This is best illustrated by an example. Let's say you buy 100 shares of a company for $100 in September. A month later the stock price declines to $80. You write a $79 call on the stock. This is considered an ITM qualified covered call as per IRS rules since it isn't deep ITM.

You then close the call position by buying it back for some price. Two days later, let's say the stock goes ex-dividend and you receive a dividend payment. You then sell the stock the following month. Here's how taxation will work in this scenario.

First, your dividend payment will not be treated as being qualified under any circumstances. With respect to dividends, qualified ones are taxed at long-term capital gains rates. In this case you did not hold the stock for 61 days during the prior 121-day holding period before the dividend was paid. Therefore, you'll pay ordinary income taxes on this payment.

Your total holding period was around two months (slightly less than 60 days). However, the period during which you held the ITM call will be subtracted from this since it is a qualified call. In this particular scenario, it doesn't affect your taxation rate. However, imagine a scenario where you hold a qualified ITM call for 90 days and the stock for 400 days and then sell the stock.

Your stock leg will be taxed at the short-term capital gains tax rate since your effective holding period will be (400 - 90) 310 days. If you had written an OTM call, the stock holding period will be 400. This impacts your dividend taxation as well. The number of days for which you hold the ITM call detracts from the necessary holding period to qualify for lower dividend taxation rates.

However, writing OTM calls doesn't reduce your tax liability. If anything, it complicates it. This is because such positions will be subject to tax straddle rules.

If a non-qualified covered call is written on a stock position that is held for less than a year, the holding period for the stock is reduced by the period of time for which the call is held.

If the stock and option are closed at the same time, the gains are treated as short-term. If the call is closed first, the holding period for the stock resumes from the day the call was closed. These rules apply upon assignment as well. When calculating the gains and the appropriate tax rate, you need to take the holding period of the stock into account.

As long as your calls aren't deep ITM, your stock holding period will not decrease or be reduced. If the covered call isn't qualified, then your stock holding period will reduce and you'll end up paying the appropriate tax rate based on the shortened holding period.

The good news is that if you're writing options in an IRA, then you don't need to worry about any of this stuff. However, as we've mentioned earlier, you should not be using the money in your IRA to jeopardize long-term stock holdings. If you do choose this option, do so wisely, with conservative OTM strikes. If you wish to exit a position, then you need to line up another potential investment instead of letting cash lie dormant in your account.

THE BOTTOM LINE

Covered call taxation hinges mostly upon the strike price of your call. If it's deep ITM, then you're potentially creating a short-term capital gains tax situation for yourself. If you're looking to exit a sideways-moving stock position, make sure you've held onto the stock for at least a year before looking to let it go. This way the ITM call won't affect your holding period.

Consult a tax professional to determine which strikes would put you past the threshold of being qualified. If this is the case, you'll need to take higher short-term taxes into account when calculating the overall profit of your strategy. Dividends are also affected thanks to qualified/non-qualified covered calls due to the 61 day holding rule.

We also recommend you read all about options taxation at the CBOE's website. It might not be the most exciting thing you do today, but it is something which will save you future headaches.

You can access the relevant file at this link:

https://freemanpublication.com/optiontaxes

17

SETTING YOURSELF UP FOR SUCCESS

It's one thing to read this book, but it's entirely another to achieve success in the markets. This is because executing a method well depends on your mindset and on your preparation. Many traders and investors think that making money in the markets is as simple as learning a strategy and then setting it up on autopilot.

This is not the case. We could provide two people with the same strategy and see one do well and the other fail to implement it. Mindset and the way you approach execution is extremely important. This is why $20,000 trading seminars exist after all. Many people attend such seminars but don't make any progress. Why is this?

THE PROBLEM WITH HOW MOST PEOPLE SET GOALS - AND HOW TO FIX IT

Goal setting is something everyone should do if they wish to get anywhere in life. The problem is that most of us aren't taught how to set goals. We invariably set goals that are measured by outside factors and influences. A typical financial goal is to "become a millionaire" or "to earn $10,000 per week" or something of this kind.

These goals are worthy, but they're not very helpful. For example, if you earned $9,000 in a given week, you've done incredibly well for yourself. However, this falls short of the $10,000 mark, so your subconscious mind knows you've failed. Many people face such situations and don't handle them well. They seek revenge on the markets and start chasing new systems that will "guarantee" $10,000 per week. This starts a downward spiral that most never recover from, which explains why so many people have a bad relationship with the stock market.

The solution to this is to change your goals instead. So which kinds of goals make the most sense? To understand this, we need to examine the nature of the market itself.

The market is a chaotic place. Over the long term, prices are driven by business quality and economic factors. However, in the short term, prices are driven by emotions.

There are methods of measuring all of these things, but you don't control anything when it comes to prices at the end of the day. You could have invested in a great business with great management, but the stock prices could remain firmly in place no matter how great the company is.

You could scream and shout at how irrational the market is, but the market is going to do whatever it wants. Attaching the success or failure of your goals to such an erratic thing doesn't make sense. Instead, you need to figure out what your processes are and attach your goals to them. This way, you'll always make progress since progress becomes as simple as doing something.

Let's look at an example of something that many people try to accomplish but fail: Losing weight and getting fit. The most common goal statement to achieve this is along the lines of "I will lose 10lbs in two months". The problem with this statement is that while it's fully measurable and time-bound, it isn't within your control. You could drink too much water one day and end up losing just nine pounds. Does this mean you've failed?

Instead of creating outcome orientated goals, how about creating process-oriented goals? Take a look at the list below:

- Exercise for one hour 5x per week, either in the gym or through another activity
- Be physically active as much as possible
- Walk instead of using transportation, where possible
- Prepare food ahead of time to prevent snacking
- Buy groceries to make sure healthy food is always in the kitchen
- Incorporate one cheat meal every week to relieve stress

None of these goals are out of your reach. All you need to do is take action. By taking action on these goals you'll automatically make progress. You won't be looking into the future, trying to figure out how much longer you have to go. You'll be in the present moment and be focused on doing what you need to do to get where you want to be.

The same principles ensure investment and trading success as well. A sample list of goals for a covered call writer would be:

- I will study 5 charts every weekday.
- I will always use the closest strike price to 0.4 delta when entering a trade.
- I will use a rules-based approach to exiting my trade.
- I will log every single trade in my trading journal.
- I will review my trades every week to see where I could improve.
- I will continue to paper trade while trading live to sharpen my sword. I will do this until I have at least 100 live trades under my belt.

All of these goals are completely within your control. Best of all, they don't depend on the amount of money you make to measure progress. In the markets, it's quite common to do all the right things and still lose money. For example, you could enter a position based on solid principles, but some unforeseen event, such as the Covid-19 pandemic, might occur and push your positions into negative territory.

Relying on results to define your goals only puts you in a position to lose your power. You'll never feel as if you're making progress doing this. How can you? You're trying to control something that cannot be controlled. Instead, always focus on what you can control. By doing this, you're stacking the deck for success.

Routines and Habits

Goal setting is one half of the success formula. The other half is a well-practiced routine that will ensure you meet with success. Most traders and investors have extremely unstructured routines when it comes to looking at the markets. The key to good performance is a structured method that is based on intelligent principles.

What a lot of unsuccessful market participants do is hear someone talking about some stock or investment idea, and they jump into it without considering its merits. They don't take the time to educate themselves on how these methods work. They don't pause to think whether this method would suit them or not.

Instead, they let promises cloud their judgment. Investors don't need to be all that active when it comes to the market. They need to put in the work upfront and then sit back and monitor their investments for validity.

When you begin involving options, your day-to-day routines are of greater importance. You cannot afford to roll out of bed on a poor night's sleep and then sit down to trade. This will only cause you to lose money. Before placing a trade or an investment, conduct a quick check of yourself. Are you a little too emotional right now? Are you making this decision from a place of rationality, or are you gambling? Where is this decision coming from?

Can you explain this investment idea in plain and simple words to someone who has no idea about it? Only when you receive suitable answers to all of these questions should you put your money into the market. If you're a trader, then instill habits that you can execute repeatedly and consistently. If you find that your routine is being disturbed, then don't trade that day.

Also, your routine after you've finished trading matters as well. As we mentioned earlier, the markets are random. At times, you will receive poor results despite doing everything correctly. This doesn't mean you're a bad trader or that you lack skills. It's just how the markets work. Conduct a thorough review of your actions, including your mental state, and remind yourself of all the good things you did. If you did some things that conflicted with your routines, make sure you don't do them again by removing the things that triggered them.

Focus on taking action and on instilling the right habits, and you'll meet with success for sure. The key is to aim for incremental success over time. Most people try to go ahead and achieve everything at once, which is impractical. What most often happens is that they end up burning themselves out and they find themselves right back at square one.

With regards to covered calls, don't try to place too many trades at once. Place one at first and see how you do. Then add another and so on until you reach a number you're comfortable with. Track your habits and processes, and over time you'll end up reaching where you want to be.

18

A PASSIVE INCOME STRATEGY WITH COVERED CALL FUNDS

The financial markets can be taken advantage of through many different strategies. All of these strategies are implemented by managed funds such as mutual funds or exchange traded funds (ETFs). You can passively adopt these strategies by buying units of such funds and pay a management fee in return. Covered calls are no exception to this.

Commonly, covered call funds carry the label "enhanced equity" in their names and these funds seek to generate returns by combining dividend investment with covered call writing. The aim of these funds is to beat the S&P 500 and to minimize the tax bill that investors face.

There is also another set of funds called closed-end funds (CEFs) that aim to achieve the same objective. Closed-end funds are an interesting breed of funds in that unlike mutual funds, they don't issue new units. Instead, the only units you can buy are from other investors in the fund. For this reason, you'll sometimes end up paying a premium to the funds' net asset values (NAV) when buying units.

Despite this phenomenon, closed-end funds don't provide the average investor with too much of an advantage. The average closed-end fund charges fees to the order of one percent of capital invested. This is the same as what a hedge fund charges its investors. As such, you're better off investing in an ETF since their fees tend to be lower.

The exception to this rule is if the CEF is trading at a discount to its net asset value. This happens from time to time, and is a useful way to offset the fund's management fee. You can screen for funds currently trading at a discount using the following website

https://www.cefchannel.com/screens/discount-to-nav/

ADVANTAGES OF COVERED CALL FUNDS

There are many advantages of investing in managed funds. Many people don't have the time, nor the desire to actively monitor their investments, and this is why passive investing strategies exist in the first place. Covered calls aren't exactly an active strategy, but you do need to be aware of what the market is doing. They also need to be up to speed with price behavior.

In some cases, a tiny dash of technical analysis might also be necessary to make sense of an investment. All of this puts additional strain on the investor, and some people might not want to take this workload on. In such cases, it makes sense to outsource money management to a professional manager who can optimize a portfolio to bring maximum benefit to an investor.

These managers will search for the best opportunities in the market and will employ an active approach to writing covered calls. Thus, the potential returns you can earn are quite high.

Lower Investment

When reviewing the poor man's covered call strategy, we hit upon one particular snag that might stop you from writing covered calls: a lack of money. If implementing covered calls using LEAPs isn't for you, you could turn to a managed covered call fund such as Blackrock Enhanced Equity Dividend Trust (BDJ).

This currently trades at $7.50, and there is no minimum investment required. It has an expense ratio of 0.8% and is actively traded with a good amount of liquidity. The fund is issued by Blackrock, which is a highly respected firm in the investment arena. This is a cheap and easy way for you to enter the field of covered call writing.

Optimization

Long-term investors will benefit from investing in covered call funds as well. If you were to implement covered calls by yourself, you would adopt a purely passive strategy. However, there are many ways to make an active covered call strategy work. These strategies seek to earn profits on both the stock as well as the option leg of the trade.

This is the approach these funds take. If you're looking to give your portfolio a little boost, then investing in such funds might make sense for you. Optimization also appears in the form of tax advantages. These funds seek to capture dividends as well as seek to minimize the tax bill you will face.

Monitoring all of this is a headache if you're an individual. It takes time and effort. Instead, pay a small fee and have your money managed for you.

DISADVANTAGES

Covered call funds offer good opportunities, but there are some drawbacks. For starters, they seek to outperform the market, and like most mutual funds with similar aims, most of them fail to achieve this goal. Market outperformance is not an easy thing to achieve, and in many cases, it's far easier to shoot for average gains instead of trying to beat the market.

These funds also experience volatility thanks to a few of their trades going the wrong way. While a well-managed fund will keep any adverse impact in check, it doesn't change the market's view of them. As a result, they tend to underperform in good times and perform worse in bad times. This is because in good times, investors rush into index funds, and in bad times, the market identifies these covered call funds as being historical underperformers and punishes them.

If you're willing to stomach a few ups and downs, then covered call funds might offer benefits for you. However, you need to hold on tight. The other disadvantage is that their fees are higher than the average index fund and ETF. Index funds and ETFs can charge fees as low as 0.03%.

Compare that to the 0.8% mentioned earlier, and you'll see the difference. These fees pose a higher hurdle for the investor to overcome, and given the historic volatility inherent in these funds, it might not be worth the risk. Our advice is that if you have the time to monitor your covered calls, then write them yourself.

A covered call doesn't require much maintenance. It takes just a few minutes to identify an optimal strike price and determine how much of a premium you want to get paid. Manage it yourself, and you won't have to pay any fees.

If you're looking to be more active as an investor, then simply buying shares in a fund is counter to your objective. After all, the point of being active is to generate more money than the market. If you cannot do this by yourself, then there's no point in investing in a fund that tries to do the same.

19

AVOIDING TRADING SCAMS

Options trading and indeed trading, in general, has acquired a "get-rich-quick" taint. As a result, there are many operators out there who promise you all the money in the world with their super-secret trading systems. All you have to do is pay their hefty fee. These self-appointed gurus can be found on YouTube and Twitter posting screenshots of 1,000% gains thanks to their simple strategies.

It's easy to fall for such scams since the people behind them are often excellent salespeople. They make various claims that are designed to convince you that you cannot do any of this by yourself and that you need their guidance to profit. They might even claim to have worked at some hedge fund or have started their own hedge fund before deciding to shutter it.

It's pretty easy to fall for such claims, so we'll now give you a list of the telltale signs that all of these scam artists exhibit. Use this checklist to avoid them.

GET RICH QUICK. REALLY QUICK.

This is the most obvious sign, and truth be told, it functions as a filter for the fake guru. People who are desperate to make loads of money fall for scams because they want to believe such claims are true. The most common claim is that the trader in question turned $1,000 into $1,000,000 in the matter of a year by trading options.

Please note that there have been traders who have turned small amounts of money into enormous amounts in the past. For example, the pioneer of computerized trading, Ed Seykota turned $5,000 into $15 million in 12 years, and commodities trader Michael Marcus turned $30,000 into $80 million in 15 years. These are extraordinary returns that are well beyond the norm.

However, the fake guru will claim such returns in the space of a single year or two years at the most. They'll tell you they started off in poverty and used trading to gain access to a life of helicopters and champagne. They'll even post videos of them in a bathrobe at their Ritz-Carlton penthouse suite. The markets have the ability to make you rich, but it's close to impossible to earn such massive returns in such a short period of time without assuming huge amounts of risk.

LEVERAGE

One of the ways that these scammers justify such large returns is through the use of leverage. They'll regularly highlight that they use 100x leverage on their trades and that this is the only way for you to make money. This is a bit like a real estate guru who claims to have a multimillion dollar real estate empire, but really has only has millions of dollars worth of mortgages on their balance sheet.

Just like how you need to stay away from companies that utilize a ton of debt to boost returns, you need to steer clear of traders who use excessive leverage to boost returns. This phenomenon is well-known in the institutional trading industry. For this reason, traders pay attention to risk-adjusted returns instead of outright returns.

The best metric for this is the Sharpe Ratio. This number takes the leverage used into account and presents a good picture of how skillful a trader really is. A Sharpe Ratio greater than one is considered pretty good. Risk-adjusted return metrics such as these can help you differentiate between a trader who risks 100% of their capital to generate 30% returns versus another that risks just 2% of their capital to generate 15% returns. It's pretty obvious who the better trader is in this case.

NO AUDITED RECORDS

It's straightforward to establish an audit trail for your trading records. Even if you're a retail trader, it's as simple as downloading them directly from your broker software or website. However, this is an extremely tough task for most fake trading gurus. They'll do their absolute best not to disclose their trading account balances or their trade histories.

They'll provide all kinds of excuses that their broker doesn't connect to online auditing platforms or that they have too much money in their accounts, and they're afraid this might make them a target. This argument is a bit odd since the very premise of getting you to sign up with them is that they make a lot of money.

Some gurus are aware of this dichotomy and post screenshots of trades on Twitter and YouTube. However, they'll obscure whether this account was a demo account or a live one. They won't disclose the account number or the account balance, so you won't have any way of knowing whether this example was chosen in retrospect or in real-time. Some gurus even use market simulation software to replay the market and then present it as a real-time trade.

The easiest way to spot such scammers is to ask them what their Sharpe Ratio is. If they cannot give you this number, run away from them. Every professional trader knows this number by heart. It's how they're evaluated at the end of the day.

Another branch of audits concerns the fake hedge fund gurus. The phrase hedge fund is tossed around very quickly these days because most retail traders have no idea how a hedge fund works. A "hedge fund" can be a single person with a Bloomberg terminal shacked up in their garage, or it can be a financial behemoth with 1,500 employees headquartered in a multi-million dollar skyscraper in Manhattan.

Whatever the situation is, anyone operating a hedge fund needs to have a license from the SEC. This securities-dealing license needs to be renewed periodically, and anyone who has traded for an institution possesses one. Ask the scam artist to show you their securities-dealing license. Pay attention to the type of licenses as well.

You can even check the validity of their license on the Financial Regulatory Authority's website (https://www.finra.org/investors/protect-your-money/ask-and-check). No excuse is a valid explanation for not having a FINRA or SEC license. If they claim to have run or traded for a hedge fund, they need to possess one of these, even if it's expired.

Ask them which broker-dealer they traded through. Hedge funds cannot trade through regular brokers since the compliance requirements are different. They need to trade through so-called Prime Brokers. These brokers are the ones that hold their license certifications and monitor them for any violations.

If a guru promises you an offer where your trades can be routed to certain brokers in their network, ask to see their broker-dealer agreement. If there is no agreement, the guru is probably bucketing your orders and is trading against you. In this scam, what happens is that your orders (along with the other students') are grouped together, and the guru then takes the opposite side of those trades.

Most moves lose money, so it makes sense to teach students some bogus system and then trade against them. Over the long run, the scammer will make money. You'll see this happen quite a lot in the world of Forex trading. So always ask for official documents and double-check their validity as much as possible. Excuses or simple screenshots which show no identifying information are not good enough.

GIMMICKS

Gurus usually push their strategies as being super-secret. They may even make you sign an NDA before enrolling in their program. You'll see a very active blog with comments mentioning how amazing their system is. The same goes for their YouTube channels and other social media. Needless to say, many of these comments are fake.

Ethel McKeown 3 weeks ago

Bitcoin's halving is now in the past, and stock-to-flow formulas predict that the asset is ready to rocket out from current lows. But that's yet to happen, and the crypto market is even crashing currently. this why it's advisable to trade with the help of expert traders like Kevin Mccarthy He is always one step ahead of other traders, he fully monitored all my trades to avoid me making mistakes and losing my money. My earnings have increased drastically from 1.2 Bitcoin to 6 Bitcoin in just 4 weeks and some days. I have full confidence in his tradin abilities. You all can reach out to him through [<< Tele-grm >> Mccarthytrade

Figure 17: An example of a fake guru testimonial posted on a YouTube video. Tell tales signs of fakery are: Using an American name but typing in broken English, mentioning the guru by name (in this case, one "Kevin McCarthy"), claiming they made huge amounts of money in a short time, and advertising the guru's Telegram channel or WhatsApp number

There is no secret formula or information that anyone is hiding from you. It's all there in plain sight. The problem isn't with the information, it's with the way you expect to run your trading operations. If you expect to get rich quick, nothing is going to work for you. Aim to get rich slowly, and you'll be surprised at how friendly the markets are in terms of making money.

Here's a simple checklist for you to follow when evaluating a trading guru:

1. Conduct proper research about the trading service and compare it with its peers. Take special note of the refund policy; many of these scam services do not even have one.
2. Investigate whether the service you are considering is regulated by the SEC.
3. Learn the basics of the stock market by reading entry level books like William O'Neill's *How to Make Money in Stocks* or our own *8 Step Beginner's Guide to Value Investing* before subscribing to any service.
4. Carefully read all the terms and conditions.
5. Consider online and offline reviews on an unbiased website like Trustpilot.

6. And finally, make sure the company is 100% transparent in their fees and policies.

We must note that courses offered by trading gurus don't fall under the purview of the SEC or FINRA. Use online review sites and the previous tips mentioned to avoid scam artists.

WHERE YOU GO FROM HERE

The final question this all boils down to is, do you want to make your existing investments work for you?

We've discussed asymmetric returns and how the market trades (both the total index as well as individual stocks) flat the majority of the time. This is what makes covered calls such a great way for you to generate additional income in your stock portfolio.

There are two ways to approach it. You could use them as a generator of synthetic dividends on your long stock holdings, or you could use them as a speculative strategy where you can try to capture the gains from the stock leg as well as the option premium. If you can generate an additional two to three percent over and above any dividends you're earning in your long stock portfolio; you're giving yourself an extra gain of five percent per year.

Once this amount is reinvested and compounded, you'll end up doubling your money over your holding period when compared to generating no income from it. Many investors discount the power of cash flow, and we hope this book has opened your eyes to how powerful it can truly be for your portfolio.

Covered calls aren't a silver bullet. You need to follow some simple principles to make sure they work for you. You need to take note of the deltas of the options you write. Stick to writing options with a delta of 0.4 as much as possible, and you'll be just fine. If you're writing calls for investment purposes, then sticking to lower delta values makes more sense. Your premiums will be lower, but you won't be in any danger of losing your long stock position.

When prices are increasing massively, you're probably better off only buying the stock and then writing far OTM calls against it instead of earning a premium by writing a put and waiting for it to fall, which might never happen. The capital gains you give up will far outweigh whatever premiums you earn from the put.

This is why covered calls are best written when the market is moving sideways or slightly upwards. If you're in it for investment purposes, then pretty much any condition will work for you except a wildly bullish one. If you're in it for speculative purposes, then you need to avoid bearish markets. The capital losses on your stock leg will outweigh the premiums you earn.

You could roll your options down and reduce your cost basis, but there's no guarantee that you'll ever be able to overcome the capital loss. You'll also need to carefully choose your rolled strikes since you don't want to inadvertently take a loss on the stock leg.

Despite all of these factors, covered calls are a simple income strategy. The only instance in which they turn complex is when you deal with taxation. We've covered this in detail but still advise you to consult a tax professional, especially with regards to writing ITM calls.

Beware of any scammers and use the tips we've given you to steer clear of them. Before jumping into covered calls, take some time to note your gains and losses on paper. This way you'll reduce your downside risk.

Many ordinary investors have grown their financial portfolio by using covered calls in addition to their long stock holdings. That's the beauty of them, because you can profit even when the stock is going nowhere. When used smartly and in moderation, options transform from a gambling tool, to an intelligent investor's best friend.

With the rise in discount brokers, and affordable access to great information, there has simply never been a better time to be an investor, so you should feel thankful that you're living in the times you are.

To demonstrate this, let's run some numbers one last time.

We'll take $25,000, and to that, we'll add $2,500 every year. At a compounded rate of 15% (10% from your long stock holdings + an additional 5% generated by covered calls).

At this rate, you can turn that $25,000 into $1 million in twenty three years.

Are you up for the challenge?

One final word from us. If this book has helped you in any way, we'd appreciate it if you left a review on Amazon. Reviews are the lifeblood of our business. We read every single one and incorporate your feedback into our future book projects.

To leave an Amazon review, go to
https://freemanpublications.com/leaveareview

REFERENCES

Baird, J. (2007, September 28). How M&G played CDOs to profit during the crisis. *Reuters*. https://www.reuters.com/article/mg-crisis-cdos/how-mg-played-cdos-to-profit-during-the-crisis-idUSL2783735020070928

Belvedere, M. J. (2019, December 13). *How the Icahn-Ackman "Battle of the Billionaires" on CNBC became a defining moment of the decade*. CNBC. https://www.cnbc.com/2019/12/13/reliving-the-carl-icahn-and-bill-ackman-herbalife-feud-on-cnbc.html

Case Study - Warren Buffett Writing Put Options To Obtain A Lower Stock Purchase Price. (2019, May 20). The Options Manual. https://optionsmanual.com/secondary-informational-articles/case-study_-warren-buffet-writing-put-options-to-obtain-a-lower-stock-purchase-price/

Ferreira, J. (2019, April 10). *US Inflation Rate Rises Above Forecasts in March*. Tradingeconomics.Com; TRADING ECONOMICS. https://tradingeconomics.com/united-states/inflation-cpi

Graham, B., Buffett, W. E., & Zweig, J. (2013). *The intelligent investor: a book of practical counsel*. Harper Collins.

History of Options Trading - How Options Came About. (2017). Optionstrading.Org. https://www.optionstrading.org/history/

Mackay, C. (2014). *Extraordinary popular delusions and the madness of crowds*. Maestro Reprints.

Nagarajan, shalini. (2020, May 1). *Bill Ackman turned a $27 million bet into $2.6 billion in a genius investment. Here are 12 of the best trades of all time. | Markets Insider*. Markets.Businessinsider.Com. https://markets.businessinsider.com/news/stocks/best-trades-of-all-time-big-short-soros-ackman-bass-2020-5-1029198259

Russel, J. (2009). *Prevent Losses in Your Forex Trading*. The Balance. https://www.thebalance.com/why-do-forex-traders-lose-money-1344936

Schatzker, E. (2020, May 7). *Bloomberg - Are you a robot?* Www.Bloomberg.-Com. https://www.bloomberg.com/news/articles/2020-05-07/paul-tudor-jones-buys-bitcoin-says-he-s-reminded-of-gold-in-70s

Schroeder, A. (2009). *The snowball: Warren Buffett and the business of life*. Bantam Books.

Smith, S. (2019, May 15). *What Percentage of Options Expire Worthless?* Stocknews.Com. https://stocknews.com/what-percentage-of-options-explore-worthless-2019-05/

Wathen, J. (2013, November 16). *3 of Warren Buffett's Weirdest Investments*. The Motley Fool. https://www.fool.com/investing/general/2013/11/16/3-of-warren-buffetts-weirdest-investments.aspx

What Are The Tax Implications of Covered Calls? (2020, January 20). Www.-Fidelity.Com. https://www.fidelity.com/learning-center/investment-products/options/generating-income-with-covered-calls/tax-implications-covered-calls

CREDIT SPREAD OPTIONS FOR BEGINNERS

TURN YOUR MOST BORING STOCKS INTO RELIABLE MONTHLY PAYCHECKS USING CALL, PUT & IRON BUTTERFLY SPREADS - EVEN IF THE MARKET IS DOING NOTHING

INTRODUCTION

As the stock market continues its improbable rise from the lows caused by the pandemic earlier in 2020, a new retail trading phenomenon is taking hold. Thanks to the creation of zero commissions and zero fee options trading, everyone with a Robinhood account seems to be buying out of the money (OTM) call options on stocks and profiting massively. The tech stock driven rally fueled this boom, and suddenly, everyone was "trading" options successfully.

As with stocks, it's easy to make money with options in a market that goes up all the time. However, when the tides turn, it turns out that just writing calls on momentum stocks doesn't work so well. We witnessed this in September 2020 when companies such as Tesla and Apple that had been going up without any end in sight, suddenly began going the other way. Resulting in many investors left holding onto worthless OTM calls.

In an ideal world, you'd always face one of the following two scenarios.

1. You buy a stock (or buy a call option), and the price immediately skyrockets.
2. You short a stock (or buy a put option), and the price immediately plummets.

However, in the real world, stock prices don't work like this. In fact, they don't experience too many strong trending moves. While it's easy to point at the previous decade and say that the markets have been rising all the time, this rise was punctuated by long stretches of sideways movements.

The kind of exponential rise that most novice investors expect rarely happens in reality. For the most part, around 80-85% of the time, markets tend to move sideways or slightly upwards. This lack of movement makes directional trading extremely difficult.

Both long-term investors and more active traders can find these sideways periods boring. For investors, the fear of missing out sets in as you see stocks you don't own rising in price, while the ones you do own remain flat. For traders, these periods are when they shoot themselves in the foot because of their compulsive need to do *something*. Being an active trader requires you to participate in all market conditions, and this automatically means making consistent profits is a lot harder. Most active traders resent sideways moves since these moves make it impossible to profit from price differences. You can't buy low and sell high (or vice versa) in a sideways market, after all.

HOW TO WIN CONSISTENTLY

Active traders have a problem with sideways markets because their default approach is to try and predict the market's direction. This means they spend their time looking for directional cues and use all the tools at their disposal to figure out the short-term direction of the instrument they're trading. When presented with the fact that the markets move sideways, for the most part, they simply shrug and look at sideways markets as obstacles to be overcome.

We contend that if the markets are sideways-bound for the most part, surely it makes more sense to use *non-directional* trading strategies. After all, why should you attempt to swim against the tide when you can make money swimming with it.

Every investor and trader's wish is to generate more consistency in their results. A secondary wish might be to show screenshots of 2,000% gains to their family and friends. We're sorry to say, none of the strategies inside this book will net you 2,000% on a single trade. Instead, this book will help you generate consistent returns month after month while not losing sleep over your positions. In our opinion, that's the acid test that every strategy has to fulfill. This means, whether you're an investor looking to generate additional income from your portfolio, or a directional trader looking for strategies to employ in a sideways market, you're in the right place.

It's fully possible to build a non-directional trading strategy that generates reliable profits using options. That is our aim with this book. You don't need to learn a ton of complicated chart patterns or 100 different indicators to make the strategy presented in this book work. *Credit spreads* might sound like a complicated name for a strategy, but once you understand how they work and how they can be best structured, you can implement them in no time at all.

BEING *ALMOST* CORRECT IS EASIER THAN BEING *EXACTLY* CORRECT

The core reason these strategies work well is that it's far easier to guess a price range than guess a specific price that a stock will rise/fall to.

Think of it this way. If someone were to ask you what a Rolls Royce Phantom costs, would you be able to guess the price correctly, down to the last cent? Unless you happen to be mad about luxury cars, probably not. However, you can think of an approximate price range quite easily. Even if you only have a cursory knowledge of cars, just the Rolls Royce brand alone is a good indicator. So you could guess that this particular model of car cost "around" half a million dollars.*[1]

What if you could make money guessing stock prices in such approximations? That's the essence of building credit spreads. You can build spreads to take advantage of any market condition, even highly bullish and bearish ones. However, one of the main benefits is that credit spreads also work well in sideways markets. As the markets move sideways most of the time, these strategies will help you take advantage of them.

Many investors want to generate reliable income every month using simple strategies. We will present simple strategies later in this book, which anyone with a basic knowledge of options and the markets can use.

When we say "basic knowledge" we mean that you don't need to understand the specifics of Option Greeks or know 200 different chart patterns. But you will need to know what a call option is and how it's different from a put option. If you are a complete beginner, then you can get up to speed quickly with our free guide *Options 101,* which you can find in the bonus resources section at https://freemanpublications.com/bonus

But don't worry. We will immediately define any new terminology that we introduce throughout this book. So we hope that generating steady and even boring returns is far more appealing to you than generating rockstar-like returns punctuated by severe drawdowns. If a stable, consistent monthly income is what you're after, you've come to the right place.

Once you make these simple strategies a part of your overall investing skillset, you'll realize that you probably won't need many other options trading strategies.

---

1. *For those of you who are into specifics, the base price of the 2020 Rolls Royce Phantom is $457,750

1

WHY SELLING OPTIONS THROUGH CREDIT SPREADS IS THE BEST APPROACH

If you've traded options before, you probably remember the first time you bought them. We emphasize the word "bought" because this is the typical way in which novice investors use options. Their affinity for buying options is a holdover from the way they think about the stock market. In stocks, buying comes more naturally than selling.

On the surface, shorting a stock seems a lot less complicated than shorting or writing an option. When you short a stock, you're betting on its price to decrease, and you wait for it to hit lower price levels. With options, there is more risk to shorting. Technically, a stock can rise forever, while your downside risk is capped at the stock falling to zero. For this reason, many brokers explicitly display the warning that shorting or writing options is risky, and you should carefully consider the terms before choosing to do so.

This leads beginner options traders to conclude that selling (also known as writing) options is always risky when this isn't the case. It's true that writing options naked is an unintelligent move and is extremely risky. A naked option is a position where your downside risk isn't covered. However, if you cover your downside risk, writing options is one of the least risky things you can do in the markets.

For example, in our previous book, *Covered Calls for Beginners* we highlighted the covered call strategy, which is another way to make extra cash when the market is doing nothing. This strategy requires you to write a call option while holding a long position on the underlying stock (this can also be an index or ETF). If the stock price goes up above your call option strike, you sell the stock at a profit, plus get the extra option premium. If the price goes down or stays the same, you get to keep your option premium.

Options offer many opportunities to build flexibility into your overall investing approach. It's why we favor using them in sideways markets. Writing options under the right conditions and within the right strategies is a good move because it allows you to take advantage of how options contracts are built.

If you're entirely new to the idea of selling options, here is the crucial point to remember at this stage; Buying options requires you to predict prices, but when you sell options you don't need to do so.

THE ADVANTAGES OF SELLING OPTIONS

The fact that you don't necessarily need to predict prices when writing options means you only need to predict if the underlying instrument (be it a stock or an index) will finish within a range. With the Rolls Royce example, we saw that predicting a price range is easier than an exact price. There are other advantages to writing options as well.

Time Decay is in Your Favor

Options contracts have a defined expiry date and have premiums attached to them. The longer there is until the option expires, the greater is the value of the premium. Therefore, options sellers are always in a position to capture the highest premium - no matter what happens to the underlying stock.

Upon writing an option, the seller keeps the premium, irrespective of what happens to the underlying. On the other hand, the buyer forfeits the premium, which forms a hurdle they need to overcome to make a profit. It's true that the underlying could always move to such an extent that the premium paid is negligible. However, that's moving into the world of directional trading. If you're going to be right predicting the direction of the market, you're just as likely to be wrong.

The option seller can be wrong as well, but there are ways to remove this directional dependency. First, the premium you pocket provides a cushion against losses. The key part of selling options is to cover the risk of the underlying moving against you. While it takes a little more understanding than your average stock trade, covering your downside risk means you can focus on predicting a price range, an approximate band within which the underlying will end up in, instead of needing to predict exact prices.

The second major advantage of this approach is you don't have to worry about whether you need to exit the trade or not. For example, if the underlying moves in an extremely volatile manner and reaches within a dollar of your profit target, you don't have to debate whether you should take a profit or not. In fact, by using the rule-based exit strategies we'll explain later, you don't need to even consider this scenario.

You Can Build Spread Trades

The strategies highlighted in this book are net credit spread options trades. These trades are part of a larger universe of trades called spread trades. Despite their ominous-sounding name, believe it or not, they're not as complicated as they sound.

We already discussed how by using options, you can bet on the markets' direction within a fixed period of time. Whether it will go up, down, or remain sideways. With net credit spreads, you remove the need for a directional bias in your predictions.

A huge benefit of no longer needing a direction bias is that your trades win more often. It isn't unheard of for spread traders to have eight, nine, or even 10 winning trades in a row.

This is because the profit amounts you earn are small but steady. Compare this to the boom and bust cycle that follows most directional traders, and you'll see how spread traders sleep much better at night.

Most directional traders have win percentages of 30-40%, or three to four winners out of 10. This is a stressful way to trade since win and loss distributions don't follow pre-ordained patterns. With a win percentage of 40%, it's incredibly likely that a trader will experience 10 losses in a row at a certain point. Losing money repeatedly and being able to still stick to one's strategy is tough to do. How many of us can genuinely claim to not care about 10 losers in a row?

Contrast this to the world of the spread trader. Your losses might be larger than your average wins, but they're far less frequent. This makes it easier to absorb from a mental standpoint. The probability of a long losing streak is close to zero, while an extended win streak is much higher. From a psychological point of view, spread traders find it easier to stick to their principles and make more money over the long term.

You Don't Have To Be Right

Credit spread trades don't require you to be right. You can guess a range of prices that the underlying will land in at the expiry date, and still make money. This alleviates a lot of pressure on your shoulders. If you've ever traded directionally, you'll know that one of the first rules of good risk management is to let go of the need to be right.

Successful directional traders truly let go of the need to be right and end up making a lot of money. However, the average trader who aspires to be successful finds this extremely tough to do. While it isn't an impossible target to achieve, it takes a lot of mental training and awareness to trade from true detachment from profits. The choice facing someone new to options is quite simple. You can choose to scale the directional trading mountain, or you can opt for an easier goal.

If there's an easier path to take, why not choose that instead of making things harder for yourself?

Lower Capital Requirements

Unlike other strategies which require a lot of capital to get going, it's relatively easy to get started trading credit spreads. You don't need to have much money in your account.

While this claim certainly isn't unique to credit spreads, in fact many stock and options strategies will tell you that you can get started with a small account. However, this is just a surface-level view and somewhat misleading. Dig a little deeper, and another picture emerges.

While you don't need too much money to open a brokerage account and start trading stocks directionally, you'll eventually run into the Pattern Day Trader rule (PDT). The PDT states that anyone who places more than four trades in a consecutive five-day period needs to maintain at least $25,000 in their trading account. This is an extremely high amount of money that the average retail investor doesn't have.

Most credit spread trades run for around 30 days. This means you can enter two or three trades over a week and have them run for a month. You won't be adding to these positions or subtracting from them in the interim. Most of them will close themselves out at expiry by expiring worthless, so there's no trade you need to place.

This keeps well away from the clutches of PDT. Plus, unlike covered calls, you don't need to buy underlying stock to cover your risk of writing options. This means you truly can earn a steady income with a small amount of capital and with a few trades every month. Your trade setups will cover your downside risk automatically, so there's no need for you to post a maintenance margin, unlike with short stock trades.

You can get started trading credit spreads with as little as $1,000 in your account (theoretically, even starting with $500 is possible – although your choices will be more limited)

Win Probabilities

The success rate of credit spreads is high, as we mentioned earlier. It's not unheard of to have more than eight winners in a row. By our estimate, the hit rate of a solid net credit spread strategy is somewhere between 65-85%. Your precise win rate will depend on how you set up your trade and the kind of spreads you create. However, you can reasonably expect to land somewhere in this spot. As we highlighted earlier, this makes it a lot easier for you to trade within your rules, and you're less likely to get desperate and engage in revenge trading.

Synthetic Dividends

In our previous book on covered calls, we explained how you can generate what we call "synthetic dividends" by selling options. With covered calls, we wrote OTM options that were backed by long positions in the underlying stock. The premium that we earned by writing calls gave us income every month that was akin to receiving a dividend from our shares.

With credit spreads, selling options allows you to earn income, whether you own the underlying shares or not. Whether the underlying finishes in your target range or not, you still keep the premium you earned from selling the option, which acts as a handy buffer against losses. Over the long run, the income you earn from selling options provides an excellent additional boost to the capital gains from your long-term investments. This is what makes credit spreads such a powerful strategy.

Writing options also opens up the entire world of stocks to you. Many investors, especially those approaching retirement, are keen on generating income from their portfolio. Typically you would rely on dividends to do this. However, not every stock or fund pays a dividend. On top of this, many so-called dividend darling stocks like AT&T pay large dividends at the expense of low capital gains. Writing options allows you to buy a stock, whether it pays a dividend or not. If you're buying it for increased capital gains, you can still generate income on it. This allows you to capture the best of both worlds.

Defined Risk and Reward

The strategies you will learn in this book are what are called defined risk and reward strategies. You'll know your maximum risk and maximum reward before you enter the trade. Because of this, almost all brokers will allow you to sell credit spreads without needing any extra permissions on your account.

This feature contrasts with directional stock trading strategies where your reward and downside risk are not defined. While stop loss orders may claim to provide a veneer of risk protection, they're prone to get jumped by the market in reality, which results in traders realizing larger losses than planned. Stop loss jumps often happen when markets are extremely volatile, which is a Catch-22 situation because volatile markets are the condition that you placed your stop loss to deal with in the first place

Every directional trader faces a few moments of anxiety when the market hangs around their desired profit or stop loss levels without hitting them. In such times, traders need to decide whether they ought to take a lower profit and guaranteed money or whether they ought to let the trade run for longer. The only sure result is mental turmoil.

However, selling an option works differently. A credit spread trade has fixed risk limits thanks to the strike prices of your option. Unlike stop loss orders, the market cannot skip strike prices. They're a part of your options contract, and you're guaranteed that price no matter what. As long as the option hasn't expired and your position is ITM, your strike price must be honored.

This means your downside risk is always protected, and your maximum profit is also defined. By choosing the size of your spreads you can pick and choose your desired risk to reward ratios and design setups accordingly. You can trade with much greater freedom when you choose to set up credit spread trades. A huge unexpected move in either direction is not going to affect you.

You Don't Need To Be Present 24/7

The trading terminal is a constant companion of directional traders. Even during the off hours, they need to monitor news releases and volatility inducing events that might affect their positions' value. They need to track events like this because of the chance that their risk limits might be breached. If overnight volatility creates a gap in the markets on open the next day, their stop loss or take profit levels will not matter too much. If there isn't any liquidity in the markets, these levels will get jumped, and the consequences could be fatal to their account. Meaning that the average directional trader has to constantly make decisions.

This is not how credit spread traders operate. For starters, the length of an average credit spread trade is around a month. This means there's more time to operate, and you can take your time when analyzing your positions.

FREEMAN CREDIT SPREAD RULE #1

THE BEST CREDIT SPREAD SETUPS ARE ONES WHICH DON'T REQUIRE YOU TO SPEND ALL DAY MONITORING YOUR TRADES

The bottom line is that as an options writer, you do not need to be glued to your screen. In fact, with credit spread trades, allowing your trade to ride instead of grabbing whatever profits you can get is the best approach to make more money.

Now we've highlighted the benefits of credit spreads, let's dive in and see how they work.

2

CREDIT SPREADS ARE MUCH SIMPLER THAN YOU THINK

"I fear not the man who has practiced 10,000 kicks once. I fear the man who has practiced one kick 10,000 times."

— *BRUCE LEE*

Thanks to their name and the fact that their setups appear more complex than the average directional trade, credit spreads are often tagged as an "advanced" options trading strategy. This is a mistake as far as we're concerned. Credit spreads are much simpler than you think, and trading them is no more complex than setting up a basic directional trade.

New traders often get confused because of the large number of variants within the spread trade category. All spread trades can be classified into two major categories: net credit and net debit. In this book, we're looking at net credit spreads. These are trades which will put money into your account as soon as you enter the trade. Net debit trades on the other hand cost you money to enter, much like a directional trade does.

Generally speaking, net debit trades are far more directionally dependent than net credit trades. However, as we previously mentioned, most markets and instruments often move sideways or slightly upwards. They rarely ever move forcefully in any direction. This means a net credit spread is a better option.

Within the category of net credit spreads, there are over 25 ways to set up a trade. Traditional options education material list all of these strategies and expect beginners to understand them immediately. We believe this is a mistake. No one can learn two trade setups so quickly. It also propagates the false view that you need to create complexity in your strategies to succeed. In our view, there are just three net credit spreads that you should learn to make a solid amount of extra cash each month.

TRADE SETUPS

Before jumping into the individual trade setups that will make you money, we'd like to address another point of confusion. Spread trades are also classified as horizontal or vertical. Horizontal spreads (also called calendar spreads) are actually just a few trade setups, while vertical spreads have many setups within them.

A horizontal spread is constructed by buying or selling a near month option and also buying or selling a far month option of the same strike price. The idea is to assume the opposite direction in either leg. For example, if the near month option is sold, the far month is bought and vice versa. The type of option is also the same. Usually, calls are used, but it's possible to use puts as well.

A vertical spread on the other hand, is where you buy and sell options with different strike prices that expire on the same date. They are called vertical spreads because of the way option prices are displayed. Figure 1 illustrates this point.

DIS > DIS OPTION CHAIN

DIS Option Chain

Date: January 2021 | Option: Composite | Calls & Puts: Calls & Puts | Moneyness: Near the Money | Type: All (Types)

	Calls							Puts					
Exp. Date	Last	Change	Bid	Ask	Volume	Open Int.	Strike	Last	Change	Bid	Ask	Volume	Open Int.
January 22, 2021													
Jan 22	16.85	[illegible] ▲	--	--	4	281	160.00	0.23	-0.14 ▼	--	--	100	1076
Jan 22	14.15	[illegible] ▲	--	--	10	93	162.50	0.34	-0.15 ▼	--	--	14	195
Jan 22	11.65	--	--	--	11	168	165.00	0.47	[illegible] ▼	--	--	69	1415
Jan 22	9.45	[illegible] ▲	--	--	20	79	167.50	0.70	-0.25 ▼	--	--	257	574
Jan 22	7.05	-0.53 ▼	--	--	164	705	170.00	1.07	-0.33 ▼	--	--	181	1075
Jan 22	5.24	[illegible] ▼	--	--	78	421	172.50	1.68	-0.42 ▼	--	--	79	748
Jan 22	3.90	[illegible] ▼	--	--	442	1237	175.00	2.60	-0.49 ▼	--	--	166	1085
Jan 22	2.73	-0.26 ▼	--	--	765	998	177.50	3.85	[illegible] ▼	--	--	188	557
Jan 22	1.84	-0.24 ▼	--	--	1181	2597	180.00	5.55	-0.37 ▼	--	--	85	707
Jan 22	1.27	-0.19 ▼	--	--	263	842	182.50	7.60	[illegible] ▼	--	--	8	113
Jan 22	0.85	-0.17 ▼	--	--	638	1612	185.00	9.45	-0.25 ▼	--	--	13	73
Jan 22	0.59	-0.11 ▼	--	--	85	894	187.50	11.00	[illegible] ▲	--	--	4	19
Jan 22	0.43	[illegible] ▼	--	--	228	1339	190.00	14.10	--	--	--	--	25
Jan 22	0.32	-0.05 ▼	--	--	22	576	192.50	13.10	--	--	--	--	6

Figure 1: The Disney Options Chain for September 4, 2020 (Source: Nasdaq.com)

We'll be focusing on the three basic vertical net credit spreads. These three are the easiest to implement.

BULL PUT SPREADS

The first vertical net credit spread we'll look at is the bull put spread. The setup is vertical because all the options bought and sold expire in the same month. This trade setup has two legs:

- One short ITM put
- One long OTM put

As a refresher, ITM and OTM refer to "in the money" and "out of the money." A put is ITM when the underlying price is less than the strike price. The put can be exercised for a profit in this scenario. A call is ITM when the underlying price is greater than the strike price. Conversely, a put is OTM when the underlying price is greater than the strike price. A call is OTM when the underlying price is less than the strike price.

Writing the ITM option will put money in your pocket. Since it's ITM, you'll receive a large premium for it. The OTM option will cost you less and covers your downside risk. This setup allows you to profit from moderately bullish or range-bound conditions. If the stock price rises or it moves sideways in a range, the setup makes you money. Let's look at a hypothetical example to see how it works.

Say you're interested in SolarEdge Technologies (NASDAQ:SEDG), which is trading at $280. You don't know the exact price the stock will be in 30 days time. However you think it's likely to rise to $300 over the next month at the very least and that it's unlikely to fall below $265 in the same period. This is the "guessing a range" portion we spoke about in the introduction. Let's say the options are priced as below:

290 ITM put premium = $8

270 OTM put premium = $2

Writing the ITM put will net you $8 per share, while buying the OTM put will cost you $2 per share. Your net credit on entering the trade is $6 (8 - 2), which you will receive upfront. This is also your maximum profit on the trade.

Note: Remember that each option contract represents 100 shares of the underlying. So a credit of $6 per contract equates to $600 in your account.

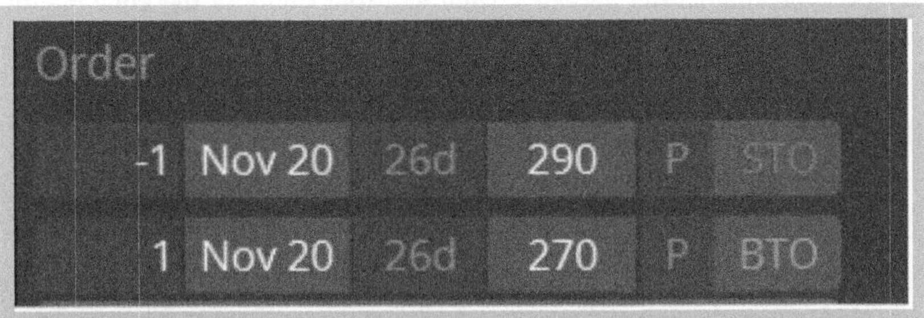

Figure 2: How a Bull Put Spread is constructed in your broker. You are selling 1 OTM put option at 290, and buying 1 ITM put option at 270. For this example, we used the November 20th options, which had 26 days to expiry at the time the screen capture was taken (source: Tastyworks)

If your maximum profit is $6, what about your maximum loss on the trade? With credit spreads, your maximum loss is always equal to the difference between the strike prices of the long and short put, minus the premium you received for entering the spread. In this case, you wrote the short put at 290, and bought the long put at 270. Which means the distance between the strike prices is 20. Because you received $6 for entering the trade, and you get to keep this no matter what, therefore your maximum loss is $14 per option contract (20 – 6). Walking through various scenarios will help you understand how these numbers come about.

Scenario #1 - Let's say the underlying closes at $310 at expiry. In this scenario, your short put has finished OTM (since the underlying price is greater than the strike price.) It therefore expires worthless, and you get to keep the full premium. Meanwhile, your long OTM put remains OTM, and you will lose the $2 premium. Therefore, your profit is fixed at the $6 per share that you earned upon entry.

If the underlying closes at any price greater than $290, this is how much you'll earn. This is the maximum profit scenario.

Maximum profit = Premium earned from short put - Premium paid for long put = (8 – 2) = $6 per share

Scenario #2 - If the underlying remains firmly in place, doesn't cross 290 and stays above 270 before expiry, here's what will happen. Your short put will remain ITM and your long put will remain OTM. Your short put will be assigned to you, which means you'll need to buy the stock from the option buyer for $290 per share. If the underlying is trading at $280, you'll carry an unrealized loss of $10 per share. You can either hold onto the stock and hope it rises back above $290 or you can sell it at the market price and eat the $10 loss. Your long put remains OTM, and you'll give up the premium paid.

Loss = Stock sale price - Short put strike price + (Premium received for short put - Premium paid for long put) = (280 - 290 + 6) = -$4

You begin to lose money on this setup if the underlying closes below the short put upon expiry.

Scenario #3 - The third scenario occurs when the underlying finishes below the long put at expiry. If our stock closes at $260, here's what our options look like. The short put remains ITM and the long put also moves ITM. We'll need to buy the stock at $290 since this is the strike of the short put. However, we can sell the stock at $270 since the long option is now ITM. This means no matter how low the underlying moves, our loss is capped to $20 per share.

Loss = Strike price of long put - Strike price of short put + (Premium received for short put - Premium paid for long put) = (270 - 290 + 6) = -$14

As you can see, the maximum profit is fixed and will be earned as long as the short put finishes OTM at expiry. This makes sense because the bull put spread is a strategy we employ when we are generally bullish on the stock's prospects.

Once again, each option contract equals 100 shares of stock, so a maximum loss of $14 per contract represents $1,400 in real terms.

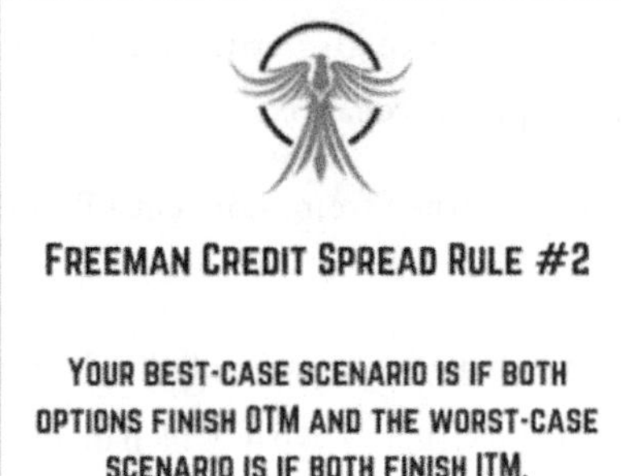

BEAR CALL SPREAD

This is a bearish spread that looks to capture slightly bearish or range-bound movements in the underlying. Like the bull put spread, this setup has two legs to it:

- One long OTM call
- One short ITM call

Writing the ITM call will net you a premium that will be greater than the premium you have to pay for the OTM call. Like the bull put spread there are three scenarios that can result in either a profit or a loss with this setup. The first is if the underlying closes above the OTM call. In this situation, both calls will be ITM, and your maximum loss is realized. You'll have to sell the underlying at the lower strike price, but you can buy it at the higher strike, thereby capping your loss.

If the underlying finishes between the range within the two calls, your loss is equal to the price of the short call minus the underlying price. Your long call will expire worthless. The third scenario is if the underlying finishes below the short call and both options expire worthless. In this scenario, you'll keep the maximum profit, which is the net credit you receive on entry.

Let's look at an example to clarify how this works. We'll use the same numbers from our previous example. This time we are bearish on SolarEdge Technologies, which is currently trading at $280. So we buy a call at $290, and we write a call at $270. Our opinion is that the stock is going to fall below $270, but is unlikely to rise above $290. Let's assume the calls are selling for $8 (270 call) and $2 (290 call).

Figure 3: How a Bear Call Spread is constructed in your broker. You are selling 1 OTM call option at 270, and buying 1 ITM call option at 290. For this example, we used the November 20th options, which had 26 days to expiry at the time the screen capture was taken (source: Tastyworks)

Scenario #1 - The underlying closes at $300. In this case, both of our calls are ITM and we'll need to sell the underlying to the 270 option's buyer. However, we can buy the underlying at 290 thanks to our long call being ITM. Therefore:

Maximum loss = Strike price of short call - Strike price of long call + (Premium received from writing ITM call - Premium paid for OTM call) = (270 - 290 + 6) = -$14

Scenario #2 - The underlying closes between the two strikes. The long call remains OTM and the short call is ITM. Your loss is limited to the difference between the underlying price (let's say this is $280) and the ITM call's strike price, minus the credit received on entry:

Loss = Underlying price - Strike price of long call + (Premium received from writing ITM call - Premium paid for OTM call) = (280 - 290 + 6) = -$4

Scenario #3 - The underlying closes below both calls, moving them both OTM. In this case, you'll keep the full credit you received on entry. This is also your maximum profit on the trade:

Profit = (Premium received from writing ITM call - Premium paid for OTM call) = (8 - 2) = $6

Risk/Reward

Another feature of these two setups is that the maximum loss is far greater than the maximum profit. In both scenarios, our maximum loss is $14, while our maximum profit is $6. This gives us a risk/reward ratio of 42%.

If you've traded directionally, you'll realize that this is a highly skewed risk-to-reward ratio. In the directional world, such a strategy isn't worth sniffing at. However, remember that this strategy's win rate is much higher than what you can expect with a directional trade.

Let's say we have 10 trades with a risk/reward ratio of 30%, and we win eight out of 10 trades, with a max profit per trade of $100 and a max loss of $300. Assuming we either capture the maximum profit or suffer a maximum loss on our trades, our overall profit would be:

- Trade 1: Win +$100
- Trade 2: Win +$100
- Trade 3: Win +$100
- Trade 4: Loss -$300

- Trade 5: Win +$100
- Trade 6: Loss -$300
- Trade 6: Win +$100
- Trade 7: Win + $100
- Trade 8: Win +$100
- Trade 9: Win +$100
- Trade 10: Win +$100

So our net profit after 10 trades is ($800 - $600) = $200. An 80% win rate might sound fanciful for directional traders, but remember that with credit spreads you're not dependent on predicting the finishing price. You can increase your win rate to this level or more by constructing OTM spreads, as we illustrated just now. Your reward-to-risk ratio will fall, but you'll win a huge number of your trades.

This doesn't mean vertical credit spreads will result in wins 100% of the time. You'll need your options to expire worthless or you'll have to buy your short options back for prices lower than what you sold them for. Of course, if the trade moves against you, you'll only be able to minimize your loss and not avert it altogether.

SHORT IRON BUTTERFLY SPREAD

This setup is the third vertical spread we'll be looking at in this book. The name of this setup is confusing and, in fact, experienced options traders disagree on how to name this. You'll find them calling this strategy the long iron butterfly as well. To dispel any confusion, we wish to clarify that we're referring to the iron butterfly setup that results you establishing a net credit on entry.

The iron butterfly is a combination of a bull put spread and a bear call spread. The setup is designed to generate a profit from a sideways move in the markets, or mildly bullish or bearish moves. Like the Iron Condor, which we wrote about in our book *Iron Condor Options for Beginners*, the trade earns a profit in a specific range on both the long and short side. However, unlike the Iron Condor, the sweet spot is smaller. The flip side is that the maximum profit you can earn is a lot higher than what you can earn on the Condor.

There are four legs to an Iron Butterfly trade:

- 1 long OTM call
- 1 short ATM call
- 1 short ATM put
- 1 long OTM put

The key feature of the Iron Butterfly is that the short call and short put **have the same strike price**. This means the bear call spread portion of the trade and the bull put portion overlap with one another. If the underlying closes right at the strike price of the two short legs, you'll realize your maximum profit. You might think that this means you need to predict price, but this is not true.

What happens is that the short legs, since they're written at the money (ATM), generate a large premium that gives you a range within which the stock can finish and still yield you a profit. It's just that to realize the maximum profit, you need to predict the price accurately. In this setup, the maximum profit isn't realized as often as on the two-legged vertical spreads we discussed earlier. However, since the trade combines two vertical spreads into one, your average profit is a lot higher than on a two-legged spread trade.

Let's look at an example to see how this works. Currently, Visa (NYSE:V) is trading at $200.99. We'll set up our Iron Butterfly as follows:

- Buy one $190 put for $1.98
- Sell one $200 put for $5.40
- Sell one $200 call for $6.10
- Buy one $210 call for $2.34

The credit we receive on entry = Premium received from writing the 200 call + premium received from writing the 200 put - cost of the long 190 call - cost of the long 190 put = (5.40 + 6.10 - 1.98 - 2.34) = $7.18 per share. Each options contract carries 100 shares of the underlying with it. This means our credit totals to $718.

The maximum loss this trade will realize is the difference in the strike prices between the long and short options legs, minus the premium received on entry. When constructing the trade, the distance between the long and short legs of the trade needs to be equidistant in both spreads. The distance between the long and short call should be the same as the distance between the long and shot put. In this case, this distance equals $10.

The maximum loss is = (Distance between strike prices - credit received on entry) * 100 shares per contract = (10 - 7.18) * 100 = $282

Since we receive a credit on entry, the trade has a buffer to it. This means our upper break even limit is the strike price of the short put plus the credit received:

Upper break even limit = Strike price of short put + net credit received = $200 + $7.18 = $207.18

Similarly, the lower break even limit = Strike price of short call - net credit received = $200 - $7.18 = $192.82.

The reward profile of the Iron Butterfly is illustrated in Figure 4 below.

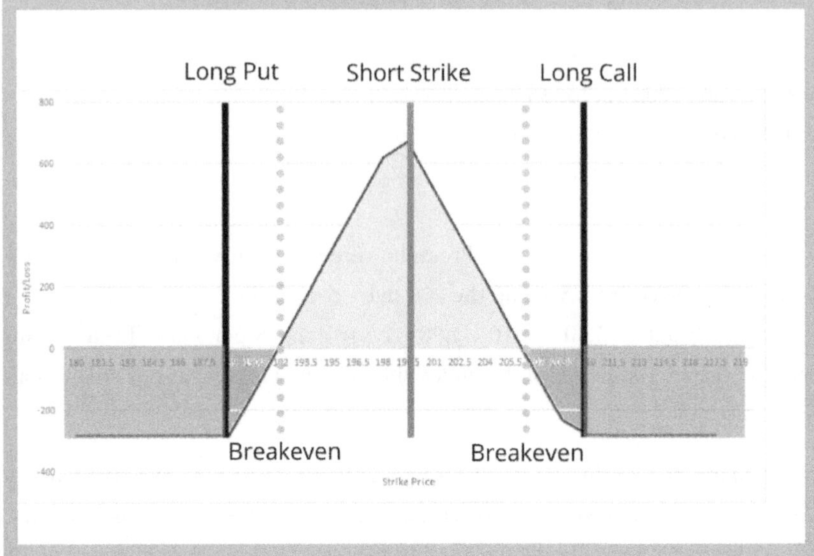

Figure 4: The Above Short Butterfly Spread Visualized

As long as the underlying finishes between $192.82 and $207.18 at expiry, this trade will be in profit. This is the profit range that we alluded to earlier. The maximum profit, which is the net credit realized on entry, is realized if the stock finishes at exactly $200 at expiry.

A more realistic scenario is that the price will finish somewhere close to it and we'll net a profit that is slightly lower than our maximum profit. The maximum loss is realized if the stock finishes outside the strike prices of the long call or put. These long positions limit our losses in the trade.

While you can set up the trade with ITM short calls, you can technically build a directional bias into the trade. For example, if you think the stock you're looking at will fall and then move in a range, you can set up the Iron Butterfly at a lower price than the current stock price and choose strike prices in such a way that your predicted range will be equal to your break even limits.

As with credit spreads, you can create wide butterflies, which increase your probability of a win, but your reward-to-risk ratio will decrease.

POINTS TO NOTE BEFORE TRADING CREDIT SPREADS

There are a few issues you need to consider before trading these three setups. The first is to see whether you can trade these within an IRA. The answer is yes, but it depends on your broker. Generally speaking, brokers allow you to trade defined risk strategies within your IRA. The above 3 setups are considered defined risk, since the long options legs limit your loss, your broker should allow you to trade them. If you are unsure, or your account doesn't appear to allow you to sell credit spreads, then call your broker on the phone and ask them to enable credit spreads in your account.

The next issue is one of trade management. What if you enter the trade and find that your assumptions are incorrect or that the trade is moving against you? We'll deal with this in great detail in the chapter on trade management. Managing your options trades is simple when you do so from a rule-based perspective. We'll give you all the rules you need to consider before changing the structure of your trade.

The next and perhaps biggest issue to consider is that of early assignment risk.

Early Assignment Risk

You'll notice that in all of these setups, we're writing ITM options. Generally speaking, options are not assigned (when the buyer exercises their ITM option and converts their option into shares of stock) until expiry. However, it's not as if this can never happen. By writing an ITM option, we're constructing a trade that requires the stock to move a certain distance before we can realize our maximum profit. This involves a certain degree of risk.

For instance, let's assume that when constructing our bull put spread, the underlying does move to a level that pushes both options OTM at expiry. However, if the ITM option was assigned to us well before expiry, at a point in time when the underlying was still in between the two strikes, we'll take a loss on this trade (Scenario #2 in our previous examples.)

Every once in a while, this will happen and will cause you to take a loss despite being right about the market's direction.

To mitigate this risk, you can construct your spreads at different levels. In the case of the bull put spread, you're assuming that the stock will rise. Since you're writing an ITM put, you need the underlying to move above the ITM put and push it OTM. What if the stock doesn't rise or if you're assigned the option before expiry? To mitigate this risk, you can construct the spread differently. Instead of writing an ITM put, you can write an ATM or slightly OTM put.

From our example, the underlying was trading at $280. Instead of writing a put at $290 (which is ITM), you can write a put at $280 or $275. The long put can be bought at $270 as in the example. In this scenario, if the stock finishes in place or if it moves slightly higher, you'll still capture the maximum profit. Early assignment won't be possible since your short put is already OTM. An ITM put can be assigned, but stock price fluctuations will likely move it OTM at some point.

Similarly, when constructing a bear call spread with the underlying at $280, you can buy an OTM call at $300 but write a call slightly OTM at $285. In this situation, the stock needs to move by at least $5 to push you into a loss. Early assignation isn't a risk since both of your calls are OTM. If you wrote an ITM call, you'd begin in a position where your trade might result in a loss if the option is assigned early to you.

The flip side is that you'll exchange a lower maximum profit for the safety that these spreads bring, because OTM options will sell for less than ITM ones. However, if you're worried about early assignment, you can opt to construct spreads like this. There is no hard and fast rule that you have to write ITM options. Doing this gives you greater profits, but you open yourself up to the slim possibility of early assignment.

While early assignment is a risk, it doesn't occur, for the most part. Why is this? It has to do with the extrinsic versus intrinsic value of options. Intrinsic value is the difference between the underlying price and the option's strike price. An option only has intrinsic value if it is ITM.

Let's use Las Vegas Sands (NYSE:LVS) as an example. The stock currently trades around $55. If we buy a $50 call for $6.50, then we have $5 of intrinsic value (because the stock is worth $5 more than the option we bought), and $1.50 of extrinsic value (the price of the option minus the intrinsic value.)

If we buy a $60 call for $1, then we have $0 of intrinsic value because the option is OTM. However, since we could resell the option for $1, it still has $1 of extrinsic value.

Therefore an OTM option has only extrinsic value since it has zero intrinsic value. What this means for early assignment is that by exercising their options contract, the buyer gives up all the extrinsic value that the option has. Which means the majority of the time, if the option buyer exercises their contract early, they only capture a fraction of the profit they could realize.

For example, let's say your short ITM call with a strike of $290 was exercised 40 days before expiry. Once it is exercised, the option has zero extrinsic value. What if within 40 days, the price of the underlying rises to $300? By exercising the option early, the buyer can capture the rise in stock price from 290 to 300. However, the option premium will likely generate them a higher profit because it will gain intrinsic value while maintaining its extrinsic value as well, to a large extent. Extrinsic value will decline sharply within 30 days of expiry. Exercising beyond this range doesn't make sense.

In fact, even within the 30 day to expiry period, it isn't as if extrinsic value evaporates. Volatility and other market conditions result in an option having some degree of extrinsic value. Giving up this profit doesn't make sense.

The key to remember is that early assignment only happens in rare circumstances. You can also mitigate early assignment risk by trading cash settled index options (like SPX or RUT).

3

CHOOSING A BROKER

As easy as it is to just trade credit spreads using your regular broker, it's worth figuring out if there is a better option.

There are a few elements you need to consider before choosing a broker. Let's look at them one by one.

COMMISSIONS CHARGED

Commissions are a considerable headwind to overcome when it comes to trading. With options, there are two tiers of commissions you need to be aware of. The first is the cost of buying and selling options. This cost is similar to the commissions you'll pay when buying or selling stocks. Brokers have different structures for them, so you'll need to check which one makes the most sense for you.

Most brokers will list per contract commissions, but some will have a model where you'll pay a fixed charge up to a certain level and will then pay additional fees when you trade above this threshold. Thanks to the rise in discount brokers, these most brokers don't charge commissions on trading options contracts. They might charge fixed contract fees, this means you won't pay commissions, but you might pay 70 cents per contract. That sounds like it could get expensive, but most brokers have a maximum price per trade. For example, the contract fees on Tastyworks are capped at $10 regardless of the trade size.

Not every broker will charge you contract fees, so this makes your choice a little more confusing. Take the time to consider your trading volume and look at the fee schedule that the broker advertises. At the very least, you can expect to pay zero trading commission fees since there are so many app-based options that charge zero commissions.

The second type of fee you'll pay when trading options is assignment fees. Once again, some brokers charge zero assignment fees, but this isn't always the case. Assignment fees are what options sellers pay. Options buyers pay exercise fees. It's the same fee, except the name changes depending on which side of the trade you've assumed.

Add these fees together to take your final commissions paid into account. One broker might charge zero commissions but higher assignment fees. Remember that these fees eat away at your profits, so you need to be aware of them before trading.

When you're just starting with 1-2 contracts per trade, your total trade fees shouldn't add up to more than a few dollars.

SOFTWARE

Broker trading terminals vary greatly. The best brokers to pick are the ones who cater exclusively to active traders. These companies have the most sophisticated tools. Having said that, the platforms that these brokers provide can be quite complex, so you don't want to choose one that requires you to go through a steep learning curve.

Avoid choosing brokers who cater to long-term investors. Long-term investment is a different game entirely, and most investors don't need sophisticated charting tools or options visualization tools. In fact, many long-term investors don't even need a real-time chart.

This is not the case for options traders. Not only do you need real-time charts, you also need risk profile visualization tools like the one we highlighted in Figure 4. These tools help you enter proposed strike prices, and you'll clearly be able to see your break even points and maximum profit and loss scenarios.

You don't need standalone desktop terminals to execute these strategies. You'll be spending perhaps a few hours every month maintaining these setups, so it's not as if you need a supercomputer to make them work. A web-based software is more than enough for your needs.

Another factor to add is to make sure your broker has a good options calculator. You'll need this to walk through various scenarios.

There are great third party calculators such as the one available at optionsplaybook.com. You can use a broker that has zero or low commissions and pair it with this calculator for maximum benefit.

If your broker's charting interface is clunky, then you can use a resource such as tradingview.com. This free software allows you to draw support and resistance zones, and use technical indicators you'll need when analyzing possible setups. We'll be talking more about these later on in the book.

One more important consideration for you to consider is your broker's experience in dealing with options trading. The more experienced brokers will allow you to enter both legs of your credit spread trades at once. This makes execution and capturing optimal prices much easier than entering each leg one at a time. It also insulates you from sudden bursts of market volatility. If you were entering your legs one at a time, you might find yourself having opened one leg with the other out of position, and the numbers on your trade will have changed.

CUSTOMER SERVICE QUALITY

This should go without saying, but you need to choose a broker with a high level of customer service. Unfortunately, these days, most customer service queries are handled by chatbots. This is frustrating because you'll need to speak to a human every once in a while. Evaluating how quickly you can access a human being is an excellent metric to measure different brokers.

You can check this by typing a few questions into the chatbot software and then checking to see how soon the bot connects you through a human. If it keeps you going round in circles, then it's a good indication that the company doesn't take customer support seriously enough. Many companies will ask you to leave your number and request a callback. This isn't good enough. If your situation is an emergency, you can hardly be expected to sit around waiting for a phone call from your broker.

Another way of evaluating their service is to send them an email and look at how long they take to get back to you. In most cases, the initial response will be quick. Send a follow-up question and wait for a response. By doing this, you're checking to see what kind of customer service process the company has. Most brokers figure that once initial questions are answered via email, the person asking them ends up opening an account. This leads them to not follow up on secondary emails.

The lack of response indicates poor after-sales service, and you should stay away from such brokers. The longer a broker has been in business, the better their customer service will be.

Choose a broker that has been around for a long time and read their reviews on impartial websites like Trustpilot. Always choose a broker that is registered with the Financial Regulatory Authority or FINRA. If you're just starting out, avoid offshore brokers since all kinds of illegal and unethical behavior is possible with them.

CUSTOMER EDUCATION

Most traders don't look at the educational resources their brokers provide, and strictly speaking, you don't need these resources to succeed. However, they're a good indicator of where the broker's priorities lie. A broker that spends resources on providing free learning tools, webinars, and other educational content clearly cares about the quality of their customers' orders.

Brokers who cater to active traders typically don't invest in such resources. This doesn't mean those brokers are bad. It's just that they cater to experienced, active traders and their platforms will probably have a certain degree of sophistication that might make it difficult for you to trade immediately. Choose a broker that offers a variety of resources and you'll be just fine.

MARGIN REQUIREMENTS

To trade vertical spread options strategies, you'll need to open a margin account. This might sound intimidating if you come from a background of "margin is always bad". But don't worry, you won't be borrowing money to trade. In this case, a margin account simply refers to having enough money in your account to cover any potential trade losses.

Margin allows you to write options, and you'll have to have enough in your account to cover any potential loss. Most brokers will automatically sell ITM options at expiry if you don't have the margin to exercise them. Assignment is also done automatically. You'll receive a notice of assignment, and your account's positions will change to reflect the situation. If you're trading index options, everything will be settled in cash since you can't own an index.

Brokers typically have four or five levels of accounts that you can open. Each level determines what sort of strategies they'll allow you to trade. Buying options and writing covered calls can typically be done with a level one account without any hassle.

Because credit spreads involve selling options on assets you do not own, you will usually need a level three account. Gaining approval to open these accounts depends on your trading experience and the margin in your account. However, this is usually as simple as answering a few questions on the phone or ticking additional boxes when you open your account. Credit spreads are a risk defined strategy, so brokers do not have many hurdles which prevent you from using them.

This is why it's essential that you choose a broker who is well versed in options trading strategies and has a good amount of resources dedicated to options traders.

FEE SCHEDULE

In older times, many brokers used to get away with hiding fees within their fee schedules. This doesn't happen anymore, thanks to increased transparency. However, a few hidden fees still sneak in. For example, some brokers may charge an account maintenance fee every month if your total margin is less than $10,000. This isn't advertised as a minimum margin penalty, of course, so most people miss this fact.

There are other little fees that add up. Wire transfer fees, account statement fees, dividend check payment and legal document fees can add up over time. A good broker will post a clear and easy to understand fee schedule on their website and will also mention it in their terms of service agreement that you'll sign when you open an account.

Pay special attention to the quality of the broker's software. If it's glitchy and regularly hangs, you'll need to phone in your trades. Most brokers charge a fee for this, and it can be as high as $25 per trade. Inactivity charges are another way that brokers will make money off you. This is especially the case with brokers who target active traders. If you're transferring your balance from one broker to another, watch out for transfer fees.

These are the primary features of a broker that you must consider before choosing one. These days it's quite easy to read reviews of brokers and to figure out what their customers are saying about them. Take special note of the negative reviews. Not all of them will be legitimate, but an unusual number of reviews that mention the same problem is a good sign of something wrong with that broker.

Many brokers offer signup bonuses. These are usually free cash deposits to your account or a few commission-free trades. It's important that you ignore these promotions when choosing a broker. They don't tell you anything about the quality of service you'll receive. Always keep the quality of service and the experience of the broker in mind when choosing one.

BROKERS WE RECOMMEND FOR CREDIT SPREAD TRADING

Note: We are not affiliated with either of the companies listed below. Brokers and fees change all the time, so be sure to double check before you open an account

- Tastyworks by Tastytrade
- $1 per contract to open (capped at $10 per trade)
- Cheaper fees for trading index options
- Zero commissions to close
- Can open/close both legs of the trade simultaneously
- Easy to set up take profit targets
- Free ACH deposits & withdrawals
- Excellent education platform
- Available to European users
- Thinkorswim by TD Ameritrade
- Commission free trading for US stocks & options
- $0.65 per contract
- No assignment fees
- Easy to use software
- US users only

"CAN I USE ROBINHOOD OR WEBULL TO TRADE CREDIT SPREADS?"

We get this question from email subscribers quite a lot, as many of them are using Robinhood or WeBull to buy stocks.

The answer is… yes, but we don't recommend it.

Newer app-based solutions such as Robinhood and WeBull are a decent starting point for investing, but they're poor choices to execute credit spreads with.

For starters, you need a computer screen to execute these setups. You cannot reliably execute them using a 6" phone screen and expect to be successful. Trying to construct and manage a multiple leg strategy on a cell phone screen isn't ideal.

Combined with the fact that neither of these platforms has phone support if anything goes wrong (as you'll see in our later chapter on Tesla options), neither Robinhood nor WeBull is a good long term solution.

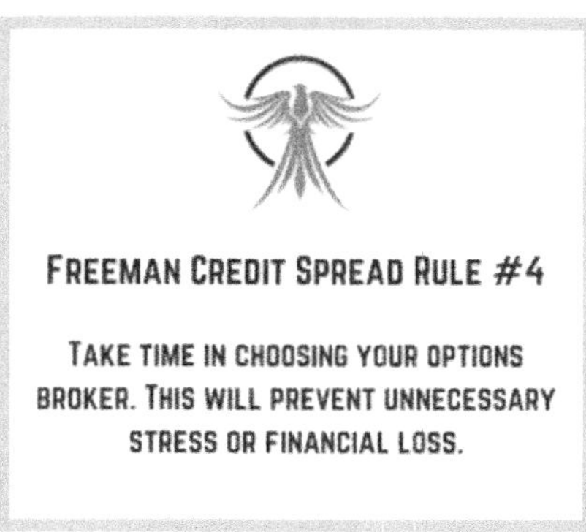

Now we've covered opening your account, let's dive deeper into understanding how to maximize your profits. First we'll cover the often-misunderstood world of option Greeks.

4

OPTION GREEKS IN 10 MINUTES

Entire books are written on option Greeks. To be frank, we could have written one ourselves. The Greeks are a great way of distilling the most important risk factors of option pricing into easily understood numbers.

By "easily understood" we speak relatively, of course. From your perspective - that is, of a market participant who has some experience with options, but isn't looking to complicate matters too much, delving deeply into all the Greeks' characteristics is pointless.

We've highlighted three strategies for you to follow in this book, and as a result we'll be highlighting just the Greeks that make the most sense for you from a trade entry and management perspective.

Keep in mind that it's possible to go even more in-depth with the Greeks than what we've covered here. Our objective is to emphasize all the relevant features that you should pay attention to for credit spreads. The first options Greek that we will use is Delta.

DELTA

Delta (Δ) measures the rate of change of an option's price relative to a price movement in the underlying.

For example, if a stock is trading at $100 and one of its calls is trading for $1, a movement in the underlying from $100 to $101 can hardly be expected to move the price of the call option from $1 to $2. That would mean a one percent move in the underlying price would result in a 100% move in the price of the call. If this were true, options would be a gold mine for everyone.

While the call might not move to that extent, it does move in some proportion to the price of the underlying. Delta gives us an exact value for how much this move will be. Delta values always range from -1 to 1 (although they are sometimes expressed as a percentage on broker platforms). Technically speaking, they range from -1 to 0 for put options and from 0 to 1 for calls. Put deltas are negative because they gain in value as the price of a stock falls.

For example, let's say we have a stock trading at $100 with a 105 strike call that is trading for $1 with a delta of 0.5.

The first thing to note is that the delta value is specific to the option, not to the underlying. Meaning options with different strike prices will have different deltas. The call with a strike price of $105 might have a Delta of 0.5, while the call at $110 might have a delta of 0.3. This means for every dollar's worth of movement in the underlying, the 105 and 110 call prices will increase by 50 cents or 30 cents, respectively.

This means if the stock moves from $100 to $101, the 105 call would be worth $1.50 and the 110 call would increase in value by 30 cents.

Similarly, if a put's delta is -0.4, the put's value would increase by 40 cents for every dollar's drop in the underlying's price. Many people make the mistake of reducing the value of the put for a price drop in the underlying due to the negative sign. However, since the value of the put increases the more the underlying drops, the put's value increases with the increase in delta.

As the price of the underlying fluctuates, so does the delta for each option. Several factors are a part of the delta calculation. The most important of them all is implied volatility or IV. This number will be listed in the option chain and is usually represented as a percentage.

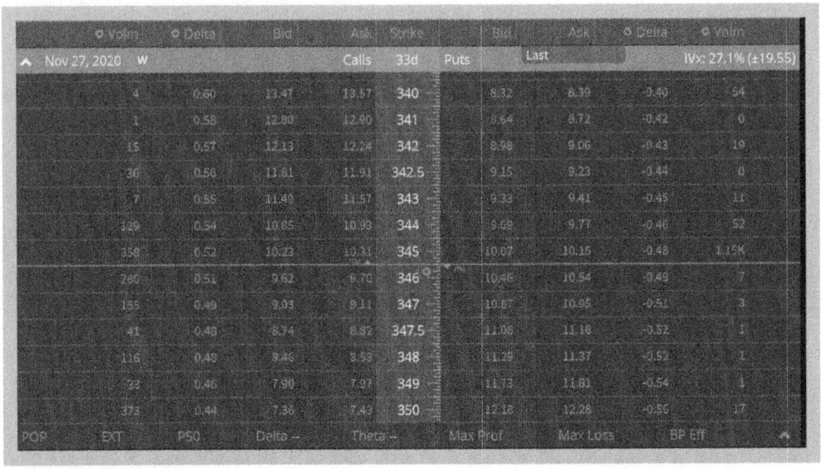

Volm	Delta	Bid	Ask	Strike	Bid	Ask	Delta	Volm
Nov 27, 2020 W			Calls	33d	Puts Last			IVx: 27.1% (±19.55)
4	0.60	13.47	13.57	340	8.32	8.39	-0.40	54
1	0.58	12.80	12.90	341	8.64	8.72	-0.42	0
15	0.57	12.13	12.24	342	8.98	9.06	-0.43	19
30	0.56	11.81	11.91	342.5	9.15	9.23	-0.44	0
7	0.55	11.49	11.57	343	9.33	9.41	-0.45	11
129	0.54	10.85	10.93	344	9.69	9.77	-0.46	52
358	0.52	10.23	10.31	345	10.07	10.15	-0.48	1.15K
280	0.51	9.62	9.70	346	10.46	10.54	-0.49	7
155	0.49	9.03	9.11	347	10.87	10.95	-0.51	3
41	0.48	8.74	8.82	347.5	11.08	11.16	-0.52	1
116	0.48	8.46	8.53	348	11.29	11.37	-0.53	1
33	0.46	7.90	7.97	349	11.73	11.81	-0.54	1
373	0.44	7.36	7.43	350	12.18	12.28	-0.56	17
POP	EXT	P50	Delta --	Theta --	Max Prof	Max Loss	BP Eff	

Figure 5: The SPY options chain with 33 days to expiry. You can see the deltas for each strike price with the call deltas on the left and the put deltas on the right. You can also see the implied volatility (27.1%) for the underlying in the top right hand corner. (Source: Tastyworks)

The IV represents the expected volatility in the stock. The greater the expected volatility is, the more expensive options traditionally are. This is because deltas increase with IV and, therefore, the price fluctuations of the options contracts increase with them. Since they're so closely tied to IV, the value of an option's delta also approximates the probability that it will finish ITM at expiry.

This means an option with a delta of 0.4 has a 40% chance of finishing ITM. We must point out that this is an approximate measurement, and there's no definitive way of predicting whether an option will finish OTM or ITM at expiry. However, you can use delta as a good proxy for figuring out how likely your option will remain OTM when you write it.

As an option moves closer to expiry, the delta of an ITM call option will move closer to 1 (-1 in the case of a put.) If the option is ATM, delta will hover around 0.5 for calls or -0.5 for puts. Once the option is OTM, delta will begin sliding towards zero. Note that the rate at which delta changes might accelerate as the contract slides towards expiry. This is especially true if the stock is volatile. In that case, you might see an option delta drop precipitously from 0.5 to 0 if it moves from being ITM to OTM.

Deltas can be extended to entire strategies as well. For example, the bear call spread is a negative delta trade since the delta of the short option will be greater than the delta of the long position. This makes intuitive sense since the setup is a bearish one that gains value if the stock slides. A bull put spread will have a positive delta because it's a bullish setup. The Iron Butterfly is a delta neutral strategy since the deltas of each leg of the trade will cancel one another.

GAMMA

Gamma (Γ) confuses a lot of traders and is often pointed to as evidence that trading options is complicated. Like every other facet of options trading, you can complicate gamma as much as you like. First, let's define what gamma is. Gamma measures the rate of change in an option's delta. Instead of measuring anything to do with the underlying price, it measures the rate at which delta changes.

For example, let's say we have an underlying stock trading at $100 and an OTM call at $105 selling for $1, with a delta of 0.5 and a gamma of 0.02. This means if the underlying moves from $100 to $101, the 105 call premium will increase from $1 to $1.50, and the delta will increase from 0.5 to 0.52. This makes intuitive sense because as the underlying gets closer to the strike price, the probability of finishing ITM increases. This means the closer the underlying price moves to the strike price, the higher delta goes. Not only does it go higher, but it also accelerates faster as well since gamma increases as well.

However, gamma's movements aren't as intuitive as delta's are. It's a second derivative of price and relating gamma back to price can get complicated. To make it easier on ourselves, we learn to think in terms of the probability of an option finishing ITM.

Gamma accelerates as an option moves from OTM to ATM. Once the option moves from ATM to ITM, it begins to decrease. Examining the behavior of delta will help us understand why this is. As an option moves from OTM to ITM, delta moves towards 0.5. It moves faster as the price inches closer to the strike price. As the option moves from being ATM to ITM, its delta moves closer to 1 (or -1 in the case of a put.) The closer it moves to 1, the shorter the distance it has to move. Therefore, its rate of change decreases as well. Hence, gamma decreases, the more an option is ITM. At some point, the delta will be 1 and it can't go higher than this. As delta stops moving, so does gamma, and it settles to 0 value.

Time also plays an important role in determining how gamma behaves. An ATM option's gamma increases as expiry draws closer. This means the probability of an ATM option finishing ITM increases dramatically as expiry draws closer. The effect of gamma decreases as we move further ITM or OTM.

In this way, we can look at gamma as a measure of certainty. The further ITM or OTM an option is as we move closer to expiry, the more confident we are that the option will finish ITM or OTM respectively. When certainty is high, gamma is low and vice versa.

Gamma tends to accelerate with less than 7 days to go before expiry. Suppose you enter the last week before expiry with options that are slightly OTM. In that case, gamma can increase rapidly, thereby pushing delta higher, which in turn indicates that the probability of your option finishing ITM will be high.

A small move in the underlying can produce exaggerated movements in the price of the option as a result. This is why it's best to avoid trading credit spreads for weekly options since gamma can leave your positions precariously placed.

Notice how gamma for Disney options changes in Figure 6 depending on the amount of time left to expiry.

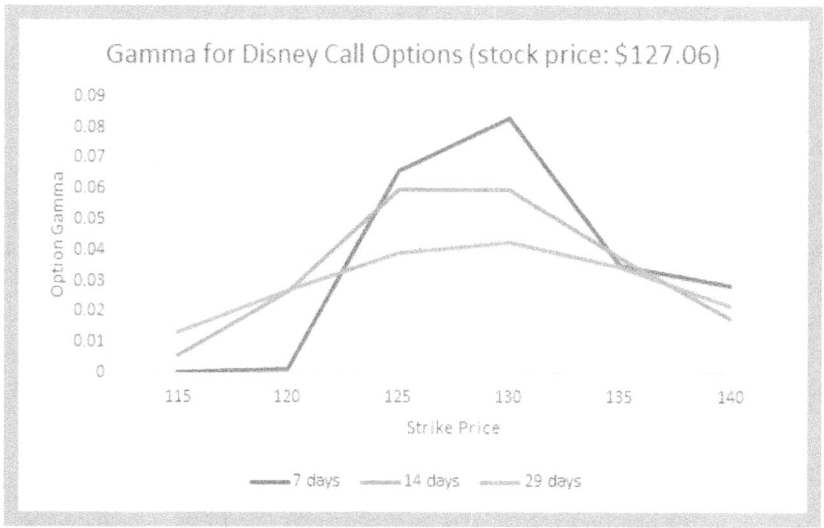

Figure 6: Gamma for different strike prices of Disney Calls at 3 different time periods

The calls that are slightly OTM at the 130 strike price and that have just 7 days to expire have the highest gamma. Note how the 130 strike has the highest gamma irrespective of how many days are left till expiry. Also notice how each curve's slope changes dramatically depending on how many days are left till expiry. The options that have just a week left will take their owners on a roller-coaster ride thanks to the degree with which gamma rises and falls.

It can take a while to fully comprehend the impact gamma has on your positions, so take some time to read this section once again. At the very least, recognize that the final week until expiry is the most uncertain time for you. If your position is near the money or not deep enough OTM, it's best to close your position and take whatever profits you have instead of trying to bet that your options will remain where they are and make you money. Closing your trade out also removes the possibility of a leg being assigned to you. We'll discuss exactly how we like to do this in the chapter on trade management.

THETA

While gamma and delta deal with the effect of the underlying on the option's price, theta measures how time affects the option's price. Theta (Θ) is used as a proxy to measure time decay, which is why you'll sometimes see time decay referred to as "theta decay." Options are intricately connected to time. Every option contract has a certain date beyond which it is worthless, which affects how it is priced.

Think of it like this. An option with 200 days left till expiry and is OTM, has more time to move ITM than an option that has the same strike price but has just one day left until expiry.

This means the latter option will be worth much less than the former. Figure 7 illustrates how this affects the way options are priced.

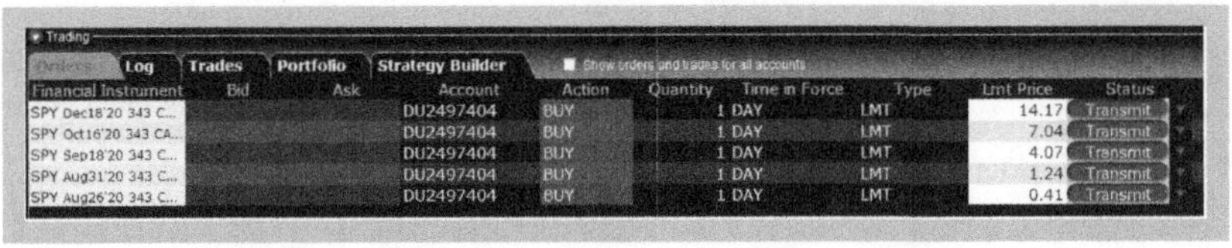

Financial Instrument	Bid	Ask	Account	Action	Quantity	Time in Force	Type	Lmt Price	Status
SPY Dec18'20 343 C...			DU2497404	BUY	1	DAY	LMT	14.17	Transmit
SPY Oct16'20 343 CA...			DU2497404	BUY	1	DAY	LMT	7.04	Transmit
SPY Sep18'20 343 C...			DU2497404	BUY	1	DAY	LMT	4.07	Transmit
SPY Aug31'20 343 C...			DU2497404	BUY	1	DAY	LMT	1.24	Transmit
SPY Aug26'20 343 C...			DU2497404	BUY	1	DAY	LMT	0.41	Transmit

Figure 7: The option premiums for an OTM 343 call option for the SPY ETF with different times remaining until expiry. (source: Interactive Brokers)

Let's look at an example. If the underlying price is $100 and its 105 call is priced at $1 with a theta of -0.2, the premium will decrease by 0.2 everyday. Theta represents a decrease in the option's price, and this is why its value is negative. Note that theta can fluctuate. As an option gets closer to expiry, theta accelerates exponentially.

Theta decay is what all options sellers look for. It's a proxy for measuring the extrinsic value an option has. The further OTM an option is, the more extrinsic value it has. As this option moves closer to expiry, the less value it has, and as theta decays, the extrinsic value drops exponentially. In fact, the last 30 days till expiry is when theta decreases the most, and we'll discuss how to take advantage of this in the next chapter.

For now, just note that as a net option seller, theta is your friend. If you write an option outside the 30 days to expiry window, you'll be capturing as much of the premium as possible. As the days go by, the premium's value accelerates to zero, and you can keep more of the premium. Since the price of the contract decreases exponentially, you can keep more of the profit even if you cover your position. It's merely selling high and buying low.

Theta accelerates, and this causes an option's price to drop significantly in the month leading up to expiry. This is why we like writing credit spreads that expire in 30-45 days since we can capture maximum theta without exposing ourselves to additional risk.

5

EXPIRATION DATES

Now that you understand how the Greeks work a little better, expiration dates are easier to address. A common concern amongst options traders is picking the correct expiration dates for their positions. Most experienced credit spread sellers choose to open positions that are 30-45 days away from expiry. This time frame is often provided as a default period as well.

Given the effects of theta and gamma we covered in the last chapter, you can now see why this period is optimal. An option that is greater than 45 days away from expiry won't witness too many price movements, and as a result you'll simply keep twiddling your thumbs waiting for something to happen. Options that are this far out often aren't very liquid either, so you might enter at prices that aren't optimal.

Once the option moves into the 45-day window, more traders start taking a look at it, which automatically boosts its liquidity and the rate at which gamma, theta, and delta move. This, in turn, brings even more traders on board and makes it easier to evaluate the case for entering a position.

Given that delta is a good measure of how likely an option is to finish in the money, it's a good idea to look at values that are as accurate as possible for it. An option that is more than 45 days away from expiry isn't going to have precise delta values, much less gamma.

Theta will remain pretty much constant since any price moves in the underlying will be negated by the fact that there's still a lot of time left until expiry. If the option moves ITM or OTM, there's still a ton of time left for the option to go the other way. Therefore, as an option seller, your money is pretty much stuck in the position doing nothing.

For this reason, we recommend that all of the positions you open be between 30 to 45 days away from expiry. This will allow you to both evaluate the option properly and you'll be able to capture the highest possible premium before theta starts rapidly decaying and decreasing the option's premium.

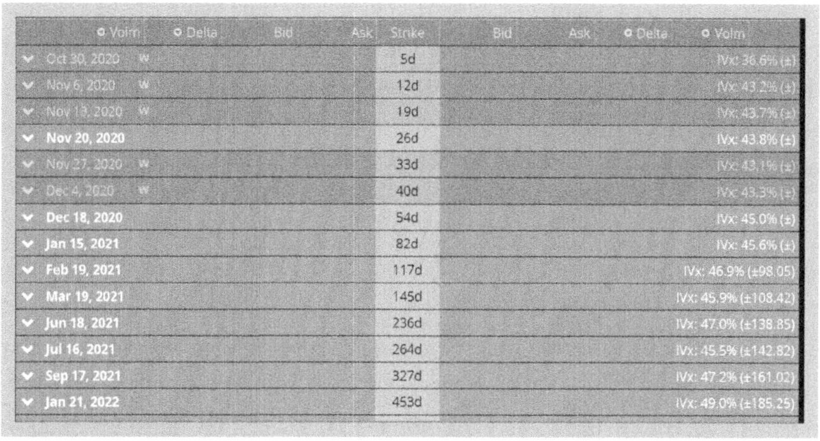

Volm	Delta	Bid	Ask	Strike	Bid	Ask	Delta	Volm
Oct 30, 2020 W				5d				IVx: 36.6% (±)
Nov 6, 2020 W				12d				IVx: 43.2% (±)
Nov 13, 2020 W				19d				IVx: 43.7% (±)
Nov 20, 2020				26d				IVx: 43.8% (±)
Nov 27, 2020 W				33d				IVx: 43.1% (±)
Dec 4, 2020 W				40d				IVx: 43.3% (±)
Dec 18, 2020				54d				IVx: 45.0% (±)
Jan 15, 2021				82d				IVx: 45.6% (±)
Feb 19, 2021				117d				IVx: 46.9% (±98.05)
Mar 19, 2021				145d				IVx: 45.9% (±108.42)
Jun 18, 2021				236d				IVx: 47.0% (±138.85)
Jul 16, 2021				264d				IVx: 45.5% (±142.82)
Sep 17, 2021				327d				IVx: 47.2% (±161.02)
Jan 21, 2022				453d				IVx: 49.0% (±185.25)

Figure 8: The Netflix options chain showing days to expiry. For credit spreads, we would look at the November 27th (33 days to expiry) and December 4th options (40 days to expiry). This allows us to capture as much of the premium as possible without holding our position during periods when options prices are doing nothing. (Source: Tastyworks)

There are some events you need to watch out for, however. It's not as if you can simply open a position 30 to 45 days away from expiry and expect it to work out. The technical state of the underlying stock matters, and we'll cover this in detail shortly. The other factors to watch out for are special events.

SPECIAL EVENTS

Special events are huge factors when it comes to analyzing volatility. When it comes to selling options, volatility is both your friend and enemy. If it turns against you, it can result in a position that was profitable for the majority of the contract, suddenly turning into an unprofitable position right before expiry.

We'll discuss the specifics of volatility in more detail in the next chapter. For now, let's look at some events that create volatility in the markets and how you need to tackle them.

Earnings Announcements

We've now established that the lifecycle of your options position is going to be between 30 to 45 days long. It is essential during this time that there be no earnings releases scheduled. The markets eagerly await earnings announcements and there's a lot of natural volatility in stock prices before them. In fact, stock prices reflect many expectations before the release is announced, which affects how the options are priced.

For example, if a stock is expected to announce record breaking earnings, its options will be priced higher than usual because the market will expect the stock price to move quickly in a given direction. If the company announces record earnings and it's a company that is followed extensively by the retail trading crowd, the price is bound to shoot higher. If it disappoints, you can expect institutional traders to pummel the stock, and the price will drop. The only thing in the markets worse than having expectations is having bad expectations affirmed. Whatever happens, the stock is going to move by a large degree, up or down. It certainly isn't going to move sideways or go anywhere slowly.

None of this fits the criteria that we need for our three setups. The vertical credit spreads require mild to sideways conditions, and the Iron Butterfly aims to capture sideways moves. Even a moribund stock that largely moves sideways isn't a good candidate during earnings season. Companies use these announcements to make other announcements regarding the future direction of the company. The reports are also accompanied by a flurry of insider trading.

In the stock market, insiders have to declare their positions and cannot trade based on insider information. If they get caught doing this, the penalties are large. A large insider move before disappointing earnings is a red flag. Therefore, most insiders schedule their trades right after earnings are announced. Of course, if earnings are great, the stock could go rocketing up on insider buying. However, we're not concerned with up or down. Volatility and consistency are what we're after. The more consistent volatility is, the easier a stock's option chain is to trade.

You can find earnings announcements calendars in your broker's software. Most often, they will be denoted with an "E" symbol in the options chain or on the stock's price graph.

Alternatively, you can visit the investor relations section on the company's website and look at the information presented there. Most brokers will have alerts set up to notify you of special events occurring with a stock you are monitoring.

Dividends

Dividends often get lumped together with earnings, but they deserve their own section. This is because, in the days leading up to the dividend payment, the amount of the dividend is accounted for in the stock price. If the stock will go ex-dividend (the date at which the stock will trade without the added value of the previous dividend amount) during the lifecycle of your trade, its calls will be priced lower to account for the dividend and you won't be able to capture as much premium.

Special Announcements

You'll need to pay attention to a company's business to figure out whether there is the possibility of a special announcement injecting volatility into proceedings. For example, pharmaceutical companies live and die by the results of their research. As a rule of thumb, you want to stay away from these companies because so much of their business hinges on approvals and lengthy drug trials working out.

The average drug spends around 8-10 years to move from inception to hitting the market (Frazier, 2015). Imagine working on a drug for close to a decade only for it to be rejected. This is a huge reason for these stocks being volatile. The pharmaceutical giants have many drugs under development, and this smooths their results, but smaller firms rocket up and down.

It isn't just pharmaceutical companies that are subject to such announcements. Announcements regarding restructuring, the results of a lawsuit or the results of a shareholder vote, create massive volatility in a stock. You don't want to be in the market using the three strategies in this book when volatility hits.

Since the predominant focus on the net credit spread strategies is to earn premiums, you need volatility to remain stable or decline. If a company is in any condition where it needs to make a special announcement that could affect its fortunes, you need to stay away from it.

Special note must be made of company CEOs who use Twitter to make major announcements instead of using the usual press release route. The rise of Silicon Valley has caused many CEOs to think they have a moral duty to disrupt everything in sight, for the sake of disruption. It's best to stay away from such scattergun CEOs who shoot their mouths off on social media. For the purpose of credit spreads, stick to boring companies with boring businesses. They're more likely to move sideways anyway.

Economic Releases

Economic releases happen all the time, so it's hard to avoid them. The ones you want to avoid are the major ones, such as interest rate announcements and jobs report releases. Both of these events occur once a month, so it may seem impossible to avoid them on a 45-day cycle. There is some good news, though.

First, these announcements are more significant for index options than they are individual stocks. They still affect company stocks but not to the extent that company-related announcements do. Therefore, you can always write options on individual stocks during these periods. If you're trading index options, try to time your positions within a 30-day window so that you can avoid these announcements.

Special note must be made of events related to the Federal Reserve Bank, such as their annual summit at Jackson Hole. These events are usually the source of major political and economic announcements, so you need to steer clear of them. While it hasn't occurred over the past decade, you also need to watch out for emergency meetings of the Federal Reserve.

This typically happens when a major bank has undertaken too much risk and is exposed to total collapse. In such situations, the markets become incredibly chaotic since the trouble hits banks directly. These events don't always make the headlines, but if you're even remotely connected to the market, you'll be aware of them. It's impossible to predict these events in advance. The best you can do is exit your positions for whatever you can get and capture as much profit as you can instead of exposing yourself to more turmoil.

Political Events

Politics interferes with everything, and the markets are no different. Election outcomes can affect the volatility of the markets. Thankfully, it's just the presidential election you need to watch out for. Of course, since 2016, sources of political volatility have been varied. While political leaders have been extremely careful with their statements regarding the stock market in the past, this isn't true anymore, with outrage fueling election campaigns. The markets don't react to every tweet or soundbite released, but you should be aware of important political dates or announcements.

As the world moves forward, the prospect of a trade war between America and China seems increasingly permanent. This means any companies that have links to China or whose business hinges on American government approval are risky. For example, many chip makers and semiconductor stocks such as Huawei have been badly affected due to their products being sourced from China but sold in the US. With these companies effectively having to pick sides in the argument, their stocks will be more volatile than ever.

These are just a handful of events that could affect your position. There are many more than can be covered here, and you'll need to evaluate how much a particular event can affect a stock's prospects. Remember that you want to err on the side of low volatility at all times. The best situation is if a stock is transitioning from a high volatility situation to a low volatility one. This will mean that premiums will be overpriced when you buy and underpriced when you sell. You'll earn bigger profits thanks to the greater price difference.

However, don't rely on such stocks all the time. It's easier to choose truly snooze-worthy ones that don't create any surprises for their stockholders, and you'll generate steady income for many years from them.

Now that we've covered events that affect volatility, let's further examine how we can use volatility levels to our advantage.

6

IMPLIED VOLATILITY DEMYSTIFIED

Implied volatility, or IV, is another concept that is central to options trading success. There are many explanations on the internet about what IV is and how options traders should use. The problem is that, like much of options trading, IV can be made as complicated or as simple as you wish. Most explanations of IV tend to focus on the mathematical explanations, which are often counterproductive.

Before we focus on how IV affects credit spreads, it's essential to understand what volatility is and how this affects stock and options prices. We've already covered the implications of volatility before, but let's revisit it. Volatility is just the degree to which an instrument's price will move in a given direction. A stock whose price jumps around all over the place is more volatile than one that moves steadily in one direction.

Volatile markets are dangerous places for traders, and as options sellers, we're not interested in operating in risky environments. In fact, all three strategies we've highlighted seek to take advantage of sideways moves and market conditions that are the enemy of directional traders. For this reason, volatility is not our friend.

The ideal situation is if volatility is high at our entry point and then decreases. This reduces the values of the Greeks and also reduces the movement in options prices. This in turn, increases the odds that our options will finish close to their original buy or sell prices, and we get to keep as much of the premium we earned as possible.

The entire market has a measure of volatility that many traders follow. This is called the volatility index or VIX. So if you're trading index options, you'll need to keep tabs on the VIX. From an individual stock's perspective, the VIX doesn't affect the price much. If you're trading individual stock options, then the stock's implied volatility is far more important.

THE ROLE OF IV IN OPTION PRICING

The phrase "implied" provides us a good idea of what IV is all about. It's represented as a percentage and is typically quoted on the option chain itself. It signifies what traders think of the current volatility levels in the stock and its future prospects. If a stock is expected to be volatile, the IV will be high. If it's expected to move sideways, its IV will be low. You can compare a stock's current IV to its historical IV levels to get an idea of where it currently stands.

On a more technical note, IV is the measure of the odds of the stock trading within one standard deviation away from its current price. That's a convoluted definition, so let's look at how it works via an example.

Disney is currently trading at $128, with an IV of 26.1%. This means there is a 68.1% chance (we'll explain why 68.1%, and why this is a crucial number later) of Disney trading within 26.1% of $128 over the next year.

The range of possible prices extends from 26.1% below the current price to 26.1% above it. These numbers are $94.50 and $161.

Note that Disney has a 68.1% chance of trading in this range. All IV numbers are interpreted this way. They give us the range that the stock has a 68.1% chance of trading in within a year. Do not confuse this with 100%. There is always a chance that Disney could trade outside this range as well. Another factor to pay attention to is that IV doesn't discriminate in terms of direction. It gives the stock an equal chance that it could trade above the current price or below it.

In practical terms this means the lower IV is, the smaller the range that a stock is predicted to trade between. When it comes to option prices, generally speaking, the higher the IV is, the more expensive that stock's options are. This stands to reason. Using our numbers from the Disney example, a call with a strike price of 160 is OTM at the moment, but it's within the IV range. This means it has a good chance of moving ITM over the next year. Therefore, as the expiry date lengthens, the premium attached to this call's strike price will increase. If we're in September right now, the October expiry will be priced pretty low. However, next September's 160 call will be priced high because it's more likely that Disney can hit that level within the next year.

The distance of the strike price combined with the time left to expiry plays an important role in the option's pricing, as you can see. Generally, deep OTM options will be priced cheaply, irrespective of their expiry date. This is because IV indicates that they're unlikely to move ITM.

As credit spread traders, we'll be buying and selling options, so the IV of one leg of the trade will cancel the other out. However, since our target is to earn as much of the premium as possible, it's in our interest to sell options that are OTM, but that can give us high premiums. This is why many traders are willing to risk selling ITM options on trade entry and risk assignment because the payoff is larger. Selling borderline OTM options is another way you can increase the premium you earn.

You must be careful though. If you do this repeatedly with high IV stocks, you're taking a high risk of the option finishing ITM. This is why it's best to target stocks that have high levels of IV from which they're certain to descend. You'll earn the resulting premium caused by high IV and will then be well placed to keep most of it as IV decreases and the stock begins to reduce in fluctuations.

It's important to note that common advice mentions that it's best to sell options in high IV environments. This is only half the story. While selling it is a good move, if IV keeps increasing, you're not doing yourself any favors. What you want is for IV to *decrease* as the trade progresses.

Ideally, you want IV to be below 50% when entering your trade. Stocks with an IV above 50% are usually too volatile to ensure consistent returns.

To give you a practical look at the kinds of IV levels to expect when analyzing stocks, here is the IV for the following nine instruments at the time of writing

- AT&T – 17.3%
- SPY (S&P 500 ETF) – 18.3%
- Costco – 25.3%
- Microsoft – 25.5%
- IWM (Russell 2000 ETF) – 27%
- Tesla – 56.3%
- American Airlines – 62.9%
- Moderna – 77.2%
- Nio – 143.1%

As you can see, more volatile stocks like Tesla, Moderna and Nio have much higher IVs than broad market ETFs or "boring" stocks like AT&T and Costco.

As you can see in Nio's case, a stock can have an IV of above 100% if it is incredibly volatile. You should never write credit spreads on a stock with an IV above 100%.

Factors That Affect IV

Calculating IV is less important than understanding the various ways in which IV can change given market conditions. The most obvious factor that affects its value is supply and demand. The higher the demand for an instrument, the higher its IV will be. Again, note that IV does not indicate direction, so if there's a lot of supply in the market, IV will be high as well.

Many people think low demand environments automatically indicate low IV values, but this isn't correct. If supply is high and there are more potential sellers than buyers, the stock can slide dramatically, increasing the option's IV. Instead, a balanced supply and demand environment is what causes a drop in IV. This is because there are an equal number of buyers and sellers in the market, so the stock is likely to move sideways.

Another market condition that creates low IV is low supply and low demand. This usually happens when a stock has been moving sideways for a long time, and traders (most of them directional) aren't interested in it anymore.

Time until expiry is another major factor in determining IV. The closer an option is to expiry, the lower its IV is. This makes intuitive sense because the closer the option is to expiry, the less time it has for the price to move significantly. The more time an option has until expiry, the higher the premium is. However, this doesn't mean you need to sell options that are expiring 100 years from now just to capitalize on higher IV. The objective is to earn as much premium as possible and capture it as quickly as we can. This is why the 30-45 day window works so well.

Market conditions also play a role. If the entire market is highly volatile, even low volatility stocks will have high IV values. In such conditions, you need to check whether the market 's volatility is likely to affect the underlying stock's price movement a lot. If the stock in question is highly connected to the market's overall health, you need to track the VIX closely.

For example, at the time of writing, the S&P 500 index is highly influenced by the stock prices of the FAANG stocks (Facebook, Apple, Amazon, Netflix, and Google). If the VIX is high, it's basically measuring the collective IV of these stocks. Even if one of them has been historically low in terms of volatility, the weight it carries regarding the overall index will push its IV higher. If you're trying to capture a premium in a decreasing volatility environment in this stock, you need to pay attention to the VIX as well as overall market trends.

That's all there is to learn about IV. If you're feeling overwhelmed at this stage, don't be. The most important thing to remember is that to profit from the strategies highlighted in this book successfully; you only need to learn where to find IV values in your broker software. You don't need to know all the intricacies of how they're calculated.

FREEMAN CREDIT SPREAD RULE #7

IF YOU'RE UNSURE ABOUT IV LEVELS, STICK TO STOCKS WITH AN IV OF LESS THAN 50%.

7

CLARIFYING MISCONCEPTIONS ABOUT TECHNICAL ANALYSIS

Technical analysis is a potent tool, but it'll be a hindrance rather than a help if you cannot use it properly.

Here is the good news, for credit spreads, you don't need complicated indicators. The truth is that it's possible to identify stocks that make good credit spread candidates using a simple moving average. It sounds impossible, but it's true.

Another piece of good news is that technical indicators tend to remain evergreen (at least most of them do) because they're closely related to the order flow of the underlying. So it's not as if you need to learn new chart patterns every other week. As a rule of thumb, the more removed a technical indicator is from price and order flow, the less reliable it will be in the long run.

But what about these super-intelligent, multi-billion dollar quantitative trading firms? Don't they use extremely complex technical algorithms to make trading decisions? Or what about these High Frequency Trading firms which come into the news every so often. Aren't they hiring the best and brightest minds to program technical algorithms all day?

There is much misconception surrounding High Frequency Trading (HFT) and algorithmic trading amongst ordinary investors and traders, so let's spend some time dissecting how these firms make money.

WHY YOU SHOULDN'T FEAR ALGORITHMS

First, we'd like to make a distinction between your average quantitative trading strategy and what a HFT firm does. Many quantitative trading strategies trade in ultra short timeframes, but this is not what we refer to when we speak of HFT. HFT firms, by our definition, are front runners. The edge that these firms have isn't technical wizardry but just deep pockets.

Here's how these firms work. They co-locate their servers as close to the exchange's matching engine as possible and rely on their orders hitting the market before the average trader's order does. Let's say you place an order to buy 100 shares of Wal-Mart at the market price. Your broker will pass this to a stock exchange clearing firm. These firms are responsible for executing the large volume of orders they receive, and that's it. They aren't brokers, and their sole objective is to find the best prices possible.

Let's say the first 10 shares of your order are filled on the NYSE at $150 each. There are still 90 shares left in the order, but there aren't any more shares of Wal-Mart available on the NYSE. This isn't a problem because the clearinghouse can search the NASDAQ. If the NASDAQ cannot fill the orders, there's BATS. If not BATS, there's the NYSE ARCA and so on. There's no shortage of stock exchanges, and it's not hard to fill orders of any size.

The HFT firm has prior knowledge of the order in which clearinghouses hop between exchanges. We'll explain why shortly. They co-locate their servers at all the exchanges in advance and lie in wait. When they see your order of 100 WMT hitting the NYSE, they know that this order will need to hop elsewhere. Before the clearinghouse hops to the NASDAQ, the HFT firm buys all the WMT available and lies in wait. As your order (via the clearinghouse) hits the NASDAQ, the HFT increases the price by a fraction of a cent and sells it to you (Lewis, 2015).

This doesn't sound like much of a profit, but if you multiply this by millions of orders a day, you'll realize that an HFT firm can clear billions every year without ever taking a loss on their trades. There's no analysis magic here, just a lot of money poured into high speed infrastructure. You might wonder how the HFT firm knows of your order size when it hits the stock exchange? After all, the clearinghouse isn't advertising the order size, is it?

Well the truth is that HFT firms buy order flow data from exchanges. It's how stock exchange companies make as much money as they do. It's also a big reason why you don't pay commissions on stock purchases or option trades anymore. Your broker is selling your order flow information to an HFT that is fleecing you fractions of a cent every time you trade. As sordid as this picture is, there's nothing you can do about it unless you open a billion-dollar fund of your own and specify which exchange you want your order to be routed to. So just think of it as the cost of doing business.

The point of all this is to show you that there's no technical analysis going on with HFT firms. They're front running your order, and that's it. Their actions have no impact on technical indicators.

What about the algorithmic traders, though?

Algorithms

Algorithmic trading firms operate in two markets, broadly speaking. These are the stock and bond markets. But what many investors miss is that the ratio of activity between these markets is roughly 95:1 in favor of the bond market. (*Bond Algos Tap into ETF Liquidity and Efficiency Gains*, 2019). Why is this? Simply that the bond market dwarfs the stock market in size by many multiples. It's populated exclusively by institutional traders, and there is next to zero retail presence. Think of it as a top-tier sports league, and the division below representing the stock market. Most algorithmic trading firms are institutions themselves.

This automatically means they gravitate towards the bond markets. There's another powerful attraction that the bond markets have. There are no insider trading laws that govern it. Many of the protections you take for granted in the stock market don't exist in the bond market. This makes it easier to trade if you have the resources. The retail side of the market greatly affects the price movement of many stocks.

Algorithmic traders by definition, are looking to trade on a rational basis. They collect large sets of data and develop models with them using sophisticated technology. The presence of a 20 year old with a brand new Robinhood account who doesn't know the difference between a long and a short corrupts this data. After all, this person isn't acting on rational principles. They're trading purely out of emotion. They're buying TSLA because they saw the price was going up and heard they could potentially double their money within a few days. No one can create a model out of that.

As a result, algorithmic trading in the stock market is restricted to market making or applying other techniques such as order cloaking. Market making is what clearinghouses do. They're straightforward execution desks and aren't concerned with technical patterns. All they're doing is getting their clients the best prices they can find.

The most important thing to note is that you, as someone selling credit spreads for extra income, have nothing to fear from these firms.

Order cloaking, or to use the illegal version of it, order spoofing, is a method by which a trader masks their true intentions. They might place an order to buy 100 shares, but their intention might be to sell 10,000. Many order spoofers and cloakers try to catch HFT firms napping and they typically do. There is no actual technical analysis going on here. Order spoofers reverse-engineer HFT algorithms, which as you've learned don't use technical analysis.

So where does this leave us? The algorithms that use sophisticated technical analysis are far fewer in number than you might initially think. You are free to develop more sophisticated methods than ever, but the truth is that as long as you stick to indicators and intelligently use them, there's no need for you to overcomplicate technical analysis. To trade credit spreads, you don't need to worry about algorithms snatching away advantages from you. Neither do you need to develop special indicators.

Despite what "professional traders" trying to sell you a $3,000 technical analysis course might tell you, the markets aren't some treasure chest that can be unlocked with a magical key. Many people try it, and a few even succeed in designing algorithms that make them daily profits. However, as we've repeatedly mentioned, it's far easier to pick trading ranges and use options to profit from them instead of trying to catch market lows and pick tops. This is what makes trading credit spreads so powerful.

HOW TO USE TECHNICAL ANALYSIS FOR CREDIT SPREADS

While many traders try to time the market using technical analysis, our opinion is that it's far better to use technical analysis to identify the periods when the market is doing "nothing" from a directional trader's perspective. These periods are greater in number, and in addition to using technical analysis, you'll be able to visually spot such periods as well.

It's not very hard to look at a chart and determine whether the instrument is moving sideways or in a particular direction. Even if this isn't clear, the technical analysis indicators you can use to determine such periods are pretty simple to plot and decipher. When it comes to making extra income with credit spreads, simplicity always wins. You can use complicated indicators, but just because an indicator is complex doesn't mean it's accurate.

A common argument for using new indicators is that no one else in the market uses them. This is falling back into the "secret key" type of thinking that dooms many traders. The markets are too random for one indicator to consistently give you spectacular returns. Instead, you need to regularly use those that help you detect patterns in the market's behavior. Counterintuitively, the indicators that do this the best are some of the oldest and simplest ones.

The next chapter will introduce you to the indicators we recommend using to trade credit spreads. Our data proves that these indicators are perfect for these setups. In our research, we haven't found any instances of a complicated indicator being more accurate in any way than the ones we will highlight in the next chapter.

8

THE THREE TECHNICAL INDICATORS YOU NEED TO KNOW

Before we dive into individual indicators, it's important to take a step back and remember why we're even using technical analysis. In our case we're merely using it to figure out whether the market is trending or ranging. Often, the market rests in between these two states.

The most common method of figuring out a trend's direction is to draw trendlines. They're intuitive and are an easy way of figuring out which points the market might touch as it moves in a given direction. Take Figure 9 for example.

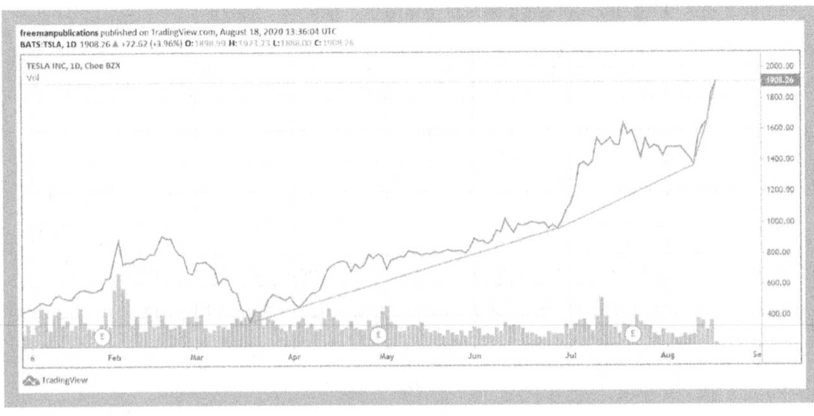

Figure 9: Trendlines in TSLA for YTD 2020 (pre-stock split). (Source: TradingView)

It doesn't take a genius to figure out that Tesla was rocketing from March to August 2020. The problem with trendlines is that they're incredibly subjective. When trends are as clear as they are in Figure 9, it's easy to connect the dips and figure out which ones are relevant.

However, the market is rarely ever this clean. If the price action is messy enough, you can reasonably draw more than one trendline through a price action sequence and have multiple trendlines indicating different trend strengths. This does nothing to help us figure out which way the stock is trending. Even in Figure 9, which is a clean set of price action, you can see that we've ignored many of the medium term dips the market made.

Choosing which dips to consider and which ones to ignore takes experience, and this is something newer traders don't have. As a result, drawing trendlines isn't the best idea. There's also the fact that the best trendlines are drawn in hindsight, which does nothing to help us predict which way prices are going to go.

Closely related to trendlines are price channels. If one trendline is hard to draw, drawing two of them to form a channel is even harder. Many trading education books depict clean channels, but these are usually the result of selective picking. In reality, you'll be hard-pressed to find stocks that lend themselves to perfect price channels.

Instead, we can start with the easiest and most reliable indicator, namely support and resistance levels.

SUPPORT AND RESISTANCE

Technically speaking, support and resistance levels are not an indicator. However, they're indispensable. The fact is that many trading authorities misrepresent them. Support and resistance levels are a great way to figure out the order flow prevalent in a stock (or any financial instrument). This helps us choose the right strike prices for our options.

The market is composed of many traders, and every one of them has a certain opinion on what prices ought to be. These traders have different strategies and are operating in different time frames. As a result, a consensus is hard to achieve.

This is why when areas on a stock chart show that many traders agree on price, it's significant. These areas are where support and resistance lines should be drawn.

An example of this is illustrated in Figure 10 where the 9 EMA acts as a dynamic support during an uptrend. The stock price continues to bounce off this level through the year-long period of price increases.

Figure 10: An Example of Dynamic Support on SPY (Source: TradingView)

Price Swings

Prices swing from one side to the next all the time. These swing points are vital since they tell us that the market was pushed in a particular direction by traders and that these traders were overwhelmed by traders from the other side of the market and that prices were pushed right back. Traders remember these levels, so when they see these levels where prices were pushed the other way in the future, you can reasonably assume that there will be another bounce.

When levels are broken, the zones where prices previously bounced will be retested from the other side. For example, a swing low that acts as a support will be broken, and prices will retest the level from below as resistance. More often than not, these levels work as strong resistance. Similarly, once a strong resistance level has been broken it acts as support. See figure 11 for a visual example of this.

Figure 11: Gold price breaks through the previous resistance level of $1,690, which then becomes the new support level (Source: TradingView)

The reason these levels are robust is because of the number of traders who look at them. The more substantial support and resistance levels are the ones that have a large number of traders waiting near them. The easiest way to spot the strength of a level is to look at the force with which price approached it and its reaction. If the price hit the level after approaching it steeply, this indicates a lot of force behind the move.

If a move with that much force can be countered and pushed back, it indicates that the traders waiting at that level are much stronger. Therefore, it's likely that there will be a secondary reaction when price retests it. When evaluating swing points, look at the angle with which price approached the level and the angle at which it left it. This is the easiest way to evaluate the strength of the traders present at the level. Figure 12 illustrates a case where prices bounced after a strong bearish move. Also, notice how they react in the future as prices moved back towards the same level over the next 6 months.

Figure 12: A Strong Swing Point in SPY (Source: TradingView)

Ranges

Ranges are periods of sideways movement in a chart, and they also provide clear indications of support and resistance levels being present. The top and bottom of ranges are areas where many traders reside. Prices usually retest these tops and bottoms repeatedly, and this only reinforces the strength of these levels. Figure 13 illustrates how powerful they can be.

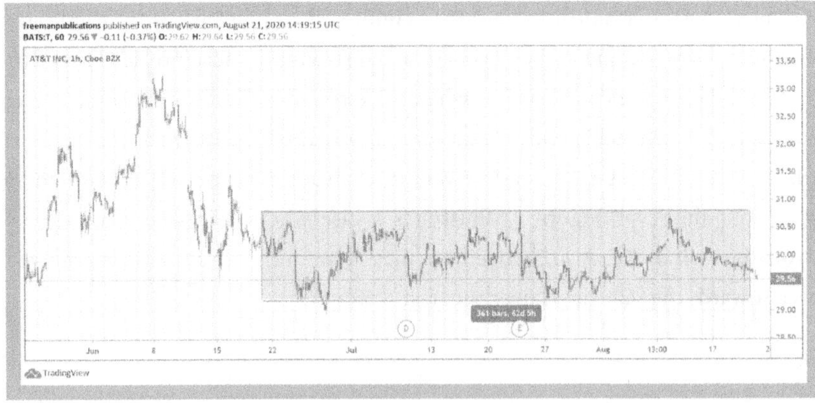

Figure 13: A Range in AT&T (Source: TradingView)

Except for one overnight anomaly, AT&T traded between $29.22 and $30.84 for 62 straight trading days between June 21 and August 17, 2020, making it a perfect candidate for both call and put credit spreads. The reason for this is the presence of strong support and resistance levels at the bottom and top of the range, respectively. This sort of price action is ideal for trading credit spreads.

Figure 13 also contains a number of swing points that act as strong support and resistance. Notice that these points by themselves don't offer much insight as to what the market is doing. In fact, swing point support and resistance levels usually form in trends. If you see a high number of support and resistance levels that are swing points, notice the length of the reactions from these levels.

In Figure 13, notice that AT&T plummeted and gapped down initially on June 10th. The swing points that it printed were small, which indicates that counter trend traders weren't present in huge numbers. This means the chances of a balanced market forming anytime soon were remote. After the gap, the stock's behavior changes. Swing points produce larger reactions, which means the buyers (counter trend traders) are stepping into the market.

At this stage you should be on the lookout for possible sideways movement forming. This eventually comes to pass as AT&T prints a clean range that you could have traded successfully for over two months. Using support and resistance in this manner helps you figure out what the order looks like right now and which way it might go. If you see swing points producing smaller counter trend reactions, it's a sign that the trend traders are getting stronger and that this environment is unsuited for our strategies.

Look for support and resistance ranges to be as stable as possible. There will be unclean price action, and that violates clean, horizontally drawn lines. Remember that support and resistance areas are zones, not single lines. The more unclean a range is, the wider your zone must be and, consequently, the more conservative your strike prices must be.

In the case of AT&T, an ideal short strike for a call spread would have been $31 (slightly above resistance) and an ideal short strike for a put spread would have been $29 (slightly below support).

Moving Averages

When trading credit spreads, we want a market that is either sideways or mildly trending. This is where the price to Exponential Moving Average (EMA) crossover system works perfectly. For bull put spreads we suggest using the 50EMA because it is the most common and available on all free charting tools and trading platforms. This is where a stock's short term (50 day) moving average crosses over its long term (200 day) moving average. This is also known as the "golden cross".

We base this choice on the results obtained during a backtest of this strategy. This backtest on SPY options between 2009 and 2019 sold 0.31 delta put spreads with 30 days to expiry, every time SPY crossed above the 50-day moving average. Using this simple system, you would have made 433% profits over the 10-year period, with a 90.5% win rate across 211 trades, provided you took profits at the 50% mark (losing trades were run to max loss).

Interestingly enough, if you pull the backtest further to include the 2007-2009 bear market, the strategy still provided net positive returns across 46 trades, because it managed to capture some of the market rallies.

This is an extremely simple system to follow and it works very well for a number of reasons. The biggest reason is that it is based on common sense. Any stock that is crossing its 50EMA is bullish in the short term, but it isn't so bullish so as to overwhelm our strategies. The stock might indeed become extremely bullish over time, but that's a risk we'll have to take in the markets when trading.

For the most part, the 50EMA crossover will highlight stocks that have broken out of a long period of sideways ranging and are beginning to establish some sort of bullishness. If you were to analyze the charts of these stocks and use support and resistance as well, you'd be able to narrow down your prospects better.

If the stock is far too bullish, you can still make money on a bull put spread. However, you will have to deal with increased volatility. Due to volatility increasing, you'll be selling options when they're cheaper and hoping that volatility doesn't grow too much so as to inflate their prices. If the trade goes against you, covering your shorts will result in a loss in this scenario.

This doesn't mean you should not take the trade at all. It's just that you need to be careful. Use the EMA crossover system we just highlighted to create a watch-list and then drill down deeper to look at whether setting up a spread in that stock makes sense.

Bollinger Bands

Bollinger bands are a great trading tool for credit spread traders. Interpreting them is also simple and this makes them a popular tool with directional traders too. From a net credit spread perspective, Bollinger Bands give us clear insight into the state of the underlying stock's volatility.

The bands are plotted at two standard deviations away from the current price. Why two standard deviations? This is because stocks have a 95% probability of trading within this band. If these percentages seem arbitrary, remember how IV levels show the stock having a 68.1% chance of trading within a range; well that's because 68.1% is one standard deviation. As a handy cheat sheet, remember that

- 1 standard deviation = 68.1% chance of being within the range
- 2 standard deviations = 95% chance of being within the range
- 3 standard deviations = 99% chance of being within the range

Bollinger Bands (2 standard deviations, 95% chance) gives us a great way of looking at how volatility changes.

Figure 14 below illustrates what Bollinger Bands look like on a chart.

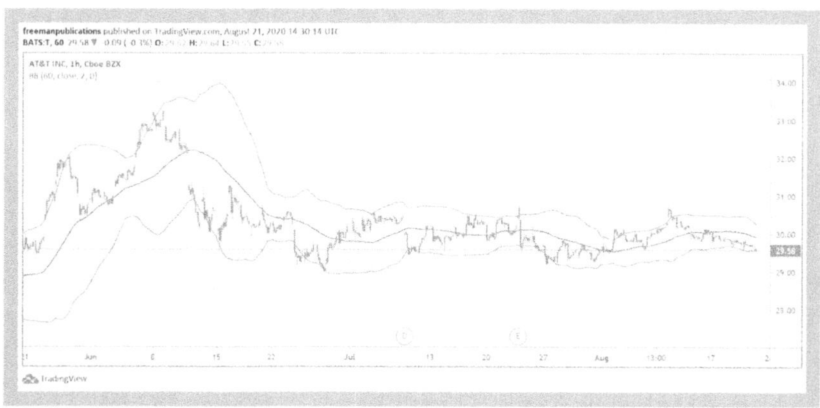

Figure 14: Bollinger Bands in AT&T (Source: TradingView)

The bands above and below price represent two standard deviations' worth of movement. The line through the center of price is the EMA. In Figure 14, we've chosen the 60-day EMA, so this represents around three months' worth of price action (because 60 trading days = 3 months real time). 60-day EMA is a stable line that isn't going to fluctuate too much.

Notice that prices rarely peek out above the bands. The minute they do so, a swift regression to the mean follows. In some cases, it's immediate, while in others, it takes more time. Notice that during powerful trends, AT&T takes a while to get back within the band envelope. It's easy to think that all you'll need to do with Bollinger Bands is to look at when the stock peeks out below or above the bands and bet on it moving in the opposite direction. This is what directional traders do.

However, for credit spreads, we like to have 30 to 45-day trade timelines. The underlying could move in the opposite direction for a short time and then reverse and continue in its original path. For example, notice the trending sections of AT&T in Figure 14.

For the purpose of credit spreads, instead of focusing on whether the stock is near the edge of the band, look at the width of the bands themselves. Notice in the trending portion of Figure 14, the bands widen massively. This indicates that IV of the underlying is increasing massively. Since we're looking for low volatility conditions, it's obvious that we need to stay away from this stock. Ideal conditions for credit spreads are when the bands are beginning to contract.

In Figure 14, notice how the upper band collapses to meet the lower band once the trend ends and as AT&T settles into a range. The tighter a range gets, the better it is for you as an options seller. It means volatility is lower and you can sell closer to the money options and capture higher premiums. Be careful of bands that are too constricted, though.

The bands often act as springs. If they get wound too tight, they're likely to explode outwards. Prolonged ranges tend to produce this effect. This stands to reason from an order flow perspective. In large ranges, traders redistribute their holdings and seek to push prices in their preferred direction once this is done. Towards the end of a large range you'll notice bar sizes reducing dramatically and higher lows or lower highs forming. This indicates that the stock is getting ready to move explosively in a given direction and begin a new trend. The bands will have been squeezed tight, to the extent that they'll constrict prices completely. Compare the relative band widths over the past 30-60 days to figure out whether you should be on the lookout for a new trend.

In Figure 14, notice how the bands come extremely close and how the price bars reduce in size dramatically. Compare the width of the bands and the bar sizes to those on the left. Since prices are below the 60EMA, we would hazard a guess that AT&T is looking to break out into a bearish trend. If we had any open bullish positions at this point, we'd wind them up and set up bear call spreads.

A bear call spread is not the most efficient setup for a high volatility environment, but this doesn't mean it's an incorrect setup. We'll still make money on it. We just won't make as much money as we could with other setups. Our point is that the bands have given us plenty of notice of the new trend possibly forming and we can take full advantage of this.

This closes our look at technical analysis indicators. Hopefully, this reassures you that you don't need to know every indicator or chart pattern under the sun to get started. By focusing on the basics like support and resistance levels, Bollinger bands, and identifying ranges, you will confidently identify good candidates for credit spreads.

If you're entirely new to credit spreads or stock charts, here is a useful practice exercise. Go to tradingview.com (you can open an account for free) and find the charts for 5-10 stocks you are interested in. Practice drawing support and resistance lines on these and identify whether the stock is trending or trading within a range. Feel free to share your results and interpretations with us. If you get stuck, you can email us at admin@freemanpublications.com and we'll help you out.

9

CHOOSING THE RIGHT INSTRUMENTS TO TRADE

The best strategies need great instruments. Without the right instruments, you will struggle to capture the highest gains a strategy can give you. When it comes to selecting instruments for credit spreads, we need to return to our investment criteria. These three strategies work best when volatility is low. Which by itself eliminates a lot of the possible candidates you can trade.

Mildly bullish or mildly bearish conditions are ideal for these setups, which you can use the technical indicators you learned in the last chapter to identify. This immediately eliminates strong trending stocks since they tend to be extremely volatile.

While the broad market has periods where it trends sideways, don't mistake overall market behavior for individual instrument behavior. For example, at the time of writing the S&P 500 is up around four percent this year (2020). While the NASDAQ is up 27%. The energy sector (as represented by the XLE ETF) meanwhile is down 37%.

This shows that every sector and stock has its own rhythms, so it's possible to find bearish conditions even in extremely bullish market environments. When it comes to writing credit spreads, you have three types of instruments to choose from, let's take a look at them one by one.

INDEX OPTIONS

The safest choice for beginners is an index option. You can trade options on broad market indexes, or you can choose sector indexes. The best indexes to focus on are the SPX (which covers the S&P 500) and RUT (which covers the Russell 2000). You can also trade the ETFs connected to these indexes. We'll discuss ETFs in the next section in this chapter. Many sector indexes don't have options tied to them, so you'll have to stick to trading their ETFs.

Index options are different from their individual stock and ETF option counterparts because, unlike the latter, these options don't cover a tradable instrument. After all, you can't buy the SPX or RUT no matter how hard you try. This means their options are cash settled. When you buy the options, you'll receive or pay the equivalent cash that the underlying movements will create.

For example, if your options finish ITM and you're assigned them, you won't have to buy the SPX. Instead, your broker will charge you whatever amount your trade will cause you to pay. You can't own the underlying as you can with other instruments. Cash-settled options are great if you're more conservative because you automatically avoid assignment fees and don't have to worry about them being exercised by the buyer.

If you find a broker that is great but charges assignment fees, you can trade cash-settled index options with them and avoid the fee completely. Take note that cash-settled options exist on a number of instruments other than just indexes. Commodity indexes and futures contract options are cash-settled, as are precious metal spot contract options.

Stick to broad market or large sector indexes since these will witness a good amount of liquidity, and you won't be caught out by unexpected volatility. Thinly traded index options are ripe for manipulation. This happens through wide spreads, so watch out for them. As a rule, the greater the liquidity is in an instrument, the closer its spread will be.

ETFS

ETFs, or exchange traded funds, are an extremely popular trading instrument since they accurately represent sector performance. ETFs have been growing in recognition since the last financial crisis. In fact, total assets under management in the entire ETF industry has gone from $534 Billion in 2008, to more than $3.4 Trillion in 2018. As a result, there is an ETF for pretty much everything now. ETFs also tend to be far more liquid than individual stocks while also providing liquidity for traders looking to speculate in obscure indexes.

For example, if you wanted to speculate on the price of gold, trading the spot option contracts would put you in a precarious position. This is because they're not the most liquid of instruments. However, by trading the options on a gold ETF you can speculate on gold's price without having to put yourself at the risk of holding onto an illiquid position. The most popular ETF for options speculation purpose is SPY. SPY and SPX options attract a lot of interest but are different. SPX options are cash-settled, as you just learned. SPY is not cash-settled and upon exercise, you'll end up owning shares of the ETF.

This means you'll pay assignment fees. There isn't much of a difference other than settlement when it comes to trading the SPX versus SPY. SPY tracks the SPX, so you'll end up gaining and losing the same amount. You might find some discrepancies in pricing for the same strike level between the two option chains, but largely the options trade for similar premiums.

There are other notable ETFs that offer great trading opportunities. IWM is the most liquid ETF, which tracks the Russell 2000 Index while QQQ tracks the NASDAQ 100 index. XLV is a popular ETF to trade if you're looking to take advantage of movements in the healthcare sector. XMB (materials), XLF (financials), XLE (energy) and VWO (emerging markets) are other popular options.

When choosing an ETF, liquidity should be your primary concern. Liquidity can be easily measured by looking at the size of the ETF. The larger it is, the more liquid it will be. There are many obscure ETFs that track similar indexes to the bigger ones, but they don't attract as much investor attention. This means their shares are not as liquid, which in turn means their options are even less liquid and spreads may widen at any time.

ETFs are a speculation tool as well. This is done through leveraged and inverse ETFs. If you want to boost your returns or profit from a drop in index values, these ETFs can provide you with that sort of exposure. However, for the purposes of net credit spread trading, they're a poor choice. This is because their volatility is inherently high. The second reason is that in periods of serious price movement, they are often suspended from trading and this throws their options all over the place.

These ETFs utilize large amounts of leverage to generate their returns, and this is why volatility is high. When trading options, you'll be leveraging your investment to a certain extent. After all, you'll be buying one contract and controlling 100 shares. To further leverage your investment by choosing a leveraged ETF is a poor choice.

Pay special attention to the trading volumes of the ETFs you choose. At the very least, stick to ETFs that have more than 500,000 shares traded every day. This will guarantee liquidity at all times. Size is a good proxy for liquidity as we mentioned earlier. You can look for any ETF that has at least five billion dollars under management. Anything below this is risky.

The prices of an ETF's options also depend on how well the manager runs the fund. Many smaller ETFs tend to be volatile because their managers are unproven. The slightest hint of trouble could lead to investors selling their units in the fund, causing its price to drop. An option holder is exposed to such price drops as well as sector performance. This is why it's best to stick to proven ETFs issued by larger companies like Vanguard, State Street and iShares by BlackRock.

INDIVIDUAL STOCKS

Individual stocks are where you'll find the most candidates for setting up net credit spread trades. The big stocks such as Apple and Google (Alphabet) are quite liquid and stable for the most part in terms of volatility. The criteria regarding liquidity applies to stocks as well. However, the size of a company isn't a proxy for its liquidity. Look at just the number of shares traded (more than 500,000 shares per day) to determine this.

Stay away from the media darlings or any stock that is being targeted by activist firms. Activist firms are usually hedge funds or private equity firms who buy controlling stakes in companies and try to force changes in their operations. Their results could be hit-or-miss, but what is guaranteed is a power struggle.

If you read news of the stock in the media, this is a good sign that it's best to stay away from it. A good example of this in the current market are stocks of Electric Vehicle companies. Everyone is jumping into these companies like there's no tomorrow despite the fact that most of them cannot profitably make cars (and for some, even generate any revenue at all). Meaning they are extremely volatile and make for poor credit spread candidates. Remember, you can use IV levels to measure this. An IV of greater than 50% is a sign you should stay away from the stock.

If you need a starting point for potential candidates, you can use free stock screeners to select appropriate stocks. We prefer using FinViz.com for this because it's free and easy to use.

We have a free Finviz tutorial on our YouTube channel, which you can find at https://freemanpublications.com/youtube

Here are the criteria we recommend:

- Stocks trading above 50-day moving average criteria
- Trading Volume > 500k shares per day
- Optionable
- Mid and large cap stocks only
- Earnings announcement in the previous week

All of these criteria fulfill certain requirements. A stock that is trading above its 50-day EMA gives us a list of stocks that can satisfy our bull put spread backtest criteria as we mentioned earlier. Alternatively, you could set up a screen that alerts you to crossovers. The trading volume criteria is so we have enough liquidity to get the best prices.

By limiting yourself to mid and large cap stocks you're insulating yourself from volatility by a large extent. Small cap stocks and stocks that are priced under $10 tend to be extremely volatile since they attract the penny stock trading crowd. Small caps also face greater headwinds in terms of business challenges, so their stock prices tend to fluctuate much more than a larger company's stock does.

Running the above scan on FinViz at the time of writing gave us 52 possible candidates, including well-known names like Barrick Gold, Draftkings, Applied Materials, Inc. and Marriott. If you have a smaller account or are only looking for stocks less than $50, 31 companies fit these criteria.

Stocks and Instruments to Stay Away From

We've told you what to choose, so it's best for us to explicitly tell you which instruments to stay away from. Here are the criteria for these:

- Instruments which don't directly track stock prices (USO)
- Inverse ETFs in which trading can be halted (SEF)
- Instruments directly related to volatility levels (UVXY)
- Leveraged ETFs (TQQQ, DWT, DUST)
- Media darlings or stocks receiving a lot of attention (NKLA, TSLA, KODK, MRNA)

All of these instruments are volatility magnets, so stay away from them. Especially, UVXY which is an ETF that tracks the short-term futures of the VIX. Volatility tends to stay relatively flat, but every now and then, it spikes massively, meaning it can throw a trade from almost certainty profitability to maximum loss in the space of a few hours.

Beyond these criteria, you don't need any other specific tool to trade credit spreads well, but one particular indicator you can add is the Choppiness Index.

Figure 15: Choppiness Index on SPY (Source: TradingView)

This indicator measures the ranging character of the markets. Values greater than 61.8 (look, it's our old friend 61.8 again) are considered indicative of a range. As you can see from Figure 15, once the indicator passes 61.8 it correctly manages to predict the existence of two ranges in the SPY ETF. The range on the left is smaller, and you can see the larger range on the right.

Once again, you don't have to use this indicator; it's merely our suggestion. However, if you find the previous chapter's indicators aren't helping you too much, then layering the Choppiness Index is a good idea.

At this point, you might be wondering if it's best to trade index options, ETFs or stock options? There is no such thing as the "best" when it comes to credit spread trading.

Indexes are far less volatile than individual stocks, so you might find that it's easier to score a high number of wins with them. However, their lower volatility means their premiums won't be mispriced, so your overall profits might be lower. If you trade cash-settled options, you'll avoid assignment fees, which can boost your profit as well. Individual stocks are more volatile, and this creates more opportunities for mispricing in their options. You'll earn a greater profit per trade, but your win rate might be lower due to additional volatility.

Try out all instrument types before choosing to stick with one type of instrument. Then choose the one that suits you the best or find the easiest to consistently win with. It's important to remember that you can make large profits by trading the same instrument over and over again. In our experience, beginners tend to prefer index options like SPX or RUT.

10

SELECTING THE RIGHT STRIKE PRICES

Your choice of strike prices directly affects the profitability of your trades. Selecting the right strike prices is tricky because you want to be close enough to the money that you'll earn a significant profit, but you also want to be far enough away from prices so that your options finish OTM. When we highlighted the strategies in detail in an earlier chapter, we first mentioned that the short option legs will begin ITM and finish OTM.

This kind of a trade setup will bring in huge premiums since ITM options will be priced higher than OTM ones. We then mentioned that if you wish to minimize the risk of early assignment, you ought to write further OTM options. This reduces the premium you'll receive, but the probability of winning the trade is much higher. There's also zero risk of early assignment because both legs will be OTM.

There's no clear-cut method of determining the right strike price every time. A lot depends on your own risk profile. If you're someone who doesn't mind losing more to make more money, then writing ITM options might make sense to you. Many people justify the increased risk through the higher premiums earned. Figure 16 illustrates why this is.

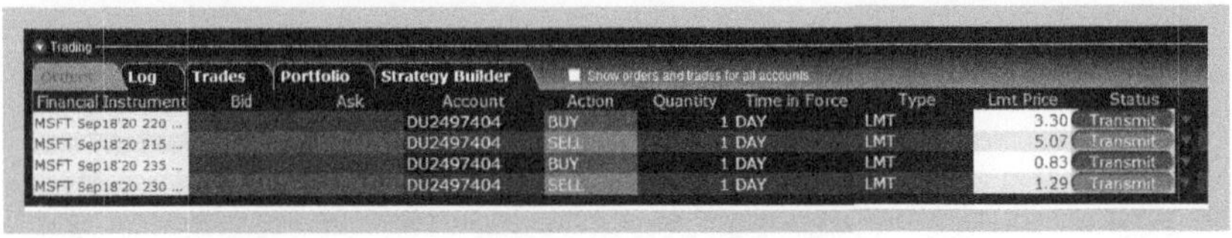

Financial Instrument	Bid	Ask	Account	Action	Quantity	Time in Force	Type	Lmt Price	Status
MSFT Sep18'20 220 ...			DU2497404	BUY	1	DAY	LMT	3.30	Transmit
MSFT Sep18'20 215 ...			DU2497404	SELL	1	DAY	LMT	5.07	Transmit
MSFT Sep18'20 235 ...			DU2497404	BUY	1	DAY	LMT	0.83	Transmit
MSFT Sep18'20 230 ...			DU2497404	SELL	1	DAY	LMT	1.29	Transmit

Figure 16: Differences in Strike Prices for Disney (Source: Interactive Brokers)

Figure 16 shows the option prices for two spreads on Disney. Disney was trading at $211.50 at the time we took the screen capture. The options listed are calls.

We have two choices for a $5 wide spread. We can either select the 220-215 or 235-230 strikes for our bear call spread. Since the 215 call is closest to the money, you can see that it has the highest premium. However, the 220 call is also more expensive.

Our net credit from this pair of strikes will be $1.77 per share (5.07 – 3.30) or $177 per contract. Our maximum risk will be the difference between the strike prices minus the premium earned. This is $323 per contract, giving us a risk/reward ratio of 54.7%

In the case of the second spread, our premium earned will be $0.46 per share (1.29 – 0.83) or $46 per contract. Our risk will be $454, giving us a risk/reward ratio of 10.1%.

As you can see, the differences in profit versus loss amounts are large for both spreads. The former spread brings us a larger premium of $177 per contract, but the trade itself has a higher probability of a loss. The second spread brings us a far lower premium, and the maximum loss is also higher than the former. However, there's a higher probability the trade itself will be a winner. As you can see, there's no one-size-fits-all answer to this.

What we can do is reverse-engineer the process. To do this, we start with avoiding loss, which begins with the probability of the trade finishing ITM. If you wish to avoid losing money, the amount of premium you can earn should be of no consequence. As long as you're earning a decent amount of money, focus solely on the probability of the win. To do this, stick to writing further OTM options.

Even if you don't mind running additional risks, it is our view that capturing steady and more probable gains is a better strategy than chasing individual wins. You will earn more on individual trades, but over time the probabilities will assert themselves, and you're not going to gain too much of an advantage over someone who writes further OTM spreads. The latter method also has the advantage of being far more comfortable to implement mentally since you don't need the market to do anything other than remain where it is.

Market conditions also play an important role. If you feel that a move in the markets is almost certain to occur, you can write ITM options and wait for the move to take place. However, keep in mind that you'll still be running more considerable risks of loss in such a trade.

Before entering any trade, it's best to fix a few worst-case scenario exit points. For example, from the scenario in Figure 16, if we wrote the 215 option, we could have fixed $218 as the highest we would tolerate the stock moving. This is lower than our maximum risk point of 220 and it reduces our loss significantly. If we were aware of the increased risk we were running in this trade, fixing such exit points ahead of time in our minds is a good choice.

Of course, there is the chance that Disney might move to 219 and then fall back down to 205, in which case we would have exited the trade too quickly. However, these kinds of risks are calculated business risks you'll need to take if you wish to trade.

There is no way you'll ever select the perfect strike price every single time, so don't try to do so. Instead, focus on the probability of loss and work from there, minimizing it at every step but not minimizing it to the extent that you earn an extremely small amount of money.

Always begin by selecting your short strike first. This is what earns you money on your trade, so fix this level before moving on to selecting your long strike. It's best to keep the long option within 1-2 strikes of your short option to minimize risk. This will result in less wiggle room for your trade, but it will cap your risk significantly.

If you're going to write ITM options, it's best to buy an option that is one strike away. This will make it easy for you to decide whether you wish to remain in the trade or not. Once you gain more experience, you can play around with selecting strikes that are further away. A long strike that is deeply OTM gives your trade more opportunity to move against you and while also having more leeway to move in the direction that benefits you. Such reversals occur all the time, but the odds of a beginner finding such instances are low. Usually, if the trade moves against you and stays against you for over 15 days, it's probably going to go for a loss.

This assumes you stick to our recommended 30 to 45-day holding period. A 15-day losing period means half the time your trade has been open; it would have resulted in a loss for you. The odds of it suddenly moving into profit are low, especially if volatility is decreasing. Let's move on and see how technical analysis can help us.

USING TECHNICAL ANALYSIS TO DETERMINE STRIKE PRICES

Technical analysis offers us an easy way to determine strike prices. Support and resistance levels are obvious regions for placing our short calls. In the case of a bull put spread, it's best to place the short strike slightly below a support level. This will give the setup additional protection against unexpected bearish swings. The presence of the support level, and the traders that come with it, will ensure that a move below this level will be potentially short-lived.

Similarly, placing the short strike above a resistance level in the case of a bear call spread will offer you added protection. Take care to notice how clean the support or resistance level is. Levels are rarely clean enough for you to draw a perfect horizontal line through them. In most cases you'll find that the market hangs around in a zone. Your degree of aggressiveness determines how deep or shallow within the zone you wish to place yourself. For example, in a bull put spread, you could choose to place the short strike at a shallow level in the support zone. This will increase your premium earned but makes the option finishing ITM more likely.

A strike that is deep within support will earn you less money, but it's more likely to finish OTM. When choosing where to place the short strike, take a look at the price distribution within the zone. Areas where price regularly retreats to within the zone or areas where it bounces away from are where most traders are present. You should look to place yourself at the extremities of these areas. You'll find that these areas get redistributed in large ranges and that the new support and resistance levels might have to be redrawn.

If the idea of using technical analysis to find the best strike prices overwhelms you, then our next method may be more up your street.

USING DELTA TO DETERMINE STRIKE PRICES

We discussed earlier that an option's delta serves as a proxy for determining how likely it is to finish ITM. This means we can also use delta to determine levels at which to place our strikes, which is the methodology we taught in our book *Covered Calls for Beginners*.

A delta of 0.16 (which is a proxy for that strike price having 16% chance of finishing ITM) is one standard deviation away from the current price. This is an important number to note because it plays an important part in determining where to place your strikes.

A backtest carried out by *projectoption* tested bull put spreads on the SPY from 2008-2020 (projectoption, 2020). In this test, the participant sold puts with deltas of 0.3, two standard deviations away from price, and bought puts of 0.16 delta. The positions were entered on the first day of the month and exited on the month's final day, regardless of profitability. This strategy yielded a 74% chance of the trader having their options finishing OTM.

Note that put deltas are negative, and we've quoted positive numbers here. When speaking of put deltas, it's important to focus on the absolute value and ignore the sign. Put deltas move just like call deltas do, so the sign is irrelevant here.

This backtest highlights how deltas play an essential part in option strike prices. Combine this with support and resistance levels, and you'll manage to build pretty high probabilities into your trade working out in your favor.

Other Factors to Note when Entering Your Order

When entering your orders, you'll have the option to enter at the market rate or on limit. We usually advise entering a limit order in the middle of the spread. Heavily traded instruments generally have lower spreads, and this makes it possible to achieve a middle of the spread fill. For example, the SPY sometimes witnesses spreads as low as $0.05 for ITM options. Even one of the most heavily traded stocks such as Google has spreads as wide as $0.80 for ITM options. This is on the lower end for stocks but doesn't compare to the SPY.

However, not all indexes witness low spreads. For example, RUT options sometimes have spreads as wide as $1.50. Using a market order on such wide spreads is inadvisable since it might result in you receiving poor order fills, which makes profitability tough. Be patient, target the middle of the spread to enter trades, and never chase a trade if it moves past your ideal entry point.

FREEMAN CREDIT SPREAD RULE #10

ENTER YOUR TRADES AS LIMIT ORDERS IN THE MIDDLE OF THE SPREAD. IF YOU'RE JUST STARTING OUT AND YOUR BROKER ALLOWS IT, ENTER BOTH TRADES SIMULTANEOUSLY

Another point to note with price is that you'll find it tough to enter all 4 legs of an Iron Butterfly at once with some brokers. This usually happens with brokers who aren't well-versed with offering options trading services. An experienced broker will let you enter all four legs at once, and you'll receive quick fills. If your broker doesn't let you do this, enter both spreads separately.

This means you'll enter the bull spread and then the bear spread. Don't mix the legs together and enter short before entering long or vice versa. This will trigger all kinds of risk limit violations on your broker's side and they'll shut you down quickly.

Speaking of trade entry points, we have one final secret weapon that gives you an advantage in knowing if you should enter a trade or not.

11

YOUR SECRET WEAPON FOR TRADE ENTRY - THE VIX

Volatility can be both your best friend and your worst enemy. Many struggling options traders label volatility as being the "best" or the "worst" and use such extreme language to talk about it. In truth, volatility is what you make of it. You can't influence it, so it's best to try to stick to its good side. With respect to credit spread trades, you want to operate in low volatility environments, with the ideal environment being one where volatility is decreasing.

Many inexperienced options sellers chase high volatility environments for two reasons. The first is due to a hangover from directional trading. In that world, volatility is needed for a directional trader to make money, because they can't earn anything if the market moves sideways, so they root for highly volatile market conditions. If you're trading net credit spreads, this isn't what you want.

This brings us to the second reason for chasing high volatility conditions. Option premiums tend to be overpriced during such times, and the prospect of earning high premiums can push traders to choose to write ITM or ATM options. The increased volatility means that the difference in premiums between ATM and OTM options tends to be larger than in normal times. This creates a further incentive for people to push their luck writing ITM options.

Instead of trying to guess where they need to write options, such traders would be better served by analyzing the overall market's volatility. This is especially the case if they're operating in index options. The market's volatility is measured by the volatility index or the VIX.

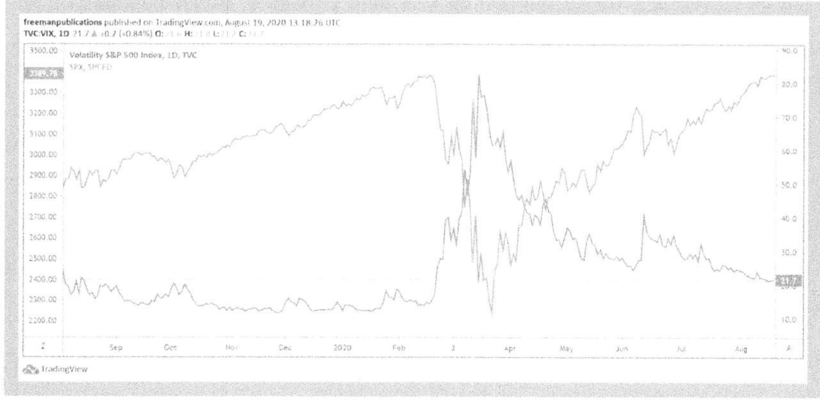

Figure 17: The Correlation Between the VIX and the S&P 500 from Aug 2019 to Aug 2020 (Source: TradingView)

Figure 17 illustrates the correlation between the VIX and the S&P 500 for a 12-month period, beginning in August 2019. As you can see, the VIX starts off low on the left of the chart and then spikes massively as the COVID-related market drop occurred. On March 18th 2020, the VIX closed at 82.69, the highest level since October 2008. Once the market settled down and began climbing again, the VIX fell back to lower levels, even though the numbers are higher than they were in 2019.

Think of the VIX as being the slope of the S&P 500's curve. The sharper the moves in the S&P 500 are, the higher the VIX will be. From a net credit spread perspective, the ideal scenario is to take advantage of high volatility to low volatility transitional periods. The entire period since the market drop has presented such a scenario. However, you need to take the levels of the VIX into account as well.

In the previous chapter, we highlighted a backtest of S&P 500 options that resulted in a 74% win rate. If we were to eliminate entering trades when the VIX was greater than 30, our win rate rises to 77% in that same backtest. A three percent bump doesn't sound like much, but under these conditions, the strategies' overall profitability increases by 50%, which is significant. A simple volatility adjustment allows us to earn an additional 50%.

While the VIX is significant when trading index options, it plays an important role in individual stocks' movements as well. However, much depends on the nature and quality of the stock. If you're focusing on obscure small cap stocks, the VIX is unlikely to affect it too much.

However, if you're operating on one of the bigger stocks in the S&P 500 index, you can bet that the VIX will affect its option prices. A good example of this are the FAANG stocks (Facebook, Apple, Amazon, Netflix, and Google). These five companies are heavily weighted in the S&P 500 and any movement in their stock impacts the overall index.

For this reason, it's best to enter trades in these stocks only when the VIX is below 30. This will ensure the odds of a win are on your side and that any sudden moves won't catch you out. It's impossible to predict what might cause the market to move, of course. However, instead of focusing on predicting market movements, it's best to focus on stacking the odds in our favor as much as possible.

FREEMAN CREDIT SPREAD RULE #11

FOR A HIGHER OVERALL PROBABILITY OF PROFIT ENTER TRADES ON LARGE STOCKS AND INDEX OPTIONS WHEN THE VIX IS BELOW 30

We've already mentioned that you need to stay away from trading options on the VIX itself. This is a bet on volatility and is an extremely risky one. On the surface, it seems like a decent trade because the VIX doesn't spike very often. However, volatility and the VIX is a derivative of the market's movement.

Which means writing options on the VIX is creating a derivative of a derivative. It's not an intuitive way to trade, and it can go wrong for you in a hurry. For this reason, stick to stock and index options.

Now we've determined the ideal time to enter trades, let's talk about how you can manage them once they are live.

12

TRADE MANAGEMENT - EASIER THAN YOU THINK

Trade management is a tricky thing to get right. You shouldn't set and forget your trades ever, but the good news is that you also don't need to remain present in front of your screen the entire time.

There are different ways of managing a trade, but to make things simple, we will focus on setting appropriate take profit and stop loss levels.

We'll begin by first looking at our previously cited backtest of bull put spreads between 2008 to 2020 by *projectoption*. In the previous chapter, we ascertained that by waiting until the VIX was below 30 before entering, the strategy's overall profitability increased by 50%.

The backtesters also added a few trade management variables to their base test, which produced some interesting results.

They tested different trade management options by implementing three take profit levels. These were set at 25% of the maximum profits as well as 50% and 75%. Which meant as soon as the trade reached 25% (or 50 or 75%) of its maximum potential profit, it was immediately closed out. This captured the profits at that level, regardless of how long the options had until expiry.

The 25% level had the highest win rate, winning 86% of all trades. However, it also had the lowest overall profitability. This is because the win amounts were so low that all it took was a single loss to cancel these out. The longer the trades ran, the higher overall profits were captured. The 75% take profit level had the lowest win rate at 76%, but it had the highest overall profit at the end of the backtest.

While this deals with take profit levels, what of stop losses? After all, stop losses are what protect you from capturing a loss. The approach *projectoption* implemented was quite novel. Remember that the way we are setting up our trades, the maximum loss is much larger than the maximum profit. To help mitigate this risk, stop losses were set at -100% gains.

When the trade moved into a position where the loss was equal to the maximum gain, it was closed out. Note that we're talking about the negative value of the maximum gain and not the maximum loss. With this strategy, we're eliminating the maximum loss from the picture with our trades.

For example, if the maximum profit was $300 and the maximum loss was $900, the trade would be closed out if the loss reached $300. Higher stop loss levels of -200% and -300% were also tested in the backtest, but these didn't yield greater overall profits.

This backtest's net result is that as a new trader, you can quickly see that micromanaging your trades isn't going to give you greater gains. In fact, you'll be overcomplicating your trades. It's best to establish sensible rules such as these that have been validated by backtests and then trade according to them.

The approach that will result in the least hassle is taking profits at 75% of maximum profits and setting up a stop loss equal to 100% of your maximum profit. This rules-based approach will help you automate your trade management to a great degree.

SETTING UP LEVELS IN YOUR TRADING ACCOUNT

Now that we've explained how we prefer setting up stop loss and take profit targets let's look at how we input these in your brokerage account. A protective stop order for an option credit spread can be established with the "trigger" for the stop being either:

1. The net premium value of the spread itself
2. The price of the underlying stock, index or ETF

The easiest way to set this up is always to use the first option. That is, to set up our stop loss based on the net premium value of the spread. The important thing to remember is we're using the *net* premium value. This means we have to factor in our initial credit when setting our stop loss order. Let's look at an example to understand this better.

Let's say we enter a $4 wide bull put spread on Oracle (NYSE:ORCL). We sell the 59 put and buy the 55 put for a net credit of $1. For this trade, our max profit is $1, and a max loss is $3 ($4 difference between strike prices - $1 credit on entry.)

Therefore a stop loss equal to -100% of max profit should be set at -$1.

We would then enter a STOP order in our broker platform. In some platforms, this will be listed as a stop order, followed by choosing "market" on the next screen. In other platforms you might simply click "stop market" order as an option.

Note that when we're buying a spread back, we are entering the opposite order to our initial trade. In the ORCL example, this means we are now buying the 59 put and selling the 55 put. This closes out our trade.

Some platforms, like Tastyworks, have a "swap" option, which automatically flips the order. Others will allow you to create a "closing order" or "opposite order" if you select both legs of your spread on the active trades tab.

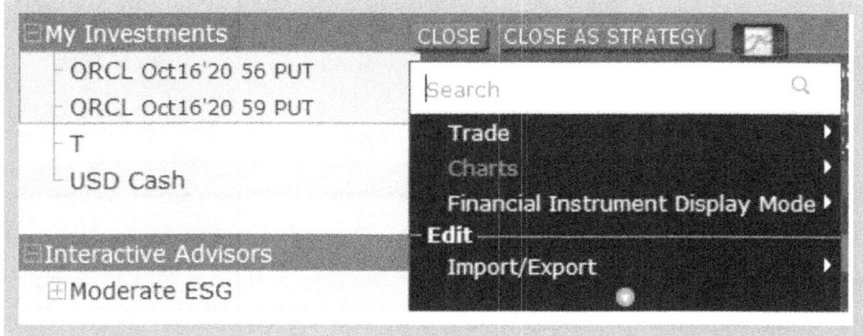

Figure 18: Order Entry Screen in Interactive Brokers

Figure 18 illustrates the order entry screen in Interactive Brokers. Here, you'll select both legs of your spread and right click on it. Click "close" after this, and this closes your spread out.

Keep in mind that you will not enter the order for a $1 value. This will stop us out when our net profit on the trade is $0. We've already received $1 in credit and ($1 - $1) = $0. Always remember that stop orders are triggered by the net premium value of the spread.

Therefore we enter our stop order for $2, because we want to be stopped out when the net premium value of the trade is -$1. To hit -$1 in losses, we need the trade to move $2 against us. Once the trade reaches this -$1 mark, our order will be converted to a market order and automatically executed by our broker.

Make sure you set your stop order as "good until canceled" or GTC, rather than one that expires at the end of the day. This is key because default stop orders in most platforms expire at the end of the day.

Lastly, remember that you will pay commissions for this stop order, so remember to consider your overall P&L calculations.

Setting up Take Profit Levels

Setting up a take profit order is a lot simpler than setting up a stop loss order in most platforms. We simply set a stop order at 75% of whatever our initial credit was since this is the level we wish to exit our trade at. In our ORCL example, our initial credit was $1. This means we set our stop order at $0.75. Note that this stop order refers to your take profit and not your stop loss. It's simply a stop order that causes you to exit for a profit. Figure 19 illustrates what the take profit order setup looks like in Tastyworks.

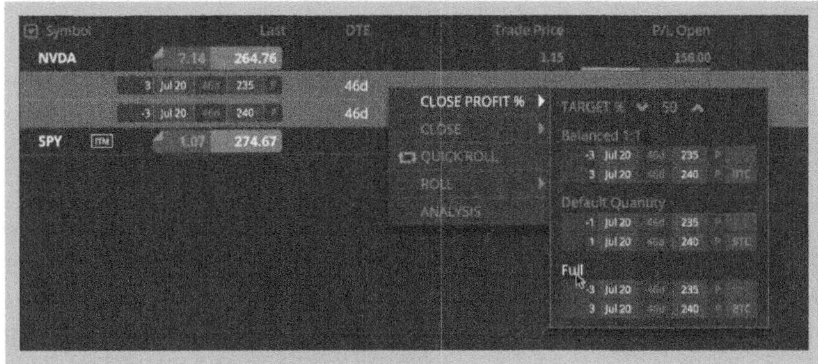

Figure 19: Setting up a Take Profit Order in Tastyworks

One advantage of Tastyworks is that you can set up your take profit orders based on percentages automatically. This means you don't have to calculate your take profit target yourself.

If some of this sounds confusing, don't worry, we have a number of video explanations for how to set up these orders on our YouTube channel which you can find at https://freemanpublications.com/youtube

Note that every brokerage account has a different layout. If you can't find the exact steps to set your orders up on your broker's website, it's best to call their customer support and have them walk you through the process.

If you're just getting started on a new platform, we recommend first trading using a paper account before jumping into live trading. This will help you become acclimated to how your platform works, and you'll avoid losing money due to fat finger errors or other errors caused by incorrect order entry. These mistakes are far more common than you think, so take care to avoid them.

MANAGING BUTTERFLY SPREADS

Managing Iron Butterflies is a bit more complex than credit spreads. This is because of the way the trade is structured. The sweet spot for an Iron Butterfly is pretty well defined. If the underlying doesn't trade at the exact price at which you wrote your short options, the maximum profit isn't realized. This means we ought to be more prudent with our stop loss and take profit targets.

One method is to ignore the top third of the profit range because of the low probability that the stock will trade in this range at expiry. As a result, we're focused just on the bottom two-thirds of the profit range and we aren't mentally anchored to the max profit level.

The easiest way to manage the trade is to stick to standard take profit and stop loss levels. For Iron Butterflies, these are typically 15% for profits and 25% for max loss. 15% of maximum profits might seem small, but remember Butterflies are structured in such a way that max profit is greater than max loss. This means 15% of the maximum profit is a good target.

There are more proactive ways of managing your trade. We'll only discuss neutral Butterflies for the purposes of this book. The great thing about a neutral Butterfly is that only one side of your trade is typically in danger. After all, if you've constructed a neutral spread the underlying cannot simultaneously be above and below your short strikes. This makes trade management a bit easier.

The rule of thumb for managing Butterfly spreads is to adjust your trade before it reaches break even. Newer traders typically adjust after break even has been breached, and they tend to over-adjust, creating more risk for themselves.

Remember that with any trade, adjustments are not designed to turn a losing trade into a winner. Instead, they are meant to create a new trade with different risk parameters. There is no magic formula that will allow you to win every trade.

Scenario #1- If There Are Significant Price Movements Early and You Don't Have a Stop Loss

If you enter a trade and it looks like a loser from the outset, check if your market outlook has changed from your initial assumptions. If yes, your best bet is to buy back the entire Iron Butterfly. By doing this, you may be able to exit the trade for less than your max loss. You'll be marking this trade as a loss, and with a long way to expiry, so it's essential that you only do this if you are certain your initial hypothesis was wrong. If the price has little chance of reversing within your profit boundaries, then carry out this adjustment.

Scenario #2 - If There Are Significant Price Movements Closer to Expiry and You Don't Have a Stop Loss

Let's say you enter a trade with 45 days to expiry, and with 12 days left, the price of the underlying blows through the short strike on the call portion of the trade. Now your long put is far OTM and thus has little value. In this scenario, we can move our long put option closer to the short, to create a new profile, which is still a net credit and maintains little risk on the untested side.

Note that this strategy will only work if the new option's price is low enough that you can still maintain a net credit on the trade. If prices are high and you eat into a significant portion of your initial profits, you're now left with a lopsided trade in terms of risk/reward ratio. Let's look at this using an example.

Let's say we sell a $10 wide iron butterfly on Papa John's (NASDAQ:PZZA), which is currently trading at $99.50, for a net credit of $5.50. Our 10 point wide butterfly would consist of these legs:

- Buy $89 put
- Sell $99 put
- Sell $99 call
- Buy $109 call

Our net credit on the trade is $5.50. If the stock rallies to 115, we may have the opportunity to sell the 89 strike and purchase another put at a 94 strike for a net debit of $0.30. This means our net credit is now $5.20, but we have just a five dollar wide put spread component of the Butterfly (because our short strike remains at 99.)

We now have no risk to the downside, since the stock price could drop below 89 and our put spread would be worth $5.00 at expiration, but we've collected $5.20 and would make $0.20 overall.

As you can see here, this adjustment strategy only works if we can buy the 94 strike for less than $0.50. If it is more than $0.50, oour trade will still lose if it falls below 89.

Scenario #3 - Doing Nothing as a Trade Management Strategy

This sounds counterintuitive, but doing nothing is a legitimate management strategy for Butterflies. This is because they're a defined risk trade where you know your max profit and max loss up front. Instead of focusing on the best adjustment strategies, it would be better to focus on your entry points and the data you had available, which caused you to choose those entry points. In our experience working with people new to iron butterflies, the problem tends to be with their entry points rather than their trade management.

AVOIDING THE WORST CASE SCENARIO FOR CREDIT SPREADS

As we stated earlier, the most important factor in successful options trading is risk management. The following example is an incredibly rare trading event, where a trader was assigned an option after expiration. This resulted in massive losses for him. We'll explain how it happened, plus what you can do to ensure it never happens to you.

We should stress that the trader himself was not at fault here. He fell victim to a little known quirk of options trading, combined with his broker's poor communication.

We'll start with the basics. How is it possible a trader was assigned an option after expiration? Below is an excerpt of the rule from the Option Industry Council's website (Options Exercise, 2020):

> *Can I exercise my right to buy the stock at any time up to the expiration date?*
>
> *As the holder of an equity or ETF call option, you can exercise your right to buy the stock throughout the life of the option up to your brokerage firm's exercise cut-off time on the last trading day.* ***Options exchanges have a cut-off time of 4:30 p.m. CST, for receiving an exercise notice.*** *Be aware that most brokerage firms have an earlier cut-off time for submitting exercise instructions in order to meet exchange deadlines.*

We've highlighted the most important sentence in bold. The stock market closes at 3PM Central Time (4PM EST), but options can be exercised up to 90 minutes *after* this time. Therefore, if your stock experiences significant after-hours movement, it can mean that an option that you thought had expired OTM, might move ITM during this 90-minute period. Which puts you at risk of being assigned.

Here was the trade in question. The trader sold five contracts of the 410/409 put spreads on Tesla. Therefore his max loss was $500 ($1 wide spread * five contracts.) At market close (3PM CST), Tesla was trading at $418. That means the trader's put spreads were out of the money and would expire worthless.

However, at 4:16PM CST, Tesla had fallen to $393, sending his $410 short put ITM. The trader was assigned all five contracts. This meant he was forced to purchase 500 shares of Tesla at $410, which represents a position of $205,000.

At this point, the trader was not in any real danger, because he could still exercise his $409 long puts to cancel the losses from the $410 puts. Or so he thought...

However, his broker did not inform him of the $410 put exercise until well after the 4:30PM CST cutoff time. This meant he could not exercise his $409 put, and it expired worthless. He was left with an order of 500 shares of Tesla, which approximated to a cash position of $205,000. As his account was only worth around $30,000, his broker liquidated the position for a $30,000 loss.

Ensuring This Never Happens to You

What transpired above was a series of unfortunate events, but ones that were entirely within the boundaries of options trading. The trader in question was an experienced options trader, who had initially placed a very conservative trade. The result was a combination of a quirk in options trading rules, and poor communication from the trader's brokerage firm.

The easiest way to mitigate this risk is to close any short options a couple days before expiration, even if they aren't ITM. You'll make a slightly lower profit on each trade, but it will give you peace of mind knowing that you won't put your entire account in jeopardy if a catastrophic scenario occurs. If you take max profit at 75% like stated earlier in this chapter, you're at less risk of this scenario occurring, but you should still close out your trades a couple of days before expiration to ensure it doesn't happen.

For a full, in-depth explanation of this exact scenario occurring with the trade in question, please watch the full video at: http://freemanpublications.com/creditspread30k

Note: Since this incident occurred, it has come to our attention that this scenario has affected multiple people, most notably those using the Robinhood platform. It turns out Robinhood did not alert traders until eight hours after the market had closed. For this reason, as well as ones we stated earlier in the book, we do not recommend using Robinhood to trade options of any kind.

You can also call your broker to see what their rules are for a scenario like this. For example, the Thinkorswim platform states they will automatically exercise your protective put in this case, mitigating your risk. Always call your broker to confirm this and make sure you get any answers in written format via email if you need to refer back to them later.

13

MONEY MANAGEMENT

Money management is essential when it comes to trading. Unlike passive long-term investing, you'll be moving in and out of the markets far more regularly. You won't be establishing as many positions as a day trader would but assuming you stick to the 30 to 45-day window we recommend, you'll likely have at least one active trade open per month.

A common question that many people ask when viewing a strategy is: How much money can I make from this? The answer is that it depends on how much you risk per trade. It's possible to earn 200% per year, and it's equally possible to earn 5%.

As we've mentioned in our other books, you need to move past thinking in terms of absolute returns and focus on risk-adjusted returns instead. There are many risk-adjusted metrics that professionals use.

You can track basic risk-adjusted metrics such as the Sharpe ratio or the Sortino ratio to measure account performance. However, when it comes to successful credit spread trading, you need to begin with the amount of money you risk per trade and focus on that solely.

If you follow our previous recommendations regarding profit taking and loss levels. You won't have to worry too much about the underlying math in your trades working out in your favor. This means your biggest consideration in how much to risk per trade, is the size of your account, and the price of the option spreads. This is because you need that much cash or margin in your account for the trade to go through.

For a credit spread, the margin requirement for each spread (with most/major brokerages) is calculated as:

(Spread Width - Credit Received) x 100

If you sell a $12 wide spread for $3.22, the margin requirement would be (($12 - $3.22) x 100) = $878 in margin requirement per spread sold, as the maximum loss potential per spread would be $878.

If you're starting out, we recommend risking no more than 10% of your account per trade. If you're from the world of directional trading, this will sound like a ridiculously high number. Indeed, most directional traders should not risk more than 0.5% of their account. However, with options, we can get away with risking this much for two reasons.

First, we're implementing net credit spread strategies that have a high success rate. We're also assuming that you will paper trade strategies before jumping into the live market. This means you'll be well-versed with your strategies and won't be assuming undue risk. The second reason for a 10% per trade risk rate is that you'll be placing one to two trades per month.

We advise against placing more than one trade or trading more than one instrument as you'll shortly learn. If you're trading a low number of instruments, your per-trade risk can be much higher. Also, remember that you'll be taking your losses as a function of your credit earned, not at the max loss number. All of this means a 10% risk number is perfectly fine.

ACCOUNTS AND OTHER TIPS

Money and risk management go hand in hand, and the biggest rule to observe when trading options is that you need to separate your options trading account from your long-term investing account. Your long-term investment account has nothing to do with your trading strategies. This will allow you to remain invested no matter what, and you won't end up selling your long-term stock holdings to cover option assignments.

Selling at the wrong time is one of the biggest reasons individual investors don't make money in the markets. Driven by panic or by euphoria, they often sell at the worst moment possible and end up losing the power of compounding. To make a lot of money, you need to remain invested for long periods and keep contributing to your account regularly. This is not how money is made in trading. Hence, keep your accounts separate.

Now that you know how your account needs to be set up and how much you'll risk per trade, the question of how much you can expect to earn is easier to answer. Assuming you follow the rules we've previously outlined, you'll earn between 1-3% percent per month. This isn't the 20,000% gain that some Twitter traders like to post screenshots of. However, from an asset investment perspective, this is a fantastic return. Best of all, it's fully scalable. Many trading strategies make large returns when the capital invested is small, but they fall apart when larger sums are involved. With credit spreads, it's true that you can't expect to run them efficiently if you have billions of dollars. However, you'll probably be very happy with a trading account that is one percent of that. We can confidently say that even if you have millions in your trading account, you'll be able to generate these kinds of returns safely.

As your account size grows, it's best to dial down the risk you run with every trade until you reach a more conventional two percent. This is because you will have less of your account at risk and you'll still be able to earn a good amount of money from your trades. If your account is small, you'll probably need to risk 10% as we mentioned earlier.

What if your account is so small that even a 10% per trade risk doesn't cover most stocks' margin requirements? In such cases, you have two choices. The first is to choose lower width spreads and stick to trading them at all times. The second is to accumulate enough capital until you have enough to risk 10% per trade successfully. Set aside some money regularly every month until you have enough to meet this risk limit.

We do not advise risking more than this to trade options. This will create massive fluctuations in your account as your trade progresses and might result in you closing your trades out too early due to the fear of losing money. Stay patient and accumulate money until you have enough to trade properly.

Instruments To Trade

How many instruments should you trade? This is a tough question to answer for most traders. It depends on how much you're risking per trade. As a rule of thumb, you don't want your risk to exceed 10% per month. However, if you place five positions, you'll be risking 50% or half of your account. This isn't a good way to trade.

Therefore, the best thing to do is to limit your monthly risk to 10%. Since all of your trades will be within the 30 to 45-day period, a per trade risk of 10% means you'll have just one position active during the month. If you risk 5% per trade, you can open two positions and so on. This gives you a good way to limit your risk and tie it to your per trade risk.

When choosing instruments, it's best to begin paper trading them before going live. Every instrument has different sets of traders active in them, and it will take you some time to adjust to its rhythms. Observe your chosen instruments for at least two months before committing to trade them live. It's best if you observe them for at least six months or two quarters. This will give you an idea of how volatility changes around earnings season.

Realistically speaking, you will need to master moves in two stocks at the very least. Preferably, their earnings season will be spaced apart so that they're in different months. This way you'll always have one instrument to operate in. Do you need more than two instruments? Some traders prefer to add more as they grow, but our opinion is that two is more than enough.

In trading, it's better to go deeper rather than wide. This means if you master trading a few stocks, you'll make more than enough money. Don't get carried away or get influenced by images of traders sitting in front of 10 screens. Many successful traders visit their trading platforms once a day, trade one or two instruments, use simple strategies, and make a ton of money.

Master a few instruments instead of the entire S&P 500 and you'll make a lot of money. Do not confuse complexity for competence. Some of the worst traders are those who sit themselves down in front of multiple screens and try to make sense of far too many instruments. This is true of active traders. The strategies we've outlined in this book aren't active ones or as active as the ones that most directional traders implement. There's no reason for you to become wedded to your laptop. Specialization is the key to large profits, so make this your goal.

14

THE LONG-TERM PROFIT MINDSET

"If investing is entertaining, if you're having fun, you're probably not making any money. Good investing is boring."

— GEORGE SOROS

If we had to summarize trading into one word, we'd say "boring." That doesn't mean you won't enjoy it or that you shouldn't be passionate about it. We're trying to say that excitement in the context of the markets is a bad thing. Traders are mostly focused on the short-term prices of stocks, and in the short term, most movements are created by emotions.

Euphoria, greed, fear and excitement create more moves in the market than are strictly necessary. If your trading or investing feels like a rollercoaster, you're doing it wrong. We're not saying you should be bored to the point of dozing off in your chair when you trade. Instead, the ideal mood is one of engaged boredom. Think of it as watching a TV show you're mildly interested in. This is irrespective of whether or not you have a position in the market.

Many traders get extremely excited when they have a position because their money is now at risk. Excitement can go two ways. It can prompt extreme happiness, or it can promote extreme sadness and anxiety. This is no way to trade. Thankfully, with credit spreads you capture your entire profit upfront, and there's not much else you need to do after that. This goes a long way towards removing any source of "excitement" you might feel.

Figure 20: The above excitement vs. boredom concept visualized

To maintain as much consistency as possible, your trading routine should be geared towards minimizing as many unexpected occurrences. Let's look at how you can set this up.

THE IDEAL TRADING ROUTINE

Many elements go into your routine. First let's deal with your actions during the trading day. The markets open at 9:30AM EST, and between 9:30AM and 11AM is where the majority of trading volumes occur. You don't need to be present on the spot to place orders quickly. As we covered earlier, you'll be trading high liquidity instruments, and this means you can theoretically place orders throughout the day without any adverse consequences.

However, we advise placing your orders during the initial period because price spreads tend to contract during this time. Stay away from the opening bell since this is when overnight orders come rushing in, and volatility will be high. Let the market settle, and then enter your trades. This means you don't need to witness the opening bell. Instead, make sure your trades are placed by 11AM and leave it at that.

Once your trades are placed, there's nothing else you need to do during the day. In subsequent days, you'll monitor your position throughout the day by checking in to see its unrealized profit or loss and make adjustments according to the rule-based strategies we've already outlined. Don't get carried away and hang around in your trading platform too much since this might tempt you to place more trades.

If you've struggled with this in the past, simply log out and go do something else. Most readers of this book will have full-time jobs, so it's best to focus on that instead of remaining glued to your trading screen. Once the markets close, after-hours trading begins. You can place your orders during these times if you missed the market hours, provided you can still find a good spread. However, it's best not to make a habit of it. After-hours trading is when spreads notoriously widen. Also, if you're entering a limit order, your broker might not be able to fill your order. In fact, most brokers won't allow you to place limit orders after hours.

During market hours or when you're placing orders, stay away from social media. In fact, stay away from social media at all times unless you can practice a good deal of self-control. Following people on Twitter for trade recommendations is not a sustainable way of making money. Remember, you need just one or two trades every month. If you're trading just two instruments or even five, there's no need for you to scour the internet for more trade ideas.

Feel free to watch YouTube videos on options trading after the market is closed. Don't do so if you're entering orders or are analyzing possible trade setups. Avoid any distractions when you're placing your orders. If you find yourself in front of the trading screen for the majority of the day, either focus on it completely or walk away.

Diet, Exercise and Sleep

These three factors will do a lot more to affect your trading than any technical analysis indicator. You cannot trade well if you aren't taking care of yourself by eating good food, sleeping well and exercising enough. Let's begin with your diet. This isn't a fitness book, so we're not going to debate the advantages of the keto diet over the paleo diet and so on. Eat whatever you want, but make sure it reduces inflammation in your gut or keeps it to a minimum. Your gut and brain are linked, and research has proven this many times over (Robertson, 2018). Avoid processed food as much as possible and stick to whole food sources.

If your stomach is upset, your brain is less likely to focus, and you're going to make poor decisions. Exercise is linked directly to your appetite. Whatever your choice of staying active is, it's important that you engage in it at least four times every week. If you're someone who hasn't been active for a long time, focus on breaking a sweat at least once a week.

It doesn't matter what your chosen activity is. Make sure you're engaging in it four times every week and are giving your body a good workout. If you're completely inactive right now, start by taking a brisk walk and build from there.

Proper diet and exercise will help you sleep better. Sleep is an essential part of a healthy lifestyle. The easiest way to ruin your mood is not to sleep enough. Make sure your bedroom is dark and quiet. Keep the temperature at optimal levels, and get at least six to seven hours of sleep per night.

Hydrate yourself throughout the day. Make sure you drink your 8 glasses of water every day. Drinking enough water ensures you'll remain healthy more than taking any medicines. Also, minimize alcohol intake since this dehydrates your body. You don't have to eliminate it if you don't want to, but certainly, minimize intake prior to trading days.

Mental Health

In the post-COVID world, our workspaces have become increasingly isolated. Full-time traders are used to this since trading is a solitary activity. However, regular workplaces have also become remote these days, and mental health is a huge issue. Monitoring your mental health is crucial if you want to make good trades. Trading requires you to make a number of discretionary decisions, and making good ones is impossible if your mental health isn't optimal.

Consider joining a trading community so you can surround yourself with like-minded people. No one will understand your predicament like other traders, and sometimes it's fun just to talk shop. The other benefit of being around people with similar interests and goals is that you avoid the negative talk that society at large has about trading and the financial world.

If you're looking for a community of like-minded people, join our Facebook Group at

https://freemanpublications.com/facebook

Another fantastic tool that is universally beneficial is meditation. Meditation helps calm down your body and mind, and it acts as a tool to separate yourself from your results. This sounds nuanced, but being able to differentiate between "I made a bad trade" and "I'm a bad trader" is of the utmost importance. You can find many free meditation tutorials on YouTube as well as paid apps like Headspace and Stop.Breathe.Think.

Whatever you do, never trade under the following conditions:

- Hungry
- Angry
- Lonely
- Tired
- Under the influence of drugs or alcohol

Avoiding these conditions will put you in a good position to trade. Establish a consistent routine and repeat it over and over. That's all there is to trading successfully.

CONCLUSION

Successful credit spread trading is like building a house. You begin by laying the foundations and then build on top of it brick by brick. You'll need to keep building on the gains you've previously made and keep educating yourself. Don't make the mistake of choosing short-term gains for long-term success. You might get frustrated in the short term, but remember that delayed gratification is the key to long-term success.

As we reach the end of this book, we'd like to remind you of the importance of generating income from your portfolio, as opposed to just capital gains. Capital gains are great, but in a low interest world it's important to generate income that can bring you additional cash flow. With savings accounts and other typical modes of passive investment unprofitable, you need to implement net credit spreads and other income generating strategies into your trading routine.

Credit spreads can bring you an average of 1-3% every month. If your capital is $5,000, this amounts to $100 per month or $1,200 per year. This doesn't sound like a lot of money, but remember that credit spreads are scalable. You'll earn this income whether your capital is $5,000 or $500,000. In 10 years time, assuming you reinvest your profits and keep earning the same rate of returns, your account balance will grow to $53,825. At that stage you'll be earning an extra $1,100 per month.

Even if you pull out your initial $5,000 after a few years, so you can essentially play with house money, and still be earning a steady 4 figures per month if you stay consistent over a period of multiple years.

And remember, you don't have to be a financial wizard or have a master's degree in statistics when starting out. Here are 3 examples of ordinary people using credit spreads to supplement their income.

> *"My worst year, I had 29 wins and 4 losses, which comes out to 86.2% winning trades. My best year was last year, 28 wins, 1-loss, 95.6%. The years in between I never got less than 92% wins, so it's just been wonderful."* – **Bob M., Florida**

> *"Trading is going well. I'm currently trading just spreads each month. That'll be three months in a row with an average profit of about $1,500 per month."* – **Matt I., Indiana**

> *"I have been investing in Credit Spreads since August. I pick them based on my own analysis so that I have one spread potentially expiring every week, and I'm looking to earn $250-$1,000 per spread. Results: 51 Trades, 47 Winners (92%), $28,430 in profits after commission (about $557 average per trade)"* – **Anthony M.**

Remember to keep things simple when starting out. One of the beauties of credit spreads is that you don't need to use 15 or 20 different technical indicators to set them up. Nor do you need to spend multiple hours monitoring your positions every day.

All you need to trade well are support and resistance levels, Bollinger Bands, and moving averages. These sound ridiculously simple, but that's all you truly need to figure out what the markets are doing.

To cement this principle, consider writing down the quote below in your trading journal:

> *"I fear not the man who has practiced 10,000 kicks once. I fear the man who has practiced one kick 10,000 times"*
>
> — BRUCE LEE

Your trading routine is important, and instead of tailoring it to produce as much excitement as possible, focus on generating consistency. Do the same things over and over as long as they're producing profits for you. If you're finding yourself getting stressed or feeling burnt-out when thinking of your trading, you're probably risking too much money.

We recommend sticking to a maximum limit of 10% per trade. As your account grows, we recommend scaling this back down to 2%. Your priority should always be to maintain your capital, first and foremost. Too many market participants focus on making money and take undue risk. Focus on keeping the money you have and the gains will take care of themselves.

Lastly, keep educating yourself. There are always simpler ways to make money from the markets. Maintain your focus on mastering the process of trading instead of looking at the gains you can potentially make. As we said earlier, focus on eliminating risks and your rewards will take care of themselves. We're positive that this book will help you generate steady income from your portfolio. We wish you the best of luck in your trading!

One final word from us. If this book has helped you in any way, we'd appreciate it if you left a review on Amazon. Reviews are the lifeblood of our business. We read every single one and incorporate your feedback into our future book projects.

To leave an Amazon review, go to:
https://freemanpublications.com/leaveareview

CONCLUSION

REFERENCES

Bond Algos Tap into ETF Liquidity and Efficiency Gains. (2019, March 18). Finextra Research. https://www.finextra.com/blogposting/16827/bond-algos-tap-into-etf-liquidity-and-efficiency-gains

Frazier, K. C. (2015). *The Process Behind New Medicines.* http://phrma-docs.phrma.org/sites/default/files/pdf/rd_brochure_022307.pdf

Lewis, M. (2015). *Flash boys: a Wall Street revolt.* W.W. Norton & Company.

Options Exercise. (2020). Optionseducation.Org. https://www.optionseducation.org/referencelibrary/faq/options-exercise

projectoption. (2020). Options Trading With Credit Spreads (FULL Trading Plan w/ Results) [YouTube Video]. In *YouTube.* https://www.youtube.com/watch?v=XBxDtcPu3PA

Robertson, R. (2018, June 27). *The Gut-Brain Connection: How it Works and The Role of Nutrition.* Healthline. https://www.healthline.com/nutrition/gut-brain-connection#:~:text=The%20Bottom%20Line&text=Millions%20of%20n-erves%20and%20neurons

IRON CONDOR OPTIONS FOR BEGINNERS

A SMART, SAFE METHOD TO GENERATE AN EXTRA 25% PER YEAR WITH JUST 2 TRADES PER MONTH

INTRODUCTION

One of the things that makes the financial markets such a wonderful resource for wealth creation is the diversity of money-making strategies that an investor can implement. You can buy stocks for the long term, you can buy bonds to earn interest, you can buy funds that execute certain strategies for you and you can even speculate in currencies based on macroeconomic conditions.

Derivatives are another type of instruments that an investor can take advantage of to boost their investment returns. While there are many different kinds of derivative securities, the ones that are the most popular are options contracts. Under the category of options, there are many different kinds of contracts that investors have access to.

The large majority of these are available only to institutional traders, and our opinion is that this is a very good thing. When used incorrectly, derivative contracts can cause huge losses and have the power to bankrupt even the most well-capitalized trader or investor. The housing crisis of 2008 is a prime example of how derivatives can cause untold damage when used incorrectly.

As far as the retail market is concerned, there are two kinds of options contracts one can buy. These are the call and the put. If you've picked up this book, then the odds are that you already know what those are. You might have even traded options in the past and even found some success with them.

Options tend to receive a bad rap amongst investors since they're viewed as highly speculative instruments that can create more problems than they solve. In this book you're going to learn why that view is mistaken. To make it clear, we're not advocating the average investor go out and begin speculating in options.

Our contention is that investors can utilize options in an intelligent manner to generate a steady source of income for themselves. Income generation is something that every investor desires. One of the drawbacks of investing in stocks is that not all of them have the potential to generate cash flow.

There are dividend-paying stocks, but these yield around two to three percent a year on average. There are some high-yielding stocks that pay around eight percent, but such stocks often come with their own set of risks. Besides, chasing such high yields often results in investing in risky companies. While the capital gains that stock investing provides can be massive over the long run, it would be great if these were supplemented by cash flow on a regular basis.

This book is going to give you a great strategy to employ that will generate steady returns for you in years to come. You will learn how you can use humble *call* and *put* options to execute this strategy.

IRON CONDORS

One of the things that adds to the perception of options being complex are the names that the strategies carry. "Buy and hold" is easy to understand and conveys exactly what it entails. What do "Iron Condor" or "bull put spread" and so on mean exactly?

As is often the case, complexity is just a veneer when it comes to these strategies. There's no denying that there are extremely complex strategies that can be executed with options, but this is entirely up to you. You can choose to execute a simple strategy or an extremely complicated one.

Iron condors have the potential to generate between two to four percent of your investment principal as regular monthly income. If your trading capital amounts to $10,000, you could earn an extra $200 and $400 per month. You do not need to stick to your trading screen 24/7 since these trades require minimal management. What's more, you'll need to place just one or two trades every month to earn this kind of return.

You will notice that we're not promising millions. You cannot make $1 million in 10 days using the strategy outlined in this book. We believe no such strategy exists that can be repeated profitably and safely. The purpose of showing you how the iron condor works is to help you ultimately become a better investor.

This is because the strategy requires you to understand volatility as well as good entry points. One of the drawbacks of traditional buy and hold investing is that it doesn't take volatility into account. Investors open themselves up to the risk of receiving terrible entry prices and this skews the returns they can earn in the long run.

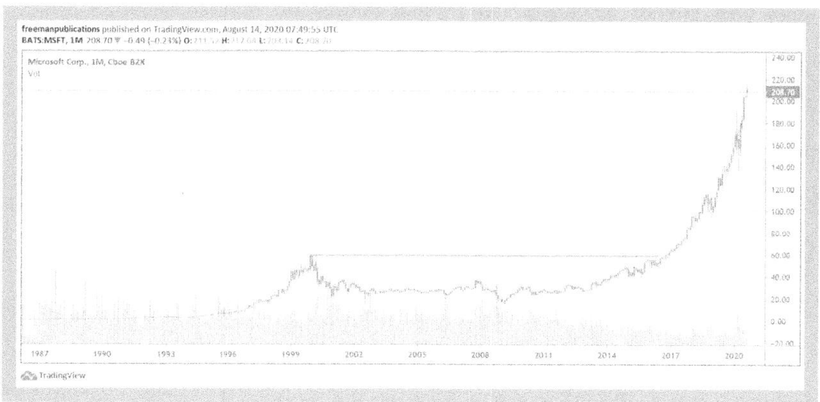

Figure 1: Entry point matters - If you had bought Microsoft at its peak on December 1st 1999, it would have taken 17 years to recover your original investment. If you had bought on June 1st 2016 for the same price ($58.95), you would have gained 302% in just 4 years.

Trading iron condors successfully will help you read volatility better and will allow you to evaluate trading entry points much better. Best of all, they're nowhere near as complex as you might think they are.

This doesn't mean executing them is child's play. You will need to understand the basics of options trading. When writing a book such as this, the authors need to make certain assumptions. We've assumed that you have basic options knowledge and understand how calls and puts work.

We've also assumed that you're up to speed with the terminology that surrounds options trading. Ideally, you will have traded options with live money previously, but it's not necessary. As long as you can understand the language used to describe options trading, that's more than enough.

You will not need to understand the ins and outs of options Greeks, although this might be helpful. Where applicable, we will highlight the elements of the iron condor that can be explained better via the Greeks. As such, there's no need for you to understand them in depth.

Above all else, we've assumed that you're here to learn and put the effort into making the strategy work. It takes time, but this doesn't mean you need to wait for years on end to be able to earn money. Follow the principles explained in this book, especially in the chapters on trading routine and mental discipline.

These chapters describe what it takes to manage your risk in the market successfully and insulate yourself from making rash decisions. While the iron condor is profitable, it requires you to understand the way it works. It's a great strategy but can create losses when used incorrectly.

Let's now dive in and try to figure out why options trading gets such a bad rap.

THE FOUNDATIONS

1

MINUS 2,387% RETURNS - WHY OPTIONS TRADING GETS A BAD RAP

Since the rise of low commission online trading platforms, options trading and investing has been gaining mainstream popularity. There have been a number of books and other literature from credible sources that have highlighted how they can be used to generate income in an intelligent manner.

Despite this, there is a large body of investors who stay away from options. They believe it to be a high-risk and high-reward means of taking advantage of the markets. There is some truth in this. There are options strategies that offer very high rewards but expose you to massive downside risk.

Then there's also the fact that most investors who use options do so in ways that break every rule of intelligent investing out there. Consider the image below which is a screenshot of an options trader's Robinhood account. Names and identifying information have been removed.

The numbers in this image are not photoshopped. That really is a 2387.84% loss they've sustained thanks to speculating in options. The story behind this number is instructive. This particular trader was speculating on the value of the VIX, which is the volatility index.

His thesis was that the VIX was behaving as if it would maintain its current levels for a long time, and consequently he sold calls of UVXY at $26. UVXY is a leveraged ETF that moves in accordance with the VIX. As Figure 1 shows, nothing of this sort happened and UVXY rocketed up to $55, thanks to its leveraged nature.

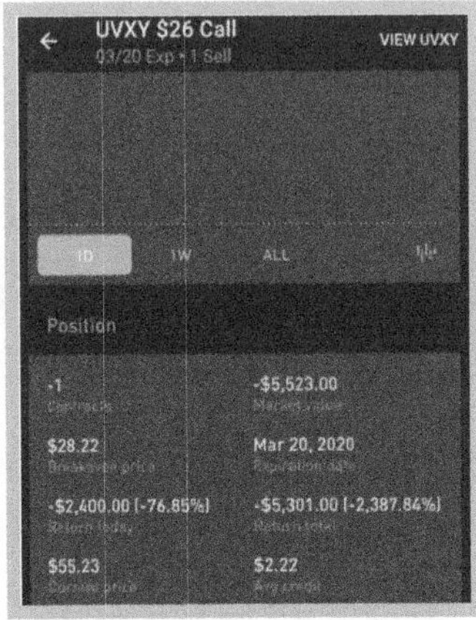

Figure 2: An Options Trader's Account

This incident is instructive in highlighting how the average trader or investor views options. Options are a leveraged instrument to begin with. Each contract covers 100 shares of the underlying instrument. To add leverage to this via an ETF is to assume an unsustainable amount of risk.

Even if this trade had worked out, we have no doubt that this trader would have met with losses down the road that would have wiped out all of his gains. Misunderstanding the role that leverage plays is an error that many options traders make. They look at its potential in terms of boosting gains but neglect the reality that they can lose many multiples of their investment capital by assuming too much of it.

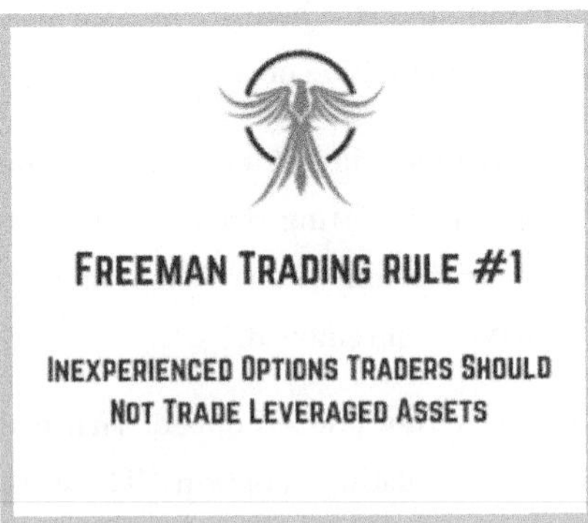

INTELLIGENT OPTIONS – YOUR UNIQUE ADVANTAGE OVER WARREN BUFFETT

When used properly, successful options investing is no different from traditional buy and hold investing, as outlined in our other books. While the instruments used and the structure of the trade might be different, the principles that underlie them are the same. They involve understanding the strategy thoroughly and picking the right conditions to take advantage of.

Take the example of Warren Buffett. He's regularly been quoted (along with his business partner Charlie Munger) as saying that derivatives are financial weapons of mass destruction (Cox, 2018). He's spoken many times about the ills of mark to market accounting and all of the procedures that surround options accounting.

Yet, he isn't averse to using options to boost his returns when the time is right. In his 2009 letter to Berkshire shareholders, Buffett explained in great detail how he had used puts to generate investment income. Here are his exact words via https://www.berkshirehathaway.com/2009ar/2009ar.pdf:

> "Our put contracts total $37.1 billion (at current exchange rates) and are spread among four major indexes: the S&P 500 in the U.S., the FTSE 100 in the U.K., the Euro Stoxx 50 in Europe, and the Nikkei 225 in Japan. Our first contract comes due on Sept. 9, 2019, and our last on Jan., 24, 2028. We have received premiums of $4.9 billion, money we have invested."

Buffett went on to explain that the options Berkshire had written were European options, so he didn't have to worry about having to cover his position in the interim. He had also taken into account counterparty risk given the massive size of these contracts. He then went on to explain why mark to market accounting that utilized the Black-Scholes model was causing a hole in Berkshire's balance sheet despite the large gains that the investment had secured.

. . .

Your Advantage

All of this can seem quite complicated, but there's good news. Thanks to your smaller size, you have many advantages that Warren Buffett doesn't. It might sound crazy to read that, but it's true.

The average retail trader focuses far too much on what they do not have (capital) instead of focusing on what they do have (flexibility and liquidity) when comparing themselves to institutional traders.

For starters, you do not need to worry about generating a satisfactory return on billions of dollars of assets. If you're controlling just $5,000 and earn $1,000 on this, you've earned a 20% return, which is great!

If Buffett earned $100 million on his option investment using the numbers he quoted above, he would have earned just 0.2%. There are far less opportunities for him to invest that sum of cash in the markets than there are available to you. While it's true that he could buy an entire company that is selling for $500 million or even a billion, this represents a drop in the bucket in terms of his overall capital.

The next advantage that you have over an institutional investor like Buffett is that you don't have to worry about counterparty risk. When executing options strategies, you need to take the credit quality of the other party into question. Think of it like this. If you make a bet with someone and the payoff is $1,000, you need to first be sure they have the money to pay you. It's no good winning your bet and then finding out the other guy is broke.

Buffett's payoff from his options play was close to five billion dollars. Not many institutions around the world have that kind of cash lying around. Still fewer would be willing to take the opposite side of a bet from Warren Buffett. If you know that the other guy is more often right than wrong, the sensible thing to do is to stay away from him.

Counterparty risk is something you do not need to worry about. The average retail investor speculates in the thousands and their brokers use clearing corporations that have liquidity and balance sheets worth billions. As such, there is zero counterparty risk.

You also don't have to worry about your reputation following you and will find that your smaller bet size will find many takers in the market. Thus, you can theoretically earn a larger return than most institutions can. Peter Lynch summarized this idea in his book *One Up on Wall Street.*

Another thing to note is that thanks to the sheer size of his trade, Buffett needed a long enough investment horizon for it to work out. This is one of the reasons why he never sells his investment unless something goes wrong with the fundamentals of the companies he buys.

In order to generate respectable levels of returns on his money, he needs to provide his investments with a large enough runway. It's unrealistic for him to expect 20% returns per year, and he has repeatedly stressed that as Berkshire's capital grows, its expected return on capital decreases as well. This is just common sense.

You don't need to write options that are 10-20 years long in terms of expiry dates. The average trade length of the iron condor highlighted in this book will be between 30 and 45 days.

The iron condor has a few more legs to it than the relatively simple-looking trade that Buffett placed, and this might lead you to think it's complicated. This isn't true and is in fact a trap that most of the "options are complicated and risky" crowd fall into.

The number of legs a trade has isn't what matters. The risk inherent in the trade if it moves against you is the true measure of how much you stand to lose. You'd think this is common sense, but it escapes the grasp of many investors.

The iron condor is a non-directional strategy that can earn you between two to four percent returns per month, provided you find the right candidates in which to execute the strategy. We'll explain how you can find these later in the book. For now, we'd like to draw your attention to another reason why many investors look at options as being far too risky, and why this is an incorrect view to adopt.

Questionable Return Claims

There are many options gurus out there whose marketing efforts center around rags to riches stories like turning $1,000 into $1 million. The spirit behind such claims is to try to convince you that options can bring unimaginable amounts of wealth. To most intelligent investors, such claims sound nonsensical.

You'll find claims of earning 20% returns every month. At such rates of returns you can turn $1,000 into a million in three years. By the fifth year, you'll have $53 million. If you believe that such returns are actually possible without a huge amount of risk, we have a bridge to sell you!

The important thing when evaluating an investment strategy is to look at how repeatable it is and what its risk profile is. The iron condor is a low-risk/low-return strategy. This means you're likely to win most of the time (the profit probability of your trades is around 80-85%) and your payoff will be low. This is right in line with the principles of successful investing.

By focusing on executing highly repeatable and scalable strategies, you can build your wealth step by step and let the rest lose their shirt over the "20% per month"-type strategies.

More importantly, the iron condor doesn't place any additional burden on your time. You can monitor your trades with little maintenance. You can easily earn a few thousand dollars per month in additional income and use this money to invest in other companies to generate more capital gains for yourself.

Central to our approach is to show you the benefits of maintaining a disciplined trading mindset and to evaluate risk correctly. There are many elements that go into this, so take the time to learn all of them. You might be tempted to dive right into the specifics of how to invest using the iron condor, but we urge you to read the chapters that precede it first.

This is what will set you up for long-term success with trading options and will augment whatever gains you make from your long-term stock investments.

Terminology

As mentioned in the introduction, we have made some assumptions about your knowledge when writing this book. We have assumed that you're familiar with the language that is used to describe options trading and that you are fully aware of the parts that constitute an options contract, such as 1 contract being equivalent to 100 shares of the underlying.

Terms such as *expiry dates, strike prices* and *intrinsic value* are hopefully familiar to you since we'll be referring to these when describing the strategy. You don't need any special knowledge beyond the basics. An understanding of how implied volatility works in determining options prices is also helpful but not necessary.

If you are a complete beginner, then it would help you to read our free *Options 101* guide available at https://freemanpublications.com/bonus. That will get you up to speed on the basics of how options work.

Throughout this book, we'll explain all terms related to the iron condor strategy as we introduce them, except when they have to do with the basics of options. In order to execute the iron condor, you don't need to understand the Greek values in detail. However a base level understanding is useful, so we've highlighted those areas with relevant explanations.

So with all of that out of the way, it's time to begin looking at the first building block of successful options trading.

2

TREATING TRADING AS A BUSINESS

Before we examine the make-up of an iron condor, it's important to go into trading with the right mindset. Many books out there mention that in order to succeed at trading, you need to treat it as a business. What does this even mean? Most people work regular nine-to-five jobs (although what constitutes as "regular" in a post-COVID world is up for debate). Which means for most people, the world of running a business is far removed. To these people, business usually signifies risk and uncertainty. Is it any wonder then that many people approach their trading with this sort of a mindset?

Treating something as a business means you need to adopt a pragmatic approach to it. Your primary aim is to make a profit (as long as it's within your moral boundaries) and your emotions about certain assets are beside the point. You might love to use a certain product or might love one particular brand. However, this doesn't necessarily make them a good investment.

Many investors and traders lose sight of this fact and blow their capital on the wrong choices. When it comes to trading, you need to protect your capital at all costs. Trading success isn't about taking a lot of risk. Instead, it's about managing this risk well and deploying your capital in opportunities that provide you with low risk and high rewards.

This is what business is about as well and this chapter is going to help you understand this point better.

WHY TRADERS LOSE MONEY

When it comes down to it, all traders and investors lose money due to one of three reasons:

1. The inability to make and stick to a trading plan
2. The inability to adjust their plan based on past results
3. A lack of personal discipline and whether they allow personal problems to affect their trading

We'll cover each of those 3 individually

The Inability To Make and Stick to a Trading Plan

While many trading educators speak about the necessity of developing a trading plan and sticking to it, most traders ignore this crucial step. Much like how every successful business needs a plan to define its goals, so does your trading. Without a good trading plan, you're a bit like a ship's captain navigating without a compass.

The reason most traders do not develop a thorough trading plan is because they get enamored with the idea of making huge profits. They look at the sky-high return numbers and think that those returns are all that count when it comes to their trading. This is obviously not the case.

No amount of promised returns, assuming they're achievable, will ever make up for poor business practices. Much like the trader highlighted in the previous chapter, you'll simply start a countdown clock that will result in you blowing up your account. Your trading plan is your business plan, and it needs to define everything you do with your business.

You'll learn more about this later in this chapter.

. . .

The Inability to Adjust Their Plan Based on Past Results

The markets are dynamic and keep changing. Over and above this, the investor and trader need to deal with shifting economic cycles as well. Back in the 1990s printing money was considered laughably stupid amongst most economists. These days, it is the norm (Connington, 2017).

Economic cycles and market behavioral patterns come together to create different sets of conditions. More often than not, these conditions are unpredictable. You might think that following some announcement, a company's stock price would rise but instead it might fall due to an unexpected reaction from a section of the market.

There are far too many variables to decipher the markets and the best way to trade them is to watch for the way in which they flow. Aligning yourself with the flow of prices is the proven way of making money since the markets have existed. This requires you to be nimble and adjust your strategies when you notice they're out of sync with the markets.

Most traders spend so much time and energy on developing a strategy that they're relieved when they finally land on one that seemingly works. They believe they've finally made it and have unlocked the market's secrets. When the strategy stops working efficiently, they ignore the warning signs because they're avoiding the pain of having to admit that they don't have the markets figured out after all.

Eventually, the strategy stops working and the trader quits in disgust. But not before they've lost most of their capital.

A Lack of Personal Discipline and Allowing Personal Problems to Affect Their Business

Here's a picture of how the typical trader approaches their trading day. They roll out of bed and pick up their smartphone. They run through a few charts on their trading app and place a trade. They then finish their morning tasks and check back in with prices. Next up is breakfast, which passes in a haze of checking prices and emotional reactions as prices jump up and down.

They go to work and occasionally sneak in a few glances at their trades. Along the way, they have alerts that keep pinging them every minute with regards to the "movers and shakers." Intelligent-sounding headlines such as "Micronesian PMI lower than expected. Depresses U.S stocks and boosts soybean kernel futures" leads them to think they're connected with the markets.

As evening nears, they check in on their trades and might even place a few more soybean kernel trades. They head back home with their minds ringing with news about some event somewhere in the world. They hop onto some forum which is filled with trading "experts" and discuss possible plays. They place a few more trades.

Right before bedtime, they place a few more trades, commit a few fat finger errors and turn in for a disturbed night's sleep. Next morning, they wake up less than refreshed and begin this cycle all over again.

If reading all of that didn't exhaust you, you're probably someone who's living it. Believe it or not, this is not how professional traders behave. They remain in touch with the markets as their strategy demands and don't assume that it's a normal state of being.

This incessant checking in with markets might seem to be disciplined action, but it's the height of indiscipline. There's no structure to this habit and the trader is simply acting out a fantasy that fulfills their self-image of being a "connected" trader.

Every single reason for trading failure can be connected back to these three basic mistakes. It doesn't matter what the market you're trading is or which instrument you're speculating in. These mistakes are universal and are committed by unsuccessful traders everywhere.

The question is: What should you be doing instead?

THE 4 PILLARS OF SUCCESSFUL TRADING

If the mistakes that traders make can be boiled down to three actions, then the right things to do can be explained as four pillars. They are:

1. Develop a trading blueprint
2. Understand your sphere of competence
3. Manage risks correctly
4. Treat losses as a necessity

Developing a Trading Blueprint

Your trading blueprint is the document that fully lists all of your trading strategies and everything that you'll be doing to make money. It will also list which instruments you will trade, how you'll choose these instruments, the hours in which you will be operational in the markets, your risk management principles and so on.

In short, it consists of everything that you will do in order to execute your trades successfully. Many traders take the right first step and establish a trading blueprint, but they make the mistake of simply listing their entry and exit strategies and leave it at that.

They fail to move forward and define their risk and money management principles, and this is a huge mistake. Successful trading isn't just about your technical strategy. Think of it as being founded on two pillars. You need a good technical strategy, but you also need to back that up with good money management.

Money management is what ensures you keep all of the money you made in the markets over the long term. It's what prevents you from inadvertently donating everything you made right back to the markets. A good trading blueprint also sets aside time for practicing your skills.

Every technical strategy relies on you being able to identify certain conditions in the market and taking advantage of them. You will need to spend time practicing these skills and getting better at them. Most traders seem to think that all they need to do is learn an indicator or their preferred entry system once and then they're automatically masters of it.

This isn't the case at all. You'll need to build a routine where you practice and evaluate your trades. The results of your trades are feedback, which clue you in to how well you're operating in the market. You'll need to track them over time and constantly review your decisions.

Your routine before, during and after placing your trades is also important. This is because trading is a mental endeavor and you need to be fresh and awake when analyzing the markets. If you're going through a tough time in your life, you need to step away since you'll only lose money.

How will you evaluate such mental states? List it out in your trading blueprint. A good idea is to give your mental state a score from one to 10 and not trade unless your psychological state is above seven, at the very least. It's better to take the time to fix what's wrong in your personal life than to try to trade your way through it.

Understand Your Sphere of Competence

How many screens do you think most professional traders use? Many traders engage in an arms race with one another and try to accumulate as many screens as possible. The stereotypical image of a trader staring at 10 screens is a nonsensical one and doesn't serve any purpose.

You do not need to follow 100 different instruments or understand every single market out there. If you're comfortable trading just iron condors on a handful of stocks, then that's more than enough to make money. The typical professional (institutional) trader focuses on just one instrument and one market. For example, a fixed-income mortgage bond trader will not start placing trades on soybean or oil futures. Such actions will likely get them fired on the spot.

As a businessperson, your objective is to reduce your risk of losing money. The best way to reduce this risk is to focus on depth rather than breadth. Get to know one instrument and market well and specialize in it. This will make you more money than any amount of diversification will.

Most traders don't do this because they wish to make money as quickly as possible. Specializing in one instrument or even a handful means they'll have to give up opportunities in other instruments and they incorrectly view this as being an opportunity cost.

They fail to realize that it is impossible to capture each and every single opportunity out there. It's like an NFL athlete trying to score a touchdown on every single possession. It's simply not going to happen. Instead, you need to focus on executing the skills you know, in the areas you're familiar with. You can earn a steady monthly income executing iron condors just on the major indices.

This is what makes money over the long term. Stick to the things you know and you'll be in a better position to weather any storm that occurs. Whatever you do, don't mistake multiple monitors for competence.

Manage Risks

As we've mentioned previously, your capital is the most valuable commodity you have when it comes to trading. Your task is to protect it at all costs. This means you need to work towards protecting your downside before you pay attention to the upside. Risk management is a tough skill to master since so much of it goes against the way we normally function in the world.

There are some things you can do to manage risk well. For starters you should not be speculating in options with money that you cannot afford to lose. Neither should this money come from your long-term investment account. Keep your speculative and investment activities separate.

Do not ever place yourself in a position where you have to make money from the market. This is a surefire way to lose it. People who look at the markets and see a shiny new car or a fancy home are simply increasing the probability of losing money for themselves.

Another good practice to stick to is to not make options trading income your primary source of money for at least five years. In other words, you need to focus on having another source of income, a day job if you will, that will keep the funds rolling in. You should also not risk more than five percent of your overall capital on a single trade.

Make sure your position sizes are in line with how much you can truly afford, and don't let the promise of outsized returns cause you to assume leverage. Make sure you take a reward that is at least 1.5 times your risk per trade.

Above all else, make sure you follow these principles consistently over time. This by itself will ensure you make as much money as possible.

. . .

Treat Losses as a Necessity

Consider the restaurant business. There are certain costs that the owner needs to bear in order to make money. There are rent, salaries, maintenance, advertising and most importantly, food. Despite them selling food to make money, they also need to buy food in order to make the dishes they serve.

Similarly, in order to make money in trading, you need to sometimes bear losses. Losses are an inevitable part of trading because the markets are unpredictable. Every trading strategy out there functions on the basis of probabilities. There is no strategy that is correct 100% of the time.

Expecting such a strategy is the same as expecting to turn $1,000 into a million within three years. Following the odds implies that you're going to be incorrect some of the time. This doesn't matter, because over the long run, the odds of your system will ensure that you'll make money.

Remembering this key fact is an extremely difficult thing to do. Unsuccessful traders react emotionally to losses and believe them to be a reflection of who they are. This causes them to try to recover these losses from the market and engage in revenge trading.

This only results in more losses since the market doesn't care about how much money you make or lose. It's simply a collection of millions of traders making decisions all at once. It's unrealistic to expect any system to be able to predict all the actions of every market participant correctly every single time.

So expect losses in your trading business and consider them a cost of doing business along with commissions and taxes. The spread is also another cost of doing business. (The spread or the price spread is the difference between the price you pay to buy the asset versus the price to sell it. It's also referred to as the bid/ask spread.)

This covers the fundamentals of treating trading like a business. Later in the book we'll be re-focusing on how to truly master the psychological side of trading, but for now, let's examine what makes the iron condor a profitable trading strategy.

I

THE MECHANICS OF IRON CONDOR TRADING

3

UNDERSTANDING WHAT MAKES THE IRON CONDOR A PROFITABLE STRATEGY

Ask any trader what kind of a market they'd prefer and they'll immediately reply that a trending one is the best. What is a trending market? Put simply, it's one where prices move in a certain direction. Looking from left to right, if the price chart has a bias towards the upper left or bottom right hand corner, the price is in a trend.

The thing about trends is that they can be tough to take advantage of. Prices do not rise (or fall) in a uniform 45 degree angle at the best of times. Observe the market in action and you'll see that it ebbs and flows. It takes a lot of breathers in between and sometimes dips lower before pushing even higher.

Many traders run after such directionally biased markets and end up losing money. The fact is that markets are range-bound for the most part. Range refers to sideways movement in the market. If you see prices hovering between two price points, this is a range.

Figure 3: Trend and a Range

Figure 3 illustrates an uptrend in AAPL. Notice that despite price being in a strong trend for such a large period of time, and despite the final angle that price makes from the bottom left to the top right being roughly 45 degrees, there's a large sideways movement in between. Not only is this present, there are also sections where AAPL moves against the uptrend. Directional traders tend to get stopped out in such times since their stops get triggered.

Some options traders adopt a directional bias in their strategies, but even with these there isn't any guarantee of success. The loss on a trade will be limited to the option premium and this is a better prospect than losing your entire risk capital on a trade. However, these losses do add up.

The beauty of options is that you can take advantage of a sideways movement in the market. You don't need to worry about how high the price will rise or how low it will fall. As long as it's within a certain range, you'll make money. The iron condor is such a strategy, and it's an extremely profitable one.

The probabilities of the iron condor succeeding are also extremely high, around 85-90%, since markets are range-bound for the most part. As long as you're able to identify the correct market conditions in a stock, you can earn a steady income from this strategy every month.

RANGES

Let's dig a bit deeper into what ranges are and how you can spot them. We mentioned that these are sideways movements in the markets, but the fact is that most ranges will have a small directional bias to them.

Some traders expect perfectly sideways moves in the market and these are unrealistic expectations. The market consists of millions of traders as you've learned previously. All of them have opinions on prices. It's tough to get two people to agree on a single point completely, so expecting millions of traders to believe that a certain price is valid is close to impossible.

The best way to frame a range, or to define its boundaries, is to look at the support and resistance zones that exist at the top and bottom of the range. This opens another issue since support and resistance is also misunderstood by traders. They're often referred to as levels and this creates confusion.

Support and resistance levels aren't straight horizontal lines you can draw neatly on a chart. Instead, they're zones within which price meets opposition. In the case of a support zone, buyers step in to push prices higher. In the case of resistance, sellers step in and push them lower.

We've assumed that you understand the basics of support and resistance and can identify such zones with reasonable accuracy. Swing points, areas of prior price reaction and higher time frame zones are examples of good candidates for support and resistance.

When trading directionally, the task of finding relevant zones is important. This is because prices won't respect every single zone on a chart. The force with which prices are moving dictates which zone will hold and be relevant. A non-directional strategy removes this need completely since you don't care about the direction or which level (we're using this word interchangeably with zones) is going to break.

Instead, you're looking for already established zones that have shown they have a good number of traders present to defend it. This removes the guesswork inherent in a directional strategy.

Going back to Figure 3, notice that when considered by itself, the range in AAPL has a slight bearish bias to it. This is normal and most ranges will exhibit such characteristics. Some of them will have their resistance levels defined clearly while some will have well-defined support. Some will have both and are easy to trade.

Letting go of the need for perfectly horizontal ranges will open a greater range of possibilities for you when implementing the iron condor. There are two types of ranges you'll typically see in the markets. There are those that form in the middle of trends and those that form at the end of a trend.

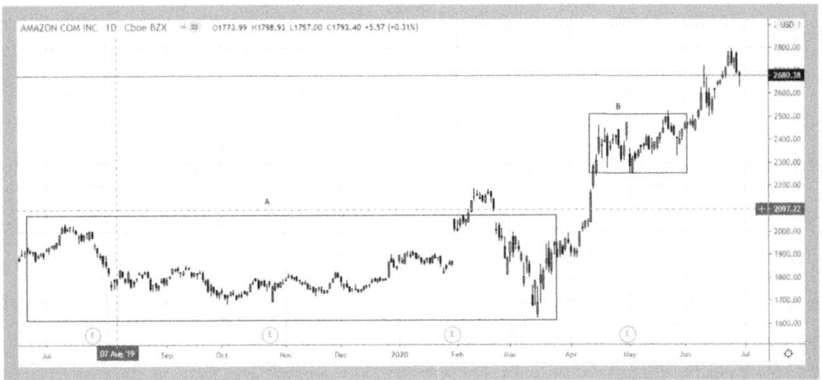

Figure 3a: Two Kinds of Ranges

Figure 3a illustrates the two types of ranges. This is the daily chart of Amazon and you can see that the range marked with the letter A occurred when prices took a huge breather after trending upward for a long time. In fact, they began moving the other way for a long time and this range was printed after this countertrend movement.

The range that forms on the right, marked with B, is what you'll usually see in the middle of trends. These are a lot smaller in size and, as you can see, even these last for close to a month. Generally speaking, you'll be setting up iron condors on such price action.

The larger ranges give you the opportunity to set up longer-term trades. With regards to the iron condor, you don't need to set anything up for longer than 45 days. Beyond this, there isn't much to be gained, as you'll shortly see.

Large ranges might result in stock prices turning the other way around. They also happen to be quite difficult to mark in terms of boundaries. This is because they last for so long that they'll contain smaller ranges within them. Zoom in close enough and you'll find that they might even contain some smaller trends.

Now that you've looked at the two types of ranges you'll be encountering, it's time to look at how the iron condor strategy works.

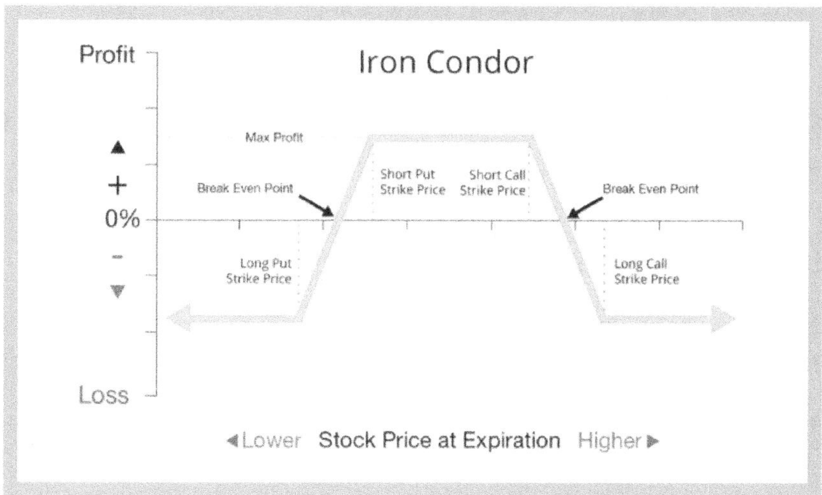

Figure 4: Risk Profile of an Iron Condor

ANATOMY OF AN IRON CONDOR

Figure 4 illustrates the risk profile of an iron condor strategy. The trade is profitable within a certain band of strike prices (we'll explain the legs of the trade shortly). There are a few characteristics of this that we would like to point out.

First, notice that the peak value (which indicates the maximum profit) is lower than that maximum loss value that lies below the zero level. Some traders mistake this for a skewed risk to reward profile. When trading stocks or any other instrument other than options, you want the reward to be at least 1.5x the risk on your trade.

When trading options, though, you can set up your trade to be a net credit or a net debit one, as you know. Net credit trades pay you your maximum profit upfront while net debit trades help you realize a profit once the expiry date goes by. The example we highlighted earlier of Warren Buffett selling puts on indices is an example of a net credit trade. He received his cash up front.

The iron condor is also a net credit trade. You will receive your maximum profit upfront and will then ideally wait until the expiry date and see the options expire worthless. This allows you to fully capture all the premiums you received in full.

There are two break-even prices as indicated in Figure 3 and we'll explain these shortly. For now, understand that since the probability of the trade working out is high, a skewed risk to reward profile isn't a problem. Going back to the examples we looked at in the chapter on risk management, a system that wins 90% of the time doesn't need to have an average win to average loss ratio of greater than one.

Let's look at how the trade is structured.

LEGS OF THE TRADE

The iron condor is composed of two vertical spreads:

1. Bull put spread
2. Bear call spread

These two legs are full-fledged strategies by themselves if you have a directional bias. The bull put will help you take advantage of markets that are rising while the bear call will help you make money in falling markets. As both of them are net credit trades individually, when combined together in an iron condor, they give the trader a net credit trade.

A common question that most options traders have is with regards to deciding between net debit and net credit trades. For example, a bull call spread takes advantage of rising markets just as the bull put does. When would you choose a bull put versus a bull call? The answer lies in volatility.

Market situations that have high implied volatility (implied vol) levels tend to favor net credit trades. This is because options tend to be overpriced in highly volatile environments, and as a result you'll capture a higher premium value when selling options. If you happen to buy options during such times, you'll end up paying a higher than normal price for an option.

In contrast, low implied vol environments indicate that option prices are likely at their correct levels. Thus, you can initiate a net debit trade since you're paying what is likely reflective of the true price of the option.

An ideal scenario would be to capture as much profit as possible if price remained perfectly stationary or between two points. A net credit trade works better in such instances. In an iron condor, we want to see high implied vol levels not just with the underlying stock but also with the VIX in general.

A common point of confusion for beginner traders is the difference between the implied vol and the VIX. Implied volatility is one of many factors that goes into the formula to determine an options price. It isn't something that can be observed and is derived from the option's price. It's a measure of the volatility of the underlying.

Many traders automatically assume that the VIX equals volatility. This is partially true. The VIX is a futures contract that is the measure of the implied volatility of the S&P 500. It's a measure of the implied volatility of the entire market and not just a single instrument.

The two volatility levels might not match one another. You might see high VIX levels and low implied vol on the stock. There's no easy way to address these scenarios. Usually, historically high values of implied vol will override low VIX levels. Choosing whether to implement the iron condor in such conditions comes down to how aggressive the trader chooses to be.

For example, a conservative trader might want to see historically high implied vol levels in case the VIX is low. An aggressive trader might not need such conditions. Another method to mitigate such risk is to structure the strike prices of the iron condor in such a way that volatility is taken into account. We'll address these questions in more detail in Chapter 8.

For now, let's look at an example of the first half of the trade, which is the bull put spread. The bull put spread consists of two legs, a short ITM (in the money) put and a long OTM (out of the money) put. Remember that an ITM option is one that will make you money if you decide to exercise it. OTM options will not make you money upon exercise. You'll receive the premium from the short put and will have to pay a premium on the long put. Since the short put is ITM, you'll receive a higher premium than what you pay for the long put. Both options have the same expiry date, which will be within 30-45 days.

Let's look at an example. Let's say DIS is trading at $107.50 and it's exhibiting low implied vol levels. The stock is in a range with the support coming in at $105. Here are the two legs of the bull put spread:

1. Buy an OTM $100 put expiring in a month at a $2 premium.
2. Sell an ITM $105 put expiring in a month for $4 premium.
3. The net credit, i.e., +$4-$2= +$2, i.e., $200 ($2*100 shares per contract)

Remember that the bull put is a bullish strategy. By executing this leg you're expressing a belief that the stock will remain above $105 in the near term (one month or however long your options have till expiration.)

Let's say the stock expires at $95. At the time of expiry, value of the put depends on its intrinsic value, which is the difference between the market price of the underlying and the strike price of the put.

The $100 put's intrinsic value will be:

= $100 – $95

= $5

Since we are long the $100 put by paying a premium of $2, we would make:

= Intrinsic Value – Premium Paid

= $5 – $2

= $3

In the case of the $105 put it has an intrinsic value of $10, but since we've written this option at $4:

Payoff = $4 – $10

= -$6

Overall strategy payoff would be:

+ $3 – $6

= -$3 or a loss of $300 per contract.

What if the underlying expires at $100? In this case the 100 strike put will not have any intrinsic value and we'll lose all the premium that was paid, i.e., $2.

The 105 strike put's intrinsic value will be $5.

Net Payoff would be:

Premium received from writing 105 put – Intrinsic value of 105 put – Premium lost on buying 100 put

= $4 – $5 – $2

= -$3

Now, let's assume the underlying expires at $105. The intrinsic value of both the 100 strike put and 105 strike put would be 0, hence both the options would expire worthless.

Net Payoff would be:

Premium received for 105 put – Premium Paid for 100 put

= $4 – $2

= + $2

What if the underlying expires at a higher price such as $108? Both the options, i.e., the 100 strike put and the 105 strike put, would expire worthless, hence the total strategy payoff would be:

Premium received for 105 put – Premium Paid for 100 put

= $4 – $2

= + $2

As you can see from the above scenarios, the trader will always make money as long as the underlying price remains between the two legs upon expiry. If the underlying finishes outside the two legs upon expiry, this results in a loss.

Let's now take a look at the second half of the iron condor, which is the bear call spread. Like the bull put spread, this is a net credit strategy that is best applied when volatility is high. The setup conditions are the same as the previous half of the iron condor, you want to take both the implied vol and VIX into consideration when evaluating whether you wish to implement a bear call or a bear put trade.

The bear call spread has two legs to it. These are:

1. A long OTM call
2. A short ITM call

Both legs have the same expiry month that is ideally 30-45 days away from the current date. A pertinent question is: Why do we insist on this time frame till expiry? The reason has to do with time decay.

An option's price has two elements to it: Intrinsic value and time value. You've already seen how intrinsic value works. Time value is not something that can be quantified. The Black-Scholes model is used to determine this particular element and has a huge effect on price.

You don't need to understand the model to figure out how time value works. The simple explanation is that as an option approaches expiration date, its time value decreases. The closer an option is to expiry, the less time an investor has to make money. This means the probability of making money is lower and the time value decays or decreases to reflect this. Within the last 30 days till expiration, time value decreases exponentially. Thus, by writing an option that is outside this expiry window, you capture as much of the time value as possible.

An option writer wants to see accelerating time decay. This makes the 30-45 day window till expiry perfect for this since time value is still a major part of the option's premium. As it approaches expiry, its premium declines rapidly, thus allowing you to capture a higher profit. Which is why through backtesting this 30-45 day period is proven to offer the best combination of time decay and strike price.

Like with the bull put, let's look at a few scenarios to see how the bear call works. We'll stick with the example of DIS, which is trading at $107.50 with overhead resistance at $110. The bear call is set up as below:

1. Buy an OTM 115 strike call by paying $2 as premium.
2. Write an ITM 110 strike call and receive $4 as premium.
3. The net cash flow is the difference between the debit and credit, i.e., $4 – $2= +$2.

Let's say the underlying sells for $120 at expiry.

At $120, both call options would have an intrinsic value and hence they both would expire in the money.

- The 115 call would have an intrinsic value of $5; since we've paid a premium of $2, we would be in a profit of $5 – $2= $3
- The 110 call would have an intrinsic value of $10; since we've sold this option at $4, we would incur a loss of -$10 + $4 = -$6
- Net loss would be -$6 + $3= -$3

What if the underlying sells for $115 upon expiry?

At $115, the 110 call would have an intrinsic value and hence would expire in the money.

- The 115 call would expire worthless, hence the entire premium of $2 would be written off as a loss.
- The 110 call would have an intrinsic value of $5, since we have sold this option at $4, we would incur a loss of $4 – $5= -$1
- Net loss would be -$2 + -$1 = -$3

What happens when the underlying is at $110 at expiry?

At $110, both the call options would expire worthless, hence it would be out of the money.

- The 115 call would not have any value, hence the premium paid would be a complete loss, i.e., $2.
- The 110 call will also not have any intrinsic value, hence the entire premium received, i.e., $4 would be retained back.
- Net profit would be $4 – $2= $2.

If the underlying expires at $105, both the call options would expire worthless. While we treat the premium paid for the 115 call, i.e., $2, as a loss, we will retain the entire premium received for the 110 call, i.e., $4, as a profit. Hence the net profit from the strategy would be $4 – $2 = $2. Clearly, as and when the market falls, the strategy tends to make money, but it is capped at $2.

Combining the bull put spread and bear call spread results in the iron condor strategy where the trader is expecting the stock to expire between $105 and $110, and if that happens, the trader will keep the entire premium from both option spreads. In our example this would be $4 ($2+$2), or $400 ($4*100 shares per contract).

To sum it up, here's how the iron condor is structured:

- Buy an OTM put, strike A
- Sell an ITM put, strike B
- Sell an ITM call, strike C
- Buy an OTM call, strike D

When constructing this spread, you want the underlying price to be somewhere between B and C ideally. If you don't do this, there will be a bullish or bearish tilt to the strategy. This isn't bad by itself, but since the objective is to profit from a range movement, you want it to be as close to the middle as possible.

The distances between strikes A and B versus C and D are usually the same. However, this depends on the range that the underlying is in as well. If prices happen to be closer to the range support, you want to wait until it drifts back to the middle of the range. Similarly, you don't want to initiate the trade when the price is hovering close to the resistance.

The simple reason is that the premiums you'll pay on the options will be skewed and this will skew your risk profile curve for the trade. The ideal scenario is if the underlying ends up somewhere between B and C upon expiry.

Given this requirement, some traders prefer to widen the sweet spot between B and C. However, by doing this you'll reduce the peak of your risk profile curve and will thus reduce your overall profit. The flip side is that by widening your sweet spot you'll be far more likely to capture the maximum gain in the trade.

Beginners to the iron condor should place their strikes B and C at the support and resistance zones respectively. Once you've gained experience, you can experiment with moving these strikes outside or even inside the range support and resistance zones.

While you want to be looking at high volatility stocks (stocks with high implied vol) for this trade, understand that volatility can potentially knock this trade into a loss. A highly volatile stock is more likely to violate support and resistance and create a ton of false breaks.

For this reason, it's a good idea to implement this on index options at first. Indices tend to be far less volatile and the movement of their component stocks tend to cancel one another out. Scaling into individual stocks is the best approach since you'll be able to give yourself time to adjust to the volatility in the markets.

Some traders also look for B and C to be at least one standard deviation away from the underlying stock price. This does increase your chances of capturing the premium and if the VIX happens to be high, this is a good approach to take. Such conditions increase the price sensitivity of the trade and requiring B and C to be at this distance gives you a good margin of safety.

Since you'll be looking to capture the highest amount of premium, you might want to look at high theta options. Theta is one of the Greek variables and the one which quantifies the value of time decay in an option. Theta measures the change in the value of an option for every day we move closer to expiry.

An option with a theta of 0.06 will gain six cents every day compared to another option with a theta of 0.04 that gains four cents. Because theta measures daily change in an option price, some traders equate theta to their daily profit/loss numbers.

For the purposes of the iron condor, because it is a credit spread, meaning that you are a net seller of options, you want to aim for a higher theta because we want to collect a larger premium up front, and then buy the options back later at a discount, giving us a net profit on the trade.

Since theta in an iron condor is usually positive, because time is working in your favor, you should focus on the absolute value of the number (0.06 is higher than 0.04.). This is because you want to achieve a higher profit on your trades.

All of this information will be listed in your trading software provided by your broker, along with a calculator that will allow you to model different scenarios.

MAXIMUM PROFIT AND LOSS

The above scenarios make it clear that the maximum profit is paid upfront upon trade entry. This profit is maintained and earned if the underlying expires between the strike prices of the two short ITM options.

The maximum loss on the iron condor is earned when the underlying moves beyond strikes A or D. Since these legs of the trade are covered by the legs at B and C, the maximum loss is limited to the difference in strike prices between A and B, and C and D less the net credit earned in the strategy.

4

THE 5 MAJOR ADVANTAGES OF THE IRON CONDOR STRATEGY

There are many advantages to the iron condor strategy. In this chapter, we're going to highlight some of them.

NON DIRECTIONAL

This is perhaps the biggest advantage of the iron condor, and one that sets it apart from other options trading strategies. You don't need to try and predict the direction of the market or try to figure out the exact distance that the stock will move. You're giving yourself a range within which the trade will work out.

What's more, the range you give yourself can be decided upfront. This range is the distance between strikes B and C. While there is a tradeoff in the distance between the two strikes and the profit you'll earn, remember that the wider the spread between B and C, the higher the likelihood of earning a profit.

This means you control the probability of the trade working out in your favor. The higher the probability you choose, the lower your profit potential is. However, since this is guaranteed money, the low payout isn't really a disadvantage. The only thing to watch for is the lack of liquidity when you establish a really large range between B and C.

For regular range-bound conditions, the ability to vary the distance between B and C means you can build additional margins of safety into your trade. For example, if DIS is fluctuating between $100 and $105, this is an extremely small range. The risk profile of your iron condor will have a high peak but small width.

You can choose to set up a profile such as this or you can set one up with more conservative strikes. You could place B and C at one or two standard deviations of price away from $100 and $105. If you happen to be more technically-minded, you could take a look at the monthly average true range of the stock and place strikes B and C outside those limits.

The flexibility and higher probability of profit with the trade makes it a steady income earner for most traders. Best of all, it ensures that you'll effectively earn rent on your stock portfolio.

You don't need to implement iron condors on the stocks you own. In fact, we discourage you from doing this. However, in terms of constructing an overall portfolio, you could have the long-term buy and hold stock investments generate capital gains for you while the iron condor generates steady monthly income.

Resist the temptation to chase high yields of five percent or more. Instead, aim for a range between two to four percent since this will bring steady income over time in a repeatable and scalable manner.

CONSISTENT INCOME SOURCE

The repeatability of the iron condor across all kinds of market conditions means it's a great strategy to utilize no matter what the overall market is doing. Be it a bull or bear market or even a largely sideways one, the strategy will always work and will produce income for you.

You will need to increase the distance between strikes B and C when markets are heavily directional. This is especially true if you're speculating using index options. However, during such times options tend to be overpriced and as a result you'll find that increasing this distance won't reduce your overall profit potential too much.

While you ideally want to deploy this strategy when the underlying instrument is moving sideways, remember that even trending markets have large sideways movements within them. The case with AAPL as illustrated in figure 2 proves this.

Remember to think of the support and resistance areas as zones and place strikes B and C accordingly.

DOUBLE PREMIUM

The iron condor is the sum of two net credit spread trades and this gives you the opportunity to earn two premiums, from a call spread and a put spread. Given that both sides of the trade cancel the directional bias of the other, this is a great deal. You're effectively being paid to maintain a neutral spread in the markets.

The lack of directional bias is also what creates the lower maintenance requirements in the trade. While there are some adjustments that you can make in the iron condor, you'll find that if strikes B and C are in the sweet spot, you won't have to check in more than once daily on the trade.

What's more, you can check in on it, but you won't need to adjust it. No matter what the price does, the two sides of the setup will cancel one another out. Your maximum loss is capped and you don't need to worry if the underlying moves too far outside the A to D spread.

Viewing the earning of the double premium from this context makes it an even better deal.

GUARANTEED PROFIT ON HALF THE TRADE

No matter what prices do, you'll earn a profit on at least half the trade. This is because a stock price can't simultaneously be below strike A and above strike D. Of course, this depends on you structuring your spread well without a directional bias to it.

Assuming you do this, if prices rise and break beyond resistance, the bull put spread will be in a profit. If prices crash through support the bear call will be in a profit. Either way, one half of your trade will make money. So how should you structure the spread? The best way to do this is to ensure the underlying price is in the middle of the range or as close to it as possible.

This way strikes B and C will be equidistant from one another and you'll ensure full neutrality. If the distance between the underlying and B is lesser than the distance between the underlying and C, then you've built a long directional bias into the trade. You'll need prices to rise and remain within B and C to capture the premium.

Some traders are comfortable with this and set up such spreads if they deem the range boundaries to be strong enough. For example, if you witness a range that is occurring at the end of a trend and if there is no evidence of a breakout pattern forming, then you could set up an iron condor no matter where the underlying price is as long as it's in between the range boundaries.

EASY TO MANAGE

As we mentioned earlier, the iron condor requires minimal maintenance. Most traders don't directly maintain the trade. Instead, they choose to set up price alerts within their trading software when the underlying moves close to strikes B and C. This gives them the chance to evaluate whether they need to adjust the spread or not.

Iron condors usually don't need to be adjusted too much. Even if adjustment is necessary, it's often a case of widening the spread. Traders will take a short-term loss by doing this, but the next few trades usually tend to recover the cost of adjustment.

Compared to other options trading strategies this makes the iron condor especially easy to trade. You don't need to have specialized knowledge. The only Greeks you need to have a strong understanding of are *delta* and *theta*.

The iron condor also reduces your cost of trading since you don't need to place too many trades per month. It reduces your chances of overtrading, as well, since you'll be mostly focused on a single trade. All of this reduces market participation costs over the long run, and you'll end up keeping more of your money.

5

9 FACTORS TO CONSIDER BEFORE ENTERING AN IRON CONDOR TRADE

There are a few important factors for you to consider before entering an iron condor. Ensure that you pay attention to these points and you'll likely not need to adjust your trade as the underlying price moves.

ENTRY PRICE

We've mentioned previously the importance of constructing as neutral a spread as possible. This is best achieved by initiating the trade when the price of the underlying is as close to the middle of the range as possible. A directional bias within your trade isn't a bad thing, but it does mess with the prices you'll receive for your written options.

While you won't be entering any trades on the underlying, its price plays an important role thanks to the intrinsic value that the executed options will have. When placing orders on the options legs, make sure you receive as competitive a price as possible. It's here that the iron condor's spreads can go awry.

We've mentioned previously that the best situation is to maintain strikes A and B at the same distance from one another as between C and D. To pull this off you might find that the option premiums don't quite line up with one another.

Some strikes might have greater time value built into them despite having the same intrinsic value (if price is equidistant from B and C).

One way of ensuring you receive prices that are most beneficial for you is to utilize limit orders. Limit orders don't entirely remove the risk of receiving poor prices, but they do reduce the possibility significantly. When you enter a limit order, you'll have to enter a trigger price as well.

Your broker will get you the best price for the instrument above or below the limit (depending on whether it's a short or long order.) The best way to determine the location of the entry trigger is to place it near the middle of the bid/ask spread. In case of a short, you want to place it closer to the bid but still near the middle. In case of a long, you want to be closer to the ask than the bid but still close to the middle.

It might seem like just a few cents to you, but remember that you're placing an order for 100 shares of the underlying per contract. Those few cents add up massively in the long run.

IMPLIED VOLATILITY

This is perhaps the most important part of the iron condor trade. When looking at implied vol, you want to aim for environments where it's high but not on the way up. Ideally, you'll set it up in instruments where implied vol is declining from a peak. This applies to both the individual instrument as well as the VIX.

As we mentioned earlier, there's no template you can use to deal with disagreements between the individual implied vol and the VIX. There will be disagreements between the two. As a rule of thumb, the individual stock's implied vol will rule the short term, but if your expiry date happens to be more than 31 days away, then you want to follow what the VIX says.

When comparing implied vol, you should be looking at current values in relation to historic values. For example, the current Covid-19 crisis has prompted the VIX to jump upwards significantly. If you were to set up an iron condor when the VIX was on the way up, you're increasing the risk of your setup being violated.

Options tend to be fairly priced in low volatility environments. As volatility increases, there is an amount that gets added to their prices and this causes inflated premiums. As a result, if you happen to be short, you're likely not going to gain too much since the premiums you receive upon writing an option are not going to be high.

You've already read about how theta decreases rapidly once the expiry date comes within 30 days. Capturing theta is of the utmost essence. You also want to be aware of *vega,* which is another Greek. *Vega* is a measure of how much an option's premium changes given a change in its implied vol.

When the overall implied vol is rising, *vega* rises as well. In an iron condor setup you want *vega* to remain neutral or decrease over the life of the trade. The only exception is if the underlying prices come near A or D. In these cases, you want to see higher volatility since this implies a greater chance of prices swinging back in between B and C. However, that's after you've entered.

Prior to trade entry look for declining VIX values and declining implied vol values, with both ideally descending from new highs.

A backtest by *projectoption* on 71,417 iron condor trades on SPY found that trades entered at the VIX levels in the 75th percentile and above (VIX of >23.5 in their test) had the highest overall profitability when compared to trades using entry levels in the other 3 VIX quartiles.

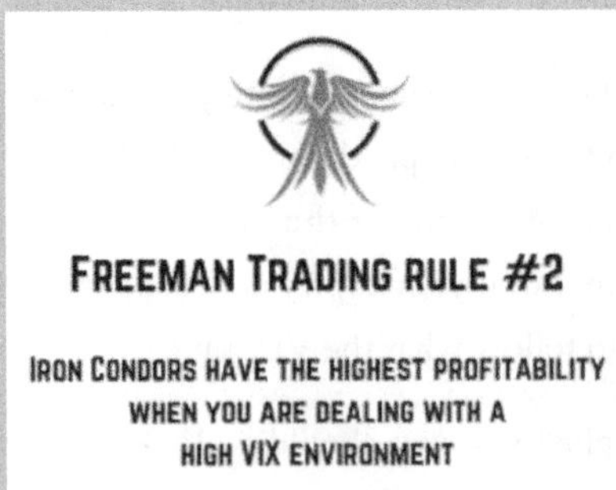

EXPIRY DATE

This one has been covered, but we'll mention it again. You want to get theta on your side when you're setting up the iron condor. Theta is what will ensure that you'll receive high premium prices when writing the two options and that they'll decline in value significantly as time progresses.

A good way to do this is to screen for high-theta stocks. Theta and the Greeks fluctuate over time and special situations such as lawsuits, earnings announcements and dividend cuts can change their values significantly. Look to stay away from such special situation stocks since you want volatility to decrease over the course of your trade not increase.

You might be thinking, if time decay is in our favor, and time decay increases closer to expiry, then why not trade weekly options? The answer lies in another Greek variable, namely *Gamma*. Gamma is the measure of the change of an Option's delta value with respect to a one point move in the price of the underlying instrument. When it comes to iron condors, because they are nearly always positive theta (benefitting from time decay), they as also nearly always negative gamma (adversely affected by gamma increase).

Gamma stays relatively flat when your options have more than 15 days left to expiry. With less than 15 days left, gamma spikes. This is a problem if your strike prices are near the money because your options are now increasingly sensitive to price changes. What this means for your trade is that because gamma has spiked with less than 15 days to go, your long strikes can no longer offset the decreasing prices of your short strikes and your trade quickly becomes a loser. This is a major issue with weekly options because of the gamma risk involved, and the very limited adjustment period.

Which means when entering iron condors, the sweet spot is between 30-45 days left to expiry. Do not speculate in options that have just a week left to expiry or those that are within the 30 days period. Theta accelerates in this time and this causes premiums to decrease exponentially. For someone new to options, you will be taking on extra risk, without being adequately compensated for the risk you're taking.

It might sound tempting to earn a return for just a week's worth of work, but this is hardly a steady way to earn money in the long run. Not to mention the fact that the commissions will add up over time thanks to the greater number of trades you're placing. This will reduce your returns significantly.

STRIKE PRICES

We've briefly mentioned that strikes A, B, C and D need to be placed on the basis of the relevant support and resistance zones nearby. This much is true for strikes B and C anyway. What about A and D? Also, what if the zones aren't clear? What should you do then?

To solve these issues we've developed a simple system that will ensure you pick the right prices every time. It begins by understanding option delta. Delta is a third Greek variable that is connected to options. It measures the amount by which an option's premium will change for a dollar's worth of increase in the price of the underlying. The sign attached to the delta depends on whether the option is a call or a put. Put deltas are usually negative since an increase in price means a decrease in the value of a put.

As time moves on and as the time value in an option decreases, deltas increase for ITM options and decrease for OTM options. This means that as time progresses, the option behaves more and more like the underlying, responding to every dollar's worth of price changes in proportion to the intrinsic value's change it has experienced.

Thus, as time moves on, the value of the delta is often seen as a substitute for the probability that an option will finish ITM. With the iron condor you want the short options to remain OTM. At expiry, the best-case scenario is for the underlying to be greater than B but less than C. This allows the short put at B and short call at C to expire worthless.

When presented with the option chain for the stock, choose the strike prices with deltas that are on the lower end of the scale. Keep in mind that you need to watch what the premiums are as well. Pick deltas that are close to zero, and you won't receive much in premiums for writing those options. Get too close, and delta shoots up and you'll likely not realize the best-case scenario.

There is no standard value that you should pick for delta. If you happen to spot a call at B with a delta of 0.1 and a put at C with a delta of -0.1, your probability of success on the trade is 80% (since there's a 20% overall chance of those options finishing ITM.)

When starting out, you can implement a strategy of finding deltas for your short strikes as close to .1616 as possible. Why this number? Because .1616 is 1 standard deviation away from the mean (in this case, the price of the underlying when you enter your trade), and indicates that this particular leg of the option has roughly a 16% chance of finishing in the money. When you combine .1616 deltas on both sides, that gives your condor around a 68% chance of finishing between the strikes at expiration. Additionally, through backtesting we have found that in higher VIX environments you can get away with higher short strike deltas at entry.

Another layer you can add to this is to look at the choppiness index. This is an oscillator that measures the degree of sideways movement in the markets. A value greater than 61.8 is considered indicative of a range-bound market. The higher the number is, the greater is the predicted sideways movement.

Figure 5: Choppiness Index and Range Behavior

Figure 5 illustrates how the choppiness index works to identify range-bound markets. SPY is on an uptrend with ranging periods in between. The range to the left of the chart isn't fully displayed, but the indicator rises above the threshold eventually. The second range on the chart is identified pretty easily by the indicator.

Combine the previous two points (deltas and choppiness index) and compare it to the closest support and resistance levels. This will give you a rough idea of which strike prices in the support and resistance zone will be suitable. As mentioned earlier, you could also add a standard deviation requirement for determining B and C, but this might overcomplicate the process.

Instead stick to the deltas, and look at the choppiness to make sure you're in a range-bound market and pick B and C accordingly. Once this is done, choose A and D at equidistant points from B and C respectively.

ORDER ENTRY

Something that trips up traders new to the iron condor is the order in which you need to enter your trade legs. Legging in is something that gets easier as time goes by. You should always enter the long legs first and then enter the short legs. This is because your broker might trigger risk warnings if you enter the short legs without covering them with the other sides of the trade. Entering uncovered or naked option positions exposes you to huge levels of risk. A short call position is the riskiest since prices can rise infinitely, creating unlimited losses. Thus, your broker will want you to cover your risk through the long legs before legging into the shorts.

For example, if you enter the trades at B and C first (short put and short call), your broker is going to send you all kinds of risk violation warnings and will possibly not allow you to even write an option if you've just opened an account. In such scenarios, A, D, B and C is the best order to leg into the trade.

Brokers who are well-versed with options might have special order entry screens and will have strategy-specific order entry mechanisms. This means you could enter all four legs of the trade simultaneously. This has a benefit in that you won't be exposed to market volatility in the time it takes to enter since all four legs will be executed at once.

However, it does mean you won't receive the best market prices upon entry. You cannot use limit orders for certain legs and market orders for others, so this might increase your trading costs a bit. Another option is to enter the bull put and bear call separately. This means you'll execute A and B and then D and C (or D and C and then A and B.)

It depends on how your broker has set up their order entry screen, so make sure you review this thoroughly before committing live money to it.

PROBABILITY

The great thing about the iron condor is that the trader can fix their desired probability of profit to a large extent before they even enter. The delta values of B and C offer a great approximation of how likely it is your trade will be successful.

You could set up an iron condor that has a high value in terms of its risk profile peak, but this automatically reduces the sweet spot you'll leave for your trade to work out. Choose a large sweet spot, and your profit (risk profile peak) decreases.

It boils down to what kind of a trader you want to be. Generally speaking, it's better to choose high probability trades that will pay you a smaller but steady amount and this will add up over time.

Another way to view probability is to look at the number of days that you'll have to spend in the trade. A trade that is 45 days long will allow you to capture the highest time decay value, but it opens you up to an additional 15 days' worth of underlying price moves that could be risky.

Every trader has a sweet spot and this is determined through experience. The individual stock's volatility and behavior also play an important role.

TRADING SPY OR SPX?

A common question that most traders ask is whether they ought to trade the SPX (the index) or the ETF that tracks it, SPY. There is no perfect answer to cover everyone's needs, but generally speaking indices are preferable due to the way commissions are structured.

If your broker charges per contract, then you will be able to trade larger underlying amounts for the same commission using an index than you would using an ETF. 10 units of SPY equal one unit of the SPX, so your commission costs will be higher with the ETF.

SPX will have lower liquidity, but still has enough for your orders to get filled at a reasonable spread. Another thing to note is that index options are often treated differently from a tax perspective. It can therefore be advantageous to trade index as opposed to ETFs.

Regarding taxes, each tax jurisdiction is different, so we encourage you to do your own research with your local tax authority.

TRADING RUT OR SPX?

Sticking with the index theme, another question that often arises is whether it's better to trade RUT or SPX. RUT is the Russell 2000 index and it behaves in a far more volatile manner than the SPX. Its volatility index is also different from the VIX. When trading RUT, you should be looking at the RVX.

Given the higher volatility levels you're likely to find the RVX throwing more peaks and declines and this gives you more entry opportunities. On the flip side, it's just as likely to turn to the other side and move your trade into unprofitable territory.

Increased volatility isn't a problem as long as you understand how to handle it well. If you're someone who panics at the mere thought of your trade moving against your setup, then perhaps trading SPX is a better choice.

Whatever you choose to trade, make sure you paper trade it first so that you have a good idea of how volatility works in that index.

THE QUIRK OF INDEX OPTION SETTLEMENT DATES – AND HOW TO AVOID ACCIDENTALLY TURNING A WINNING TRADE INTO A LOSING ONE

Many options traders overlook this particular aspect of options trading and it often causes them to lose money. Depending on the index you're trading, there could be two different ways that settlement takes place. Settlement refers to the final price that the index closes at on the expiry date.

The most common form of settlement is P.M. settlement and this is the closing price as of 4 P.M. on a Thursday (all CBOE expiry dates fall on a Thursday.) However, there's also A.M. settlement, which fixes the settlement price as whatever price the index opens at on the following Friday.

This might seem like a small thing, but more often than not it results in huge gaps being formed and in options being kicked out of the money. Using the example of the SPX below, note the difference in prices according to the two settlement methods:

The May 2020 monthly option settlement prices were as follows:

S&P 500: 2827.52

S&P 500 PM Settled Options (SPX): 2863.70

For the most accurate data on this topic go the link below:

http://www.cboe.com/data/historical-options-data/index-settlement-values

The best way to mitigate this risk is to first know which type of settlement the index you are trading uses. The second is to close your trade out if it's near breakeven the day before expiry, to lock in the smaller profit. This is especially important if there is big news (such as unemployment data) scheduled for release after the market closes on Thursday.

6

BUILDING A BULLETPROOF IRON CONDOR TRADING PLAN

If you fail to plan, you're planning to fail. The iron condor might be a relatively simple strategy to execute, but it can fail if you don't have a proper trading plan in place. A trading plan is an essential element to your trading success.

This is because it makes the strategy seem more real and you're more likely to follow it. A well-defined trading plan also removes the negative impact that emotions might have on you during times of stress. You'll always have something to refer back to and ground yourself.

This chapter is going to provide you with a great template you can use to plan your trading.

TRADING PLAN ELEMENTS

All good trading plans need to have a few elements as a minimum. Define these and you'll find that a lot of your trading problems, especially with regards to unwanted emotions, will take care of themselves.

Instruments

This one is self-explanatory. Which instruments will you trade? If you're executing the iron condor, options are an obvious instrument. Which underlying security will you trade, though? We'll expand more on this shortly, but for now simply define which asset classes you'll be trading.

In this case it will be stocks. You can trade options on FX instruments with some brokers, but this opens an entirely different can of worms, so we recommend you stick to stock options.

Another important element to define is the timeframe of choice. Iron condors work best when executed on the daily time frame. Technically you can use the lower time frames and target options closer to expiry. However, this puts you on the wrong side of time decay, so it isn't really worth it.

Besides, as we explained before, you'll end up placing more trades and your costs will increase. This reduces your overall profit, so it isn't really worth it.

Screening

How will you screen these underlying instruments? We've already mentioned that you could use theta as a screener. To make it even simpler, you can simply stick to the large indices such as QQQQ, SPX, RUT, IWM, NDX, MNX, XLF, RTH and SPY. These indices and ETFs are stable and have more than enough liquidity to take care of all your needs.

You can make a good sum of money every month trading just two or three of these regularly. So don't think you need to dive into individual stocks in order to be a successful trader. Once you're making a good amount of money every month with these instruments, you can dive lower and pick individual stocks to speculate on.

Here are the criteria you can use to screen such stocks:

1. Reasonably High Priced Underlying Asset: Low-priced stocks are not suitable because there aren't enough strike prices to make a condor work. You want as wide a range of strike prices as possible, and there

simply isn't enough space between a low price and zero to give you this. Stick to stocks that are priced above $50, at the very least.

2. Large Cap Companies: Companies that are smaller in size can be manipulated thanks to insider trading and large volumes from institutions. We don't mean illegal manipulation here. It's just that these smaller stocks react to orders differently. Sticking to companies that attract large trading volumes minimizes these movements, and you're more likely to find that they stick to their trading ranges.
3. No Recent News or Upcoming Earnings Release: As mentioned earlier, you want to avoid high volatility events when screening stocks. This means any upcoming news events such as the outcome of a lawsuit or earnings announcements should be avoided. This applies to the entire holding period. The iron condor is a neutral strategy, so you cannot use it to play earnings news. These events are binary in that the stock either goes up or down. It certainly won't move sideways.
4. High Liquidity: Without a reasonable level of market liquidity, transaction costs are likely to become higher due to larger bid-ask spreads. Thus you want to screen stocks that have a high trading volume on average. Almost every large cap stock has adequate trading volumes, so if you stick to them, liquidity will never be an issue.

Using Automatic Screening Software

Screening websites can help you find assets which tick all the boxes for entering a trade. Many brokers also have their own screening software built into their trading platform. These are a great time saver, because all the data is pulled automatically based on preset filters. However, there are a few drawbacks to using them when you are just starting out. The major disadvantage of using screening software, especially when starting out is that you're not internalizing the foundation of the strategy. You're simply picking from a list on a website. Which means if the trade goes against you, you won't fully understand where you went wrong, and what could be improved for the next time.

We recommend manually screening for opportunities and setups yourself when starting out, and only focusing on 2-3 assets to build your sphere of competence.

Remember, you can make a good living just trading the same few assets over and over again.

Strike Price Levels

Where will you place your strikes A, B, C and D? We've mentioned the various options you have when deciding the distance between these prices and how you can determine them. Keep in mind that you might want to mix and match them depending on the instrument in question.

For example, the SPY might warrant one standard deviation's distance between the underlying price and strikes B and C. As a rule of thumb the distance between A and B must be equal to the distance between C and D. This creates a balanced condor and will not cost you additional margin thanks to uneven spreads.

Choosing strike levels also impacts your profit. How much would you like to earn every month from a trade? Since one trade is going to last for at least this long, you want to make sure the strike levels line up with your earnings expectations. You also need to pick a relatively realistic number since the underlying stocks' price action needs to be able to deliver those returns.

It's best to paper trade before going live since this will let you know how realistic the numbers are for different instruments. When paper trading, look at setting up as many condors as possible on as many indices. This will give you an idea as to how volatility and liquidity works within them and how much you can reasonably expect to earn.

This process will also let you know how many trades you realistically need to place to earn your desired level of income. If one trade per month gives you a three percent monthly return, that's great. However, if you wish to increase the probability of your trades working out and want the same level of return, you'll need to place more trades.

Rules

What rules will you follow when setting up the iron condor? The first rule to follow is to only execute the strategy when the VIX is greater than 20. Also, remember that the VIX (or equivalent liquidity index) needs to be on a downward swing when you set up the condor. If you're entering a market that is experiencing increasing volatility, the options you purchase will be more expensive. Decreasing levels of volatility allow you to short options at more expensive prices and also increases the chances of prices moving within a specified range.

When choosing strike prices, will you use deltas to maintain a neutral position? Choosing to go delta-neutral involves determining a lot of things beforehand. For starters, what is the acceptable delta range for your position? This determines how often you'll adjust it as the market moves.

Also, what will be the maximum cost that you're willing to bear for adjustment? This comes out of your maximum profit, so you need to fix a certain value for this. Once your costs exceed this amount, you need to close the trade and take the maximum loss. This way you won't be stuck forever adjusting a bad position that has no chance of making a profit.

It's better to free up the capital that is stuck in that position and use it for something else. Fix the risk per trade to no more than five percent and preserve your capital at all costs.

Event Plans

This is an important section when it comes to directional trading strategies, but it assumes lesser significance when trading condors. This is because you simply avoid them. Stay away from any major announcements within the time frame that you'll be holding your options trades.

This isn't always possible when it comes to an index. Interest rate announcements and economic reports such as the Nonfarm Payrolls are released every month. One option is to simply widen the spread between B and C. Another option is to reduce your holding period to slightly under 30 days.

You will lose some of the time value, but if it keeps you away from the volatility that might be induced after an announcement, this is a good trade-off.

Mindset and Tracking

You will need to track everything with regards to your trading. The more things you track, the more you can improve. Some traders take this too lightly and tell themselves they'll record journal entries later or that they'll review them later. This is a surefire way to fail.

Another mistake some traders make is to neglect recording their mental state when trading. You need to be extremely aware of this and need to check in with yourself psychologically when you're analyzing the markets and after you've just exited a trade. These entries will help you pinpoint the areas you can improve.

Take a brief survey of yourself before you sit down to analyze the markets or screen relevant instruments to trade. If you're not feeling up to it or are struggling with some negativity that is distracting you, then do not trade the markets that day. Remember that your trades will be running for 30 days on average, so a single bad decision will keep you stuck in or force you to adjust a setup over this time.

Define how often you'll trade the markets and when you'll take a break from them. Some traders define certain months and hours to trade while others rely on monitoring themselves psychologically. Whatever you do, do not make the mistake of trading every single day that the market is open.

Take the time to also define when you'll practice your skills. To trade an iron condor effectively you need to be able to quickly identify a number of things from a range to relevant support or resistance levels to deltas and strike prices that can maintain a neutral position for you.

Building these skills takes time. There's no doubt that the more trades you place, the more skills you'll develop. However, placing trades with live money will potentially lose you a lot more than you bargained for. Therefore, paper trading and simulating your profits and losses is extremely important.

Review Session Structure

Much like how your trading routine is structured, your reviews need to be structured as well. Typically, the best time to review your trades is during the weekend. With iron condors you'll probably find that there aren't too many trades to review since you'll be placing just one or two per month or three at the most.

Placing a large number of trades has advantages for the trader in that you can receive feedback with regards to your skills. This is why it's important to continue paper trading even when you're trading live.

Look at paper trading instruments you would like to explore. For example, if you're trading indices currently, then look at individual stocks to paper trade. This way, you'll double the number of trades you're taking and you'll receive more feedback. This builds your skills faster.

When reviewing, make sure you re-examine all of your trades and look at the mental state that led you to placing the trade. Your job in this regard is to look for behavioral patterns. For example, you might find that you're taking riskier setups in an attempt to claw back some of the losses you sustained in a period of time.

Alternatively, a winning streak might have made you complacent and you're taking too much risk with your setups. You could be taking less-than-perfect ones that don't fulfill all of your criteria or risking too much per trade.

Keep an eye on your drawdown levels as well. Do not violate them under any circumstances. If you've been on a losing streak, then take a break from the markets and evaluate what you've been doing wrong. Remember that you can do everything right and still lose money, so don't go looking for evidence of a mistake.

Some traders choose to give themselves a score at the end of their review session to determine how well they performed. As long as you can keep this scale objective, then this is a good idea.

During the review session, take the time to look at potential opportunities you could have entered but didn't for one reason or another. Don't beat yourself up over them or mentally calculate how much you could have made. Instead, look at it as a learning experience and seek to improve the next time you sit to trade.

7

HOW TO CORRECTLY CALCULATE ROI ON IRON CONDORS

FREEMAN TRADING RULE #4

IN AN IRON CONDOR TRADE, ALWAYS CALCULATE YOUR POTENTIAL PROFITS & LOSSES BEFORE YOU ENTER THE TRADE

One of the advantages of the iron condor strategy is that you can know your maximum potential profit and loss up front before entering the trade. This helps us calculate the potential ROI.

However, there are a lot of numbers that will be flying around when you look to execute an iron condor, so it's worth taking the time to properly define ROI and the maximum profit and loss on the trade.

For this example, we'll use the SPY which was trading at $307.62 at the time of this writing.

We first begin by identifying strike prices B and C. Assuming the support and resistance levels are around $299 and $332, we can use these as our strike prices. Next, we need to determine the position of strikes A and D. We choose prices $291 and $340 since we think it's unlikely that SPY will move beyond these limits over the next 30 days.

So our legs are as follows:

1. Cost of buying put at strike price A = $1.80
2. Premium received writing put at B = $2.70
3. Premium received writing put at C = $1.67
4. Cost of buying put at strike price D = $0.64

The maximum profit or net credit on this trade equals the sum of these four numbers. This comes to (2.7-1.8+1.67-.64) = $1.93 per share. Remember each options contract is 100 shares.

The maximum loss is limited to the difference between strike prices A and B or the difference between D and C minus the credit received upon trade entry. This is because the strikes at A and D limit the maximum downside whether the stock rises or falls.

Because the difference between the strike prices is $8, our maximum loss is (8-1.93) = $6.07 per share.

Which means the potential max ROI on this trade is calculated as the maximum profit divided by the maximum loss so (1.93/6.07) = 31.7%.

Now this number is the ROI *before* commissions. Let's say your broker charges you $1.50 per contract. As each iron condor has 4 legs, this results in a cost of $6 (1.50*4) for all four contracts. Each contract contains 100 shares so the per share cost is $0.01.

Multiplying the per share numbers by 100 gives you the number per contract. So your maximum profit is $187 after commissions and your maximum loss is $607. Which gives us a true ROI of 30.8%.

Now let's look at a scenario where expiration is approaching and you want to lock in your profits from the trade. Let's say it's July 6, 12 days before expiration and SPY is trading at $327.5.

Given its proximity to the $332 breakeven point, you decide to buy a 332 call at $0.51 and sell your 340 call at $0.01.

Therefore your net debit is $50 (-$51+$1). You've placed two more trades, which means you have to subtract an additional $3 in commissions. So the total debit is $53.

This reduces your total profit to $187 minus the $53 debit you used to lock in the profits, giving a total profit of $134. This then results in an actual ROI of 22.07% ($134/$607).

Remember, commissions are a cost of trading, so always remember to factor them into your ROI calculations.

8

ADJUSTMENT STRATEGIES TO MAXIMIZE PROFIT POTENTIAL AFTER YOUR TRADE IS LIVE

The perfect scenario for an iron condor is that the options at B and C expire worthless and you get to capture the entire premium. This also saves you the cost of having an option assigned to you.

While this may seem like an idealistic scenario, it is one which does occur frequent when trading iron condors. A backtest by *Project Option* found that from 71,417 trades on SPY between 2007 and 2017, the no-adjustment strategy (in other words, just holding to expiration every single trade) made a higher profit per trade than the other 15 adjustment strategies they backtested using the same entry points.

However, while this is a great scenario, the fact is that 30-45 days is a long time and a lot can happen. Thus, it's imperative for you to be up to speed with adjustment strategies. The strategies highlighted in this chapter cover almost every scenario out there that you'll encounter. Adjustment might sound complicated to you, but it's really just a case of changing the profile of the iron condor's curve.

Your broker will most likely display the scenarios that pertain to hypothetical adjustment in a graph, especially if they're well-versed in dealing with options. Make sure you understand all the implications of adjustment before committing to a particular course of action.

Adjustments will add to the costs of your trade and this might rub some traders negatively. They're unavoidable, unfortunately, so there's no way to get rid of them. Generally speaking, the cost of an adjustment is far less than dissolving the trade and taking the maximum loss on it.

This puts you in a better position to capture any profits that might arise from the adjustment. Having said that, don't fall into the trap of constantly adjusting your trade. Just because you can, doesn't mean you should. Sometimes, your analysis might just have been wrong and it's best to cut the cord and try again fresh.

The principles behind adjustment are simple. Above all else, our aims are to:

1. Protect our capital and profits and not gamble them away.
2. Not allow small losses to grow into huge losses.
3. Be willing to accept losses and move on to another investment.

Let's take a look at the first option you have in case the trade moves against you.

OPTION #1 - WAIT

This isn't technically an adjustment strategy, but it's one that might work. Markets will move against your trade for certain periods of time and if you allow enough time, it usually bounces back to put your trade in the profit zone.

Discipline is the key to maintaining your calm in such situations. While it will be tough to sit tight and watch your position move deeper into the red, you should not exit the position simply because it's currently in a loss.

When trading iron condors, it's extremely important for you to determine your exit points in case the trade moves against you. Usually the strikes at A and D are these limits. At these points you'll earn your maximum loss on the trade. When you're new to trading iron condors, you should allow the market to float towards those strikes and take your maximum loss on the trade.

You might be tempted to exit prior to these points. However, as a new trader you might be prone to exiting too early and you'll potentially lose the profit you might have gained by remaining in the trade. Therefore, it's best to remain in the trade even if it looks as if you'll end up taking the maximum loss.

There's a fine line between behaving in a disciplined manner as detailed above and hoping for the market to reverse. If the underlying has already moved into a position where you're at the maximum loss level, and if there isn't much time left till expiry, you need to exit the trade or adjust it via one of the other options presented next.

Remaining in the trade without adjustment and hoping that the market will bounce back to put you in a profit is a losing proposition. Traders who do this usually cannot stand the thought of being wrong and are approaching trading as an examination at school, as we detailed previously.

Hoping is not a strategy, so don't be one of those traders.

OPTION #2 - CLOSE THE LOSING HALF

If the trade isn't working out for you, this means the market is trending in a particular direction. Since you've set up a market-neutral trade, one half of your trade will be in profit while the other will be in a loss. Let's say the stock has risen too much for your liking and this has placed your bull put in a profit, but the bear call is suffering.

You can adjust the bear call side of the trade to a higher level. This means you'll eat the loss on that half of the trade (which will be roughly half of your maximum loss). Keep in mind that when adjusting the trade in this manner, you're expressing a belief that the market will eventually go back the other way.

For example, if you spot prices trying to break out of a range and if you adjust your bear call spread higher, what you're saying is that the breakout might be a false one and that prices will spike higher and then return right back into the range. Such judgments need to be backed by solid evidence and not just hope.

So what counts as evidence? Price patterns are a good indicator of this. If you spot a series of higher lows (in case of a bullish breakout) and increasing pressure to the upside, then the breakout is likely going to hold. Increasing volumes towards the upside (in the case of a bullish breakout) is also an indicator of increasing pressure that will sustain the breakout.

However, if you spot patterns such as a large bearish pin bar forming near the resistance or if the pattern of higher lows is broken, then you can safely conclude that the breakout will likely be a whipsaw and prices will drop right back into the range. Keep an eye on volumes.

Volumes in ranges tend to be lower than in trends because directional traders cannot make money in such times. Examine the volumes when prices rise versus when they fall within the range. Rising volumes towards one side combined with the price patterns mentioned above (bearish equivalents in case of a bearish breakdown) indicate a high probability of a breakout.

OPTION #3 - CLOSE THE SHORTS

Sometimes your judgment about the sweet spot of the iron condor might be off. You might have misjudged the distance between strikes B and C when initially setting up the trade. This happens more often than you might think, especially when prices move in large ranges at the end of a trend.

You'll be operating on the daily chart, and as a result such ranges will last for months on end. During this time, prices will form smaller ranges within the larger range. Zoom into your charts too much, and you'll end up mistaking the smaller range for the larger, more sustainable one.

In such scenarios, it's a good idea to place A and D far away from B and C. This gives you a lot of breathing room to adjust B and C (the short options) in case you need to expand the distance between them. Sometimes prices will jump beyond the smaller range and will explore the boundaries of the larger range.

When this happens, you can close the options at strikes B and C and establish them at higher prices. Since A and D are safe and are outside the larger range (or in an area that is unlikely to be disturbed), you can adjust B and C to higher levels. This will result in you taking a loss on one short leg, of course, but this money can be made back if the adjusted trade works in your favor.

Make sure to adjust your trade before the expiry date or else you'll end up with an assigned option, and this will increase your costs significantly. When moving the short option levels (B and C), make sure you have technical justification for doing so. The presence of valid bullish or bearish patterns along with supporting volumes are good evidence as explained in the previous section.

OPTION #4 - MAINTAIN DELTA NEUTRALITY

You've already learned what delta is. This Greek variable measures the amount by which the option premium will move given a dollar's worth of increase in the price of the underlying. Trading positions have deltas as well. When constructing an iron condor, you will be creating two spreads that have individual deltas.

When you enter your trade, the bull put spread's delta will ideally offset the bear call spread's delta. This makes the entire position delta neutral. Why is this a good thing? Remember that since the iron condor is a net credit trade, you want the options to be worthless at expiry.

This is another way of saying that you don't want the value of your position to move irrespective of how the market moves. Since an iron condor captures the maximum profit up front, ideally you want all market conditions to remain the same.

The problem is the market never remains still. It will always move and as the days go by your position's delta will vary due to changing closing prices. Adjustment is at the heart of a delta-neutral strategy. By maintaining its neutrality you'll ensure that your maximum profit remains in place and that any additional adjustment cost will be paid for by the profits you'll collect post-adjustment.

You can think of adjusting deltas like driving a car through a tunnel. If your short position is in trouble, your car is veering left towards the outside wall. What would you do if your car was veering left? You'd turn the steering wheel to the right. In the case of options, steering to the right would be adding more long deltas by buying calls/selling puts, because these additional calls would balance out your position. The same goes if your long position is being attacked, to keep delta as neutral as possible, you would add more negative delta by buying more puts or selling more calls.

Let's take an example where the underlying is exhibiting more bullishness. In this case, the delta of the bear call spread rises while the puts decrease in delta, eventually moving to zero as they drift away from the money.

To offset the increase in the call deltas, you can sell more puts that are closer to the money and above strike B to bring in more premiums. Their deltas will reduce the positive increase in the calls' deltas.

A second option is to roll the calls forward (puts, in case of a bearish breakout). Rolling your option is as simple as closing the current month's contract and opening a contract that has an expiry date further into the future. Options that are further out in expiry have lower deltas. If the deltas of those options that are further out bring the overall delta back to zero, then you can maintain neutrality in this way. In simpler terms, you're giving your trade more time to work out.

You will incur a loss on the call position you closed and your iron condor will gain a horizontal spread element as well. This can be reduced by rolling the puts into the next month. Alternatively, you could establish a new bull put spread once the original spread expires worthless.

A third option is to reduce the distance between strikes C and D (A and B, in case of a bearish breakout) since this reduces the delta of the position. You'll need to use the options calculator and the graphing capabilities of your trading platform to visualize the effects of these events.

Since delta can never be maintained at zero, it's best to fix an acceptable delta range for yourself when entering. Look to maintain delta in this range through your adjustments. At some point, it won't be worth it to keep adjusting the trade since the maximum profit will not be able to pay for them. In this case, simply close the trade and move on.

OPTION #5 - BUY INSURANCE

We don't mean calling GEICO and having them issue you a quote. Instead, we're talking about buying further OTM options that cost pennies but insulate you from massive and unexpected market movements.

Events such as Covid-19 or 9/11 create huge shocks in the market. This results in traders' positions moving by huge amounts. During such times, adjustment is not an option because of the massive spike in volatility. You could move your strike prices as far away as possible, but there's no telling if the market might hit them.

However, an iron condor trader has the choice of mitigating such extraordinary events by buying farther OTM put options. These puts act as an insurance from extreme market moves. The markets usually tumble downwards when such extreme events strike.

By buying these puts you'll be able to cover your downside completely. If the markets do tumble, the premiums on those puts will rise astronomically and you'll be able to cover any other losses you might sustain.

Therefore, it is advisable to spend two to three percent of the income generated from iron condors as insurance buying farther OTM puts. We prefer to have a 5:1 ratio while executing iron condors, i.e., for every five lot spreads, we prefer to buy one farther OTM put option.

Let's understand this better with the help of an example:

Walt Disney is trading at $100 and you execute iron condors.

Trade Setup:

Bull Put Spread: (5 contracts of each spread)

- Buy $85 put by paying $1.2 as premium
- Sell $90 put and receive $1.5 as premium

Bear Call Spread: (5 contracts of each spread)

- Buy $115 call by paying $0.5 as premium
- Sell $110 call and receive $1.05 as premium

The net cash flow will be calculated as follows:

Bull Put Spread: $1.5 – $1.2 = $0.3

Bear Call Spread: $1.05 – $0.5 = $0.55

Cash Flow: $0.3 + $0.55 = $0.85

Net Credit: $0.85*5 option contracts*100 shares per contract

: $425

Now we'll add our insurance:

Buy 1 contract of $80 put option (farther OTM) at $0.4

Insurance Cost: $40 ($0.4*100 shares per contract)

Total net credit received: $385 ($425 - $40)

If the market dropped just after you bought your insurance, it would work out really well and might reverse your losing position into a profitable one.

However, if the market corrected somewhere close to expiry, the put option's premium won't increase much and provides less protection due to the impact of time decay.

9

LIVE EXAMPLES OF 3 IRON CONDOR ADJUSTMENTS

Trade Example 1: Short Iron Condor on Netflix

Trade Set up:

Stock Price at Trade Entry: $500 June 14th

Time Until Options Expire: 45 Calendar Days (July 28th)

Short Iron Condor set up:

- Sold the call spread 550/600 for $5.70
- Sold the put spread 450/400 for $6.50

Net Credit received: $12.20 (Final Iron condor value)

Maximum Profit Potential: $1,220

Maximum Loss Potential: $3,780

ROI: 32.37%

Breakevens:

- Call side: $562.2 (550+12.20)
- Put side: $437.80 (450-12.20)

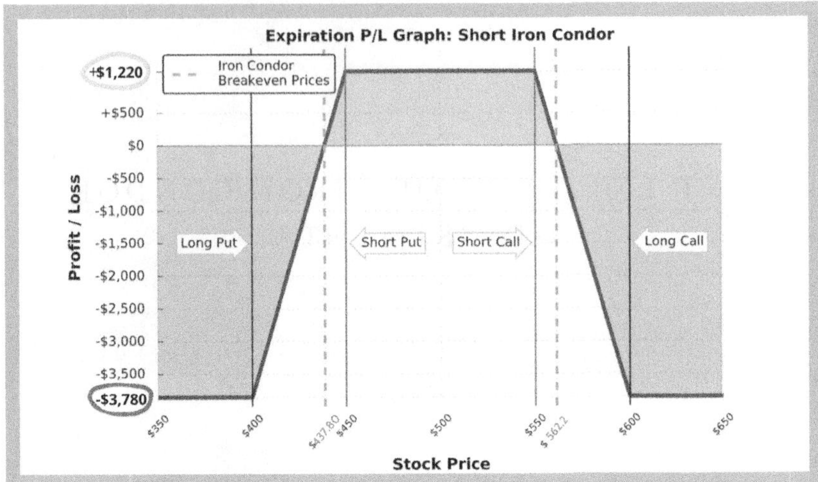

Figure 6: The pay-off chart for the Netflix Iron Condor

Trade Adjustment: Rolling the un-challenged side

3 days before expiry date the stock price moved near upper break even @ 562.20

The stock is challenging the call spread, so for the adjustment we rolling the un-challenged side closer to the new stock price. This is so we increase our upper challenged breakeven to avoid a potential big loss in case the stock continues up. Here is what that looks like visually.

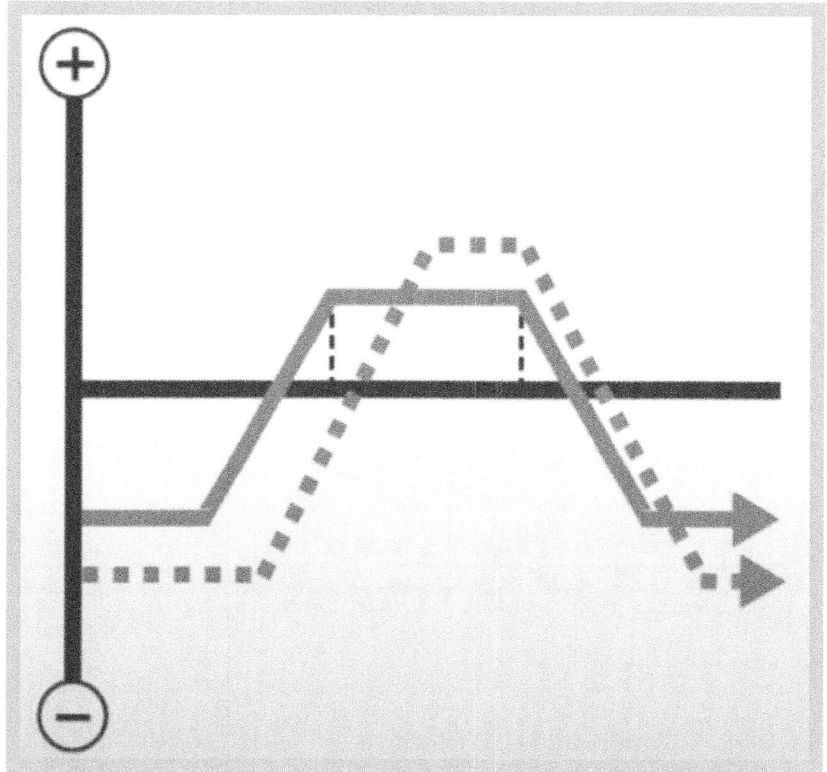

Figure 7: The revised pay-off chart now we have added the credit spread on the unchallenged side

To do this we execute a credit spread on the unchallenged side.

Credit Put spread strategy: Sold Put 510 and bought Put 450 for a net credit of $3.06

Which gives us a new upper break even of 562.20+3.06= $565.26

At expiry Date: Netflix Stock settled at 523.89 in our profitable zone

Which gives us a final Profit of $1,220 (the original Iron Condor) + $306 (credit spread hedge) = $1,526

Trade Example 2: Short Iron Condor on NIO Stock

Trade Set up:

Figure 8: The daily price chart for Nio

Stock Price at Trade Entry: $14.32 July 8th

Time Until Options Expire: 10 Calendar Days July 17th

Short Iron Condor set up:

- Sold the call spread 15/18 for $0.71
- Sold the put spread 10/7 for $0.35

Net Credit received: $1.06 (Final Iron condor value)

Maximum Profit Potential: $106 per contract

Maximum Loss Potential: $194 per contract

ROI: 54.63%

Breakevens:

- Call side: $16.06 (15+1.06)
- Put side: $8.94 (10-1.06)

Trade Adjustment: Hedging via debit Spread

3 days before expiry date the stock price moved above upper Break even and reached $16.42, leaving us at a loss on the current trade.

In order to hedge the upper side and avoid a bigger loss we bought the debit call spread 16/18 for $0.50 per contract. This means we are protected from 16.50 and our residual risk will be between $16.06 and $16.50, leaving us a small $0.44 loss if the stock settles in this zone.

At expiry Date: NIO Stock reversed and finished at $11.09 in our original profitable zone

Final Profit= $194 (original iron condor) - $50 (debit spread hedge) =$144 per contract

Trade Example 3: Short Iron Condor on Walt Disney (DIS)

Trade Set up:

Stock Price at Trade Entry: $109 June 25th

Time Until Options Expire: 8 Calendar Days July 2nd

Short Iron Condor set up:

- Sold the call spread 110/116 for $2.10
- Sold the put spread 108/102 for $2.30

Figure 9: The daily price chart for Disney

Net Credit received: $4.40 (Final Iron condor value)

Maximum Profit Potential: $440 per contract

Maximum Loss Potential: $160 per contract

Breakevens:

- Call Side: $114.40 (110+4.40)
- Put side: $103.60 (108-4.40)

Trade Adjustment: Hedging via credit spread

1 day before expiry date the stock price hit $114, which near the upper break even level.

In order to hedge our Iron Condor strategy, we decided to sell another Call spread 117/120 for $1.80. As we expected a resistance around $116, we decided to give ourselves some more leeway on the challenged side of the trade with the trade-off of a small amount of risk between $114.40 and $116.20.

New upper breakeven = 114.40+1.80=$116.20

At expiry: DIS Stock settled at $112.18 in our profitable zone

Final Profit = $440 (original iron condor) + $180 (credit spread hedge) = $620 per contract

10

HOW TO PICK THE RIGHT OPTIONS BROKER

Your broker is the one who gives you access to the markets and will even help you make sense of them through the research tools they provide. While a broker's fiduciary duty is to simply execute your trades in the market, you should carefully consider the kind of research tools and interfaces they provide you with.

A common approach that most traders take is to choose the one that charges the least amount in commissions. In a buy and hold approach this makes a lot of sense. Your trading volumes will be low and you'll be conducting your own research by reading SEC filings and so on.

However, this is not the case when trading. A broker's technical capabilities and offerings matter a lot more. For instance, you want your broker to offer you a wide variety of orders beyond the usual stop, limit and market orders. You might not need them to execute the iron condor, but it's nice to have and points to the infrastructure they possess.

We're now going to list some of the things you should look for in a good options broker. Some brokers might possess all of them while some might possess only a few of them. Make sure you conduct your research thoroughly into them and that you're comfortable with the trading environment they provide you with.

COMMISSIONS

We might as well get the big one out of the way. These days there are a number of brokers that charge zero commissions. The brokerage world has been engaged in a race to the bottom for a long time now. While commissions have reduced, fees have not entirely disappeared.

You might think those are one and the same, but brokers beg to differ. Trading usually attracts a higher amount of fees compared to buy and hold investing. Options commissions (and fees) are structured differently depending on the broker in question.

Almost every broker out there will charge you zero commissions to trade options and will boldly advertise this fact. However, they'll charge you additional options contract fees. This amount varies depending on the broker in question. Typically, this isn't more than 70 cents per contract.

The fee structure also varies depending on the broker. Some might charge you per trade fees, while some might charge you a flat fee. Others will charge you a commission plus per contract fee as just described. Still some more might charge you a fixed rate up to a certain number of contracts and then charge you a volume-based fee.

Take the time to review the fee structure in detail. The iron condor requires you to place four options trades per setup. If you execute two or three setups over the course of a month, these fees will add up to a significant amount. This doesn't include any possible adjustments that you might need to make during the month.

Something to keep in mind is that your broker might charge you zero fees but might charge you assignment commissions. If your option finishes ITM you'll be assigned the contract and you'll have to bear the fees that arise as a result of fulfilling the contract and delivering the underlying.

By now you can see that there are different fees you could be hit with when trading options. Carefully review how much it will cost you to trade since these add up over time.

TRADING SOFTWARE

Aside from commissions, the quality of the trading software provided is of paramount importance. You'll be spending time analyzing possible trade setups in here, so it's imperative that you are comfortable with the way the software works. Depending on the kind of trader the broker caters to, their software will vary in complexity.

Some trading platforms such as Tradestation can be pretty complex to navigate since they're best suited for traders who place a lot of orders and trade many different asset classes. The first choice you'll have to make is whether you'll be okay with a browser-based platform or whether you'll need a stand-alone software.

When it comes to executing iron condors and given the time involvement in executing this strategy, you don't need stand-alone software. Once you've entered the trade, you'll be spending a few hours every month maintaining the trade and evaluating it for adjustment, so your time commitment is low. A web-based software is more than enough.

One of the most crucial things an options broker must provide is an easy-to-use calculator. Prior to entering a trade, you'll need to plug in your numbers and take a look at various scenarios. Much like how we walked through the different underlying prices upon expiry, you'll need to do the same so that you can quickly grasp what your profit and loss numbers look like.

The quality of calculators vary from one broker to the next. Playing around with a demo version of the broker's software (if available) is a good idea. If you happen to love one particular broker due to low commission costs but they happen to have a poor calculator, consider using a third party calculator such as the ones available at optionsplaybook.com.

Another important aspect of the broker's software package is the charting they offer. Web-based brokers' software will provide some level of charting, but they can be clunky to use. You will need to analyze charts for support and resistance zones, so it's important that these are up to scratch.

If your broker's charts aren't good enough but you still wish to stick to them, then a resource such as tradingview.com is your best bet. The quotes might be delayed by a bit, so make sure you compare the last traded price to your broker's feed to make sure you're getting the right prices.

CUSTOMER SERVICE

This is an important area that even experienced traders overlook. As a trader, you're operating by yourself and this might cause you to think that you'll never need a high degree of assistance. These days everything is online anyway, so there isn't any need for human intervention in most cases.

We say in most cases because when things do become critical, you absolutely need to speak to a human being. A lot of brokers utilize chatbots and there's no way these programs will address your questions. For example, if your deposit didn't show up in your brokerage account, you'll need to speak to a human being to figure out next steps.

A good way to evaluate customer service is to type a few messages into the chatbot on the broker's website and look at how quickly you can get through to a person. The results will be self-explanatory. A good broker will give you quick access to a real person instead of keeping you going round in circles with a chatbot.

Another good technique to utilize is to send them an email and then respond with more questions after their initial reply to you. A lot of low-quality brokers rely on systems that highlight the first query of a customer and neglect follow-ups. This kind of behavior is a good indicator that after-sales service will be shoddy.

A good rule of thumb is to ask how long the broker has been in operation. Newer platforms like Robinhood play the disruption card very well but simply do not have the experience that older brokers have. These kinds of app-based platforms don't have the expertise or the knowledge to handle various market scenarios.

What usually happens is that during times of high market volatility they get overwhelmed and you'll find your data feeds getting cut or liquidity disappearing. Even worse is when the broker retroactively restates prices. Such behavior has not taken place recently in the United States thanks to strong regulation. However, in the international markets it has been known to happen.

So don't neglect the quality of customer service and keep pressing to have all of your questions answered before opening an account.

EDUCATION

The presence of educational tools on the brokerage platform is usually a good sign that the broker cares about the quality of clients they bring on board. Even if you never use these tools, it's a good sign nonetheless. The only exception are platforms that cater to full-time traders. Typically, those will focus their efforts on back-end technology and on order execution.

You won't need to open accounts with those kinds of brokers, so look for how well your broker delivers educational messages and tutorials. Often, it can be helpful to utilize these resources to learn more about the markets.

While it's important to not rely on your broker for investment recommendations or stock picks, you should spend some time learning how the markets work. Especially important for you to understand is how liquidity and volatility work and how market prices behave during such times.

Price spreads widen and you'll find that orders will get jumped. Limit or stop orders won't reduce your risk fully in these circumstances. It's useful to read reviews of how brokers behaved during such moments by visiting websites such as Reddit or a trading-specific forum such as Elitetrader.

HIDDEN FEES

While no broker explicitly hides their fees anymore, they can creatively draw attention away from them. For example, some brokers might mention they don't have a minimum account balance but might mention in the fine print that accounts with less than $10,000 in equity will attract maintenance charges.

All brokers these days charge fees for paper statements, and during the account setup process, you might find that this is ticked as the default option. Another area of hidden fees is the money transfer process. Most brokers will not bear money transfer charges and will hit you with correspondent bank charges.

Some brokers might have mandatory minimum withdrawal limits but won't have any deposit minimums. Check how your prospective broker will handle tax documentation. Usually, they will send you a PDF file of the relevant tax forms, but some brokers might stiff you with fees to send you the paper forms instead.

There are other fees that kick in when you call a representative to place a trade. Even if this trade is placed through a machine-based system, you will be hit with charges for simply calling that number. If the software regularly glitches or doesn't allow you to view data seamlessly, then you'll find yourself having to place calls to enter and exit trades.

If you happen to have open positions with other brokers, you might be considering switching those positions to another broker. Some brokers do this for free, but the older broker might charge you a fee for this service. In fact, some brokers will even charge you a fee to bring the positions onto their platform. So make sure you read all the fine print in regards to this.

Inactivity charges are another way brokers can charge you fees as well. Keeping all of this in mind, here is a list of the best brokers you can trade options with:

1. Interactive Brokers ($0.65 per contract with discounts for higher volume)
2. Optionshouse ($0.65 per contract)
3. Charles Schwab ($0.65 per contract)
4. Thinkorswim ($0.65 per contract)
5. Robinhood ($0 per contract) - mobile only, difficult-to-use interface for iron condor trades

Traders based in Europe will find it difficult to trade options on U.S.-based stocks. The only brokers who can facilitate this are DeGiro and Tastyworks. Be warned that the latter has complicated withdrawal and deposit procedures.

Some European brokers will offer you a *contract for difference* or a CFD as an alternative to trading in these stocks. CFDs simply mimic the underlying stock price and have nothing to do with options. You cannot execute a market-neutral strategy with them since you'll effectively be speculating on them directionally.

MARGIN

Margin is one of the most important considerations when you're trading options. Options strategies can get complex, and as a result most inexperienced brokers will simply not understand how trades work. They might end up asking you to post margin amounts that don't make sense.

With regards to iron condors, you will need to post an equivalent margin that is calculated by the difference between strikes A and B, and C and D. For example if you sell SPX calls at $332 and buy the $340 call, the difference is $8. Each contract covers 100 shares, so you'll need $800 to cover the margin requirement.

Since one side of the trade will always lose and the other will always win, you'll only have to post margin that covers just one half of the trade. However, if a broker is inexperienced and doesn't typically deal in options, they might ask you to post margin for both sides of the trade, which doesn't make much sense.

Keep in mind that the requirement to post only one half of the trade's margin assumes that your iron condor is balanced. If the distance between A and B, and C and D is the same, then it's balanced. If the distance between C and D is greater by 10 points, then you'll need to post that much additional margin ($1,000) to cover the difference.

Choosing a broker is extremely important for your options trading business, so take the time to thoroughly vet the brokers in your list. You can utilize the ones we've provided, but always do your own research to see which one fits you the best.

II

MASTERING THE MENTAL SIDE OF TRADING

11

OPTIMAL ROUTINE OF AN IRON CONDOR TRADER

Habits are what create success. This much we can all agree with. Trading is no different. Practice successful habits, and you'll end up creating success in your life. Practice the habits of unsuccessful traders, and you'll end up with their results as well.

The best routine is one that you can stick to. Contrary to popular perception, there isn't just one correct way of trading. Some traders find themselves wide awake and fully focused at night when everyone else is asleep. A few traders find it profitable to trade just five months in a year, with a deep and exhaustive focus. They spend the remaining months fine-tuning their strategy and recovering from the effort they expend.

The default approach most traders have is to trade around their full-time job in the beginning. The iron condor makes it perfectly possible to do this successfully. The point we're trying to make is not to stick to a routine just because some book told you to do so.

Instead, stick to executing the important points that every successful routine has and implement it whichever way suits you best. Here are some of the important things that every routine must have.

PLANNING THE NEXT SESSION (THE NIGHT BEFORE)

Always plan your trading session beforehand. This doesn't mean you need to map out all of the trades that you'll take ahead of time. In fact, resist planning exact trades as much as possible. Instead, focus on the steps you will take during the session.

How will you analyze the markets and at what time will you sit down to do so? At the end of every trade session and before the next day's activities, you should take the time to review your trade journal to note any areas you can improve on. What are the improvements you would like to incorporate for your next trading session?

It's never a good idea to jump right into a live session without some warming up first. Much like an athlete warms their muscles up before exerting them in action, you can practice your skills on demo charts or simulation software before analyzing the real thing.

This will put you in a good frame of mind when your trading session begins and you'll hit the ground running. Something else to remind yourself of during your session is awareness. Where will your focus be and how do you want to react to losing trades, should they occur? Do you have multiple web browser tabs open or just your trading screen open?

If you happen to hit a losing trade tomorrow, will you fly off the handle and react in an emotional manner? Or is your intention to react calmly and remind yourself that this is just the cost of trading profitably? Set this intention the previous day and constantly remind yourself of this habit that you wish to install within yourself.

What will your actions during the trading session be like? Will you behave like most traders do and check the news and browse the internet? Or will you remain focused on the task at hand? If you're someone who places their trades in the morning, near when the market opens, will you check in throughout the day?

When will you check in, and how will you safeguard yourself from executing something rashly? What kind of preparation will you undergo before checking in? The check in itself could be just for a few minutes, but it's wise to prepare your mind before exposing it to the markets.

This way you won't exit a position in a fit of anxiety or enter one in a euphoric state. When will you conduct your review, and how will you record trade information in your journal? Remember to record the specific reasons for entry and exit since this will help you analyze your performance better.

CONSISTENT SLEEP AND REST

This is the most important part of your routine and it is one that is often ignored. For some reason our society doesn't value sleep. We view it as evidence of being lazy. We glorify people who work ridiculous 120-hour weeks and praise them as being driven and motivated.

When those same people turn around and confess they don't have much of a life and undergo regular nervous breakdowns, we shrug it off and think that's the price of success. The usual picture that is painted of a trader is that of an over-caffeinated person who lives on their trading desk and has time for nothing else.

Rest is what resets your brain and allows you to function at peak levels. Without this, you don't stand a chance of making money. Let go of the Hollywood portrayals of traders and of the worship that those misguided 120 hours per week entrepreneurs receive from mass media.

Instead, make it a point to get as much rest as your mind needs. Sleep is when your mind synthesizes all the information of the day and processes it to create new habits within you. A person who has not slept for 24 hours has the same level of sobriety as someone who is above the legal blood alcohol limit (Eske, 2019).

After 48 hours without sleep, your brain will involuntarily shut down for a few seconds to get some sleep. Hopefully the message from all of this is clear to you. You need to rest and need to prioritize getting good quality sleep.

A restful night's sleep helps you achieve something else that will boost your trading performance. By sleeping at the same time every night consistently, you'll wake up at the same time as well. This will give you all the time you need to finish the tasks you need to do in order to trade well.

If you approach the markets in a hurried and rushed attitude, then you're likely going to make mistakes that will cost you money. A calm mind also has lesser distractions to contend with and you'll naturally end up making better decisions.

MEDITATION

Meditation is often lumped together with other woo-woo type practices that supposedly change you spiritually, but unlike many of those practices, it actually works. Meditation helps you build awareness of your thoughts and actions. It helps you detach from your current reality and view it as objectively as possible.

This is a skill that is extremely important for a trader to possess. Mediation literally rewires your brain for the better (Hanson & Mendius, 2009). All of our beliefs and actions are encoded within our brain through neural networks. These networks are pathways along which our brain stores information about our habits and about how we usually behave when confronted with a stimulus.

If you happen to react emotionally to a few losing trades, then there's a corresponding neural network within you that contains this information. Meditation helps you bring awareness to its existence. Changing your habits from this point is as simple as choosing to practice the right habit or action instead of choosing the familiarity of the old pattern.

It all begins with awareness. While most of us become aware of our thoughts when they cause us extreme pain or joy, it's far better to catch these troublesome thoughts earlier when they're less intense. This is what meditation helps you do. It doesn't have any religious connotations, although you can choose to chant phrases or intonations as you wish.

You can practice meditation for as little as 10 minutes every day and see a profound effect. It's as simple as sitting quietly, undisturbed, for 10 minutes and observing your breath as you breath in and out. You can also use mobile apps such as *Headspace* or *Stop.Breathe.Think* to help you with this.

The biggest effect of meditation that you will notice is your ability to remain calm, or relatively calmer than you usually are, when confronted with a mistake that costs you money. For example, if you pulled the trigger on an incorrect trade setup, instead of blaming yourself and identifying with it ("I'm a failure"), you'll be able to take a step back and view it impartially ("The trade failed. I made a mistake that I can rectify immediately.")

This separation of success and failure from your identity ("I") is critical. Trading as an endeavor will require you to take losses. If you can't handle them, then you'll likely not be successful. Meditation builds your strength in this regard.

MARKET ANALYSIS

Market analysis is a routine unto itself, and you should develop a procedure that helps you the most. Ideally, you'll perform it before the market opens so as to get up to speed with everything that happened overnight. The stock markets aren't particularly active overnight, but news items might have some effect on opening prices.

Some traders wait for the market to open before beginning to analyze it. The thought process here is that since that session's chart landscape will be different, why not analyze it after the open rather than before anything has happened? There is some logic to this, but we must caution that it doesn't work for most traders.

The best way to structure market analysis is to first take a look at any overnight news items or events that might disrupt your current positions. This will usually be reflected in the value of the open positions you have. Next, look at potential new positions and determine ideal entry prices. If you need to go ahead and set limit orders for entry, then this is the time to do this.

FREEMAN TRADING RULE #5

ALWAYS REVIEW YOUR CURRENT POSITIONS BEFORE ENTERING ANY NEW POSITIONS

If you're trading iron condors, you need to first look at the VIX to determine where the market's volatility is at. You'll also need to review whether there are any special events during that day, such as earnings announcements or interest rate announcements that might create large levels of volatility in your chosen stock.

Review what your plan is with regards to trading around these events. Iron condors don't need much maintenance, so typically you'll be able to trade right through the event. If your trade is affected by the prices of commodities such as gold or oil, then check those charts as well.

The idea is to get a lay of the land before or as the market opens so that you're in a good position to pounce when opportunity makes itself known.

REVIEW YOUR PLAN

From the previous night, you must have determined a certain course of action. Remind yourself of what these actions and intentions are before placing trades or even before the market opens. Bring awareness to everything that you do and also take a quick psychological check of where you're currently at.

Burnout is a problem that strikes many traders, and you should be very aware of it creeping up on you. You don't need to trade every single day the market is open to make money. At the very least, you need to take a month off every year to review your strategies and to consolidate everything you've learned over a long period of time.

Coming back to your daily routine, review your plan to see whether you're fulfilling all the conditions your entry system requires. Are you aware of the criteria for exits? Is your event handling plan in place? Review all of this so that you're up to speed with regards to your plan of action.

Some traders like to create watchlists in real time to track the stocks they think will give opportunities. Create these and track the prices or attributes that are relevant to your strategy. Always check whether your entries and exits are a part of your trading plan. If they are, go ahead with them. If not, stay out.

This equally applies to trades that you entered by mistake but are working out anyway. Remaining in such trades is to rely on dumb luck and is hardly a good strategy to chase. Remember that everything you do in session will form a habit within you. The more you execute poor actions, the more likely it is that you're building habits that breed unsuccessful trading.

JOURNAL

Your trade journal is the most important document in connection to your trading efforts. It is a record of everything you did throughout the day and also forms the basis of your review system. Opinion is divided as to how often you need to review your trades. The most common frequency is once a week.

Choose a frequency that allows you to learn the most from your in-session behavior. When recording trades in your journal, enter as much information as you can. Record the levels and behavior of everything that your trade depends on and also note your reasons for entry. Make it a point to note your mental state during that time as well.

This trading routine should take you no more than a couple hours every day during the week and an hour during the weekends to execute. They're small steps, but they add up to a sum that is greater than its parts. Review the actions you performed during trading sessions and you'll unearth patterns in your behavior that you can fix down the road.

YOUR SECRET WEAPON – THE COMPOUND EFFECT OF PROPERLY USING YOUR TRADING JOURNAL

There is a common saying in the business world that "If something can't be measured, then it can't be managed." The same applies to trading since trading is also a business. Whether you're an individual retail trader or an institutional trader, you have to write down as many details of your trades as you can.

In his New York Times bestselling book *The Compound Effect,* Darren Hardy states that even small changes can, if applied consistently, produce huge effects over time. This is no more true than in the case of logging your trades. This isn't a new idea, in fact, Jesse Livermore, often called the Father of Day Trading, is also one of the first men ever to be credited with recording his trades, and revisiting them to notice patterns in his wins and losses.

Unfortunately, most traders go about recording trades in a completely counter-intuitive way. If they do record trades at all, they see it merely as a process of logging profit and loss from each trade – the same way a bookkeeper logs a businesses' revenue and costs for a given month.

Technology has made this worse, because now many trading software offer an automatic import option to trading journals, meaning you don't even have to log your trades yourself.

Here's why we believe this doesn't work.

Noting entry and exit points, as well as profit and loss, only tells a fraction of the story for each trade. Any automatic import software can log numbers, what it can't log is your state of mind, or emotional reactions to price changes. Only you can do this, and it requires the utmost discipline and brutal honesty if you are to benefit from it.

"This market doesn't make any sense" might be a fair reason for a single trade going against you. But when 80% of your trades for that month fall under that category, then it's not the market that doesn't make sense, it's your strategy.

Which is why we've prepared the trading journal below and made it free to all readers. You don't need to give us your email address, just click on the link to the Google sheet and click file > make a copy and you're good to go.

By writing these details, you will train yourself to be accountable for every trading decision you make. Maintaining such a record will give an edge over the long term when you review your trades in the future and learn from your mistakes. Pay particular attention to patterns which are emerging with your losers rather than your winners. Are you making adjustments too early? Are you getting the strike prices wrong? Whatever it is, you can learn from it and iterate your trading strategy to produce better results.

You can access the journal itself by clicking the link below

https://freemanpublications.com/ICJournal

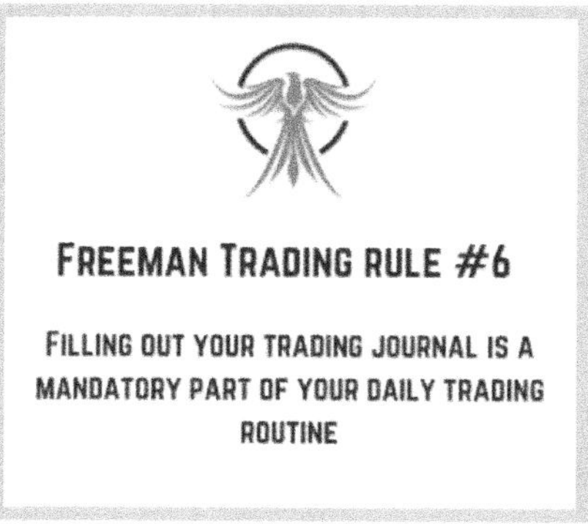

3 NON-NEGOTIABLE RULES OF SUCCESSFUL TRADERS

Aside from sticking to a routine that allows them to be successful for long periods of time in the markets, all successful traders follow three basic rules. You can view these as being the three non-negotiable rules of success in the markets. While they might seem to be obvious, the fact is that many traders underestimate how difficult the markets can be.

These rules only reinforce the fact that when it comes to trading success, your mind is your most powerful tool. It's what you use to make trading decisions and analyze all of your actions. Without prioritizing its well-being, you're only going to become a donor of money in the markets.

Rule #1 - Never Trade Under the Influence

Here's a true story. A trader we happen to know very well was quite active in the FX markets. While he was successful, his trading routine and general lifestyle caused him to absorb far too much risk. However, he managed to ride his luck for a long period of time until one day he lost 45% of his account overnight.

The reason for such a loss? He spotted a setup that he thought was golden while inebriated and told himself that he'd close his position out in the morning when he woke up. Unfortunately for him, he forgot he had a trade on when he woke up hung-over and as a result ate a 45% loss.

This might seem to be a humorous story, but it hits far too close to reality as far as we're concerned. Many unsuccessful traders do things like this and it happens because of a fundamental misunderstanding of what trading success is all about.

The average losing trader spends many months or even years seeking that perfect system or that perfect indicator that unlocks all market secrets. They spend countless hours back testing their system and running simulations. Once they find something that works, they eagerly rush into the markets to use it.

Thanks to all the effort they've expended developing this magical indicator, they think they've cracked the code. All they need to do now, they think, is to wait for the money to start rolling in. After all, they have a foolproof system!

Trading reality is far more sobering than this. All they've done is figure out a portion of one leg upon which successful trading is built. Technical systems go far beyond just figuring out the perfect entry. The perfect exit needs to be developed as well and market conditions need to be analyzed thoroughly.

The market's conditions will influence how well any trading system does and these change all the time. The trader then needs to marry this to their risk management system by evaluating their win rates and average win to loss amounts. Sitting back and hoping that some indicator does the work for you is only going to cause you to think that you can function on autopilot.

This is what leads people to begin to lose their discipline and begin to enact bad habits in the name of finding "freedom." They think they can get away with staying out all night and then rolling out of bed in the morning to trade. The net result is a 45% or worse loss to their accounts.

It's a simple rule to abide by, really. Do not trade under the influence. You need your mind to be as sharp as possible to do all of the things that we've already discussed. We haven't even gotten to identifying appropriate candidates for iron condors as yet. Your brain's analytical abilities are your biggest tool, and you should do everything in your power to maintain them.

Rule #2 - Exit All Trades Before a Vacation

Many traders get sucked into the image of being a "hardcore" trader who lives and breathes the markets, whatever that means. They think of themselves as being part of an interconnected web that makes the markets flow. They're extremely interested in what's happening with the trade negotiations between the workers and owners of a bread factory in some small town in France and think that this could impact their positions.

We're exaggerating, of course, but there are many traders who behave in this manner. They think they need to be switched on all the time and religiously follow every single tick of the market. As a result, they find that their normal lives interrupt this dream state. Their first reaction is to bend their vacation times around the market. The result is that when they're supposed to be on vacation relaxing and recharging, they're walking around trying to get a signal on their phone so that they can check their positions.

This kind of behavior is also frequent in traders who think they need to squeeze every single cent of profit from the markets. They behave as if opportunities don't come by very often in the markets and that if they miss a few potentially profitable trades, they'll end up making far less money than what they ought to make.

First off, if your trading strategy throws up just 20 or 30 opportunities every year, you need to find yourself another strategy to complement it. There are exceptions to this rule, surely, but no one ever got rich by unearthing just those few potential trades. Note that we're talking about opportunities, not final trades.

Your strategy needs to give you plenty of opportunities that you can sift through. You should only take the ones that are closest to your entry conditions and ignore the rest. If your system generates enough such entries, then there's no need for you to remain engaged with the market every day it's open.

Successful traders routinely take time away from the markets to unwind. This is because trading places a huge strain on your mind and it's impossible to perform at peak levels every single day of the year. More importantly, you also need to take the time to review your system and make sure it's still relevant for the market.

A system such as the iron condor will always be relevant, but even with this, you need to evaluate whether you're executing it properly. Are you taking the right opportunities, and are you analyzing the markets correctly? Evaluating all of this requires you to step away from the trading screen and review your skills.

You also need to enhance your skills. While you'll learn the best conditions to implement an iron condor, there are some conditions that you might be able to unearth that work just as well. Remember that the markets are constantly evolving, and there's no telling that what worked today will work tomorrow.

Time off from the markets, such as vacation, help you recharge and rejuvenate. These moments help your mind recover and also consolidate all the learning it has gone through. You'll come back refreshed and ready to attack the markets again. In the long run, this approach makes a lot more money than one where you're glued to the screen at all times.

In order to overcome market fatigue, you need to switch off completely. This means you need to close all open positions so that you have no pending liabilities in the market. The last thing you want to be doing is checking in on the markets when you're supposed to be switched off. It's one thing to check in out of interest, but it's entirely another to do so from a place of worry. If you have an open position, then you need to monitor it or else you'll lose a lot of money.

This creates a lot of disruption in your life and you'll find that once your vacation is over, you'll not be refreshed enough to trade well. So do yourself a favor and switch everything off.

Rule #3 - Take a Break When on a Significant Losing Streak

Losing streaks are a reality of trading. Whether you like it or not, they will happen. Oddly enough, no one has a problem with a winning streak, but the moment losing streaks begin piling up, everyone loses their minds. Some traders consider losing two trades in a row as evidence of a significant losing streak.

Two losses in a row is a normal day at the office. A losing streak is a string of losses that are on the borders of the probability of your trading system. What does this mean? All trading systems have inherent probabilities of losing or winning streaks. The lower your win percentage is, the higher are your chances of losing multiple trades in a row.

Most traders' problem with losing streaks occur due to a fundamental misunderstanding of how the market works. They approach trading decisions as if they were appearing for an exam in school or some assignment at work. Think back to your school days. How was success defined?

The more questions you answered correctly, the greater was your final score and the higher was your chance of passing to the next grade. We carry this behavior into the real world, but unfortunately this is not how things work out there. How many times have you done everything correctly and still failed? Even worse, how many times have you seen someone do all the wrong things and succeed?

Some of us tell ourselves that the world is unfair like that and that talentless people often prosper. Instead of adopting such a negative mindset, it's more appropriate to reevaluate the way you approach success and failure. The markets are no exception. Making money in the markets doesn't just depend on you being right or wrong on a single trade.

It isn't an examination where the more questions you get right, the more money you'll make. Trading success is built on two metrics: Your win rate and your average win versus average loss. If you were asked to pick the more successful trader between one who wins 30% of the time and another who wins 70% of the time, you would most likely choose the latter.

Well, it turns out that you don't have enough information to make this decision. The trader that wins 30% of the time can make a lot more money than the one who wins 70% of the time. How? If the 30% trader loses $1 on every loss but makes $5 on every win, they'll make a huge amount of money.

If the 70% trader loses $10 on every loss and wins just $1 on average, they'll lose money. Success in trading isn't a question of being right. It isn't linear. Instead, trading success exists on a band that is defined by your win rate and average win to loss ratio. There are many combinations of these numbers that ensure you'll make money.

As a result, winning and losing streaks don't matter. If you lose five trades in a row, at some point the probabilities will kick in and you'll run into a streak of wins. This doesn't make it likely that you'll hit a win streak right after a losing streak. However, in the long run the probabilities of your system will assert themselves and you'll emerge in the black. Of course, this assumes that your system has profitable odds to begin with.

What sabotages these chances of emerging profitably despite a losing streak is your mental state. If you view a losing streak or every loss as being a judgment of how good a trader you are, then you're going to have a tough time of it. You'll die a little on the inside with every loss and before you know it, you won't be in a position to execute your strategy as it demands.

No one likes losing money and it hurts our emotions. Even professional traders who have been doing this successfully for a long time hate taking extended streaks of losses. This is why monitoring your drawdown and fixing drawdown limits is extremely important.

A drawdown is the measure of how much percent of your account you lost from an equity high to a trough. If your principal was $5,000 and you lose $2,500, that's a (catastrophic) 50% drawdown. A losing streak that disrupts your mindset is best dealt with by taking time away from the markets.

Even a professional athlete isn't at their best day in and day out. They need time to rest and recover as well. Burnout occurs to even the best of traders and sometimes it can be tough to spot its symptoms. During such times, traders are liable to misinterpret market signals and enter wrong trades.

Thus, it's best to impose a drawdown stop limit such as the 10/1 rule. This rule states that when you hit a monthly drawdown of 10%, you'll take a month off. If you hit a 20% drawdown, you'll take two months off and so on. This will help you recover from the vagaries of the market and you'll preserve your capital better.

Drawdown limits are essential if you want to practice good risk management. Without them you're going to have a tough time adhering to your rules. Losing streaks can take over your mind and you'll begin revenge trading as a result. You'll be so desperate to make back the money you lost that you'll take anything that remotely resembles a profitable trade.

This only results in more losses, and a losing streak is born. Tragically, this streak could have been easily avoided if you had just stuck to drawdown limits. So implement this rule and always take time away from the markets when you hit a losing streak. You might miss short-term opportunities, but in the long run, you'll preserve more capital.

Every dollar of capital preserved can be turned into profits, so you'll automatically end up making more money.

This brings to a close our look at the three non-negotiable rules of successful traders. They seem pretty easy to implement, but they require a high degree of discipline to execute. Awareness is the key to ensuring you follow these rules. Combine them with your trading routine and you'll see money flowing towards you easily.

12

PSYCHOLOGICAL WARFARE - WINNING THE INNER GAME OF TRADING

What separates the traders who consistently make profits year after year, from the ones who do "just ok?" If you said better market analysis, you'd be wrong. If you said intelligence, you're wrong. If you said built-in personality traits, you're be wrong. In the case of the latter, we would argue that trading as a profession tends to attract people who naturally *would not* be good traders. More on that later.

The fact is there are genius traders who have the most detailed trading plans defining all entry and exit signals, stop loss levels, take profit levels, money management, risk management. There are those who have backtested their system until the cows come home, and know they have a clear statistical edge... and yet they still don't make money!

But here's where they are falling short: they lack the fundamental confidence to enter trades when their system tells them to, and possess an ego that keeps them in trades which are clear losers.

What does this mean in practical terms?

The 2 Primary Trading Motivations

Let's look at trading in a vacuum. There are 2 results for any trade; you can win, or you can lose. Most traders try to win every time. After all, that's logical, right? Why would you ever want a single losing trade? But here's why that mindset is the death of so many traders.

There is no way you can win 100% of the time. So you must accept that fact as absolute. Instead of trying to win every time, you must have a different goal. As a successful trader, your goal should be to develop a system which gives you the likelihood of profiting more times than not.

These 2 goals may sound the same on the surface, but the subconscious notion is totally different. The first goal involves being right every time, and as humans, we love to be right. Even more so, we hate being wrong. How often have you fumed when someone tells you "I told you so" after you made a choice which turned out to be incorrect. For many traders (and investors too – they're not immune from this), being right is more important than actually making money. The need to be right is what prevents so many from getting to the next level because being right is ego driven.

So with that in mind, if you aim to be right every time, then trading will involve a lot of being wrong, which is out of alignment with your priorities. When you consider that being wrong is synonymous with losing money, this is a double blow to your priorities.

In his book, *Vital Lies, Simple Truths,* Harvard Psychologist Daniel Goleman states that as human beings, we are more motivated to avoid pain than we are to seek pleasure. What Goleman then discovered was that our minds would retrospectively rationalize situations to divert attention away from the pain we are feeling.

In practical terms, what this means for traders is that our minds will rationalize situations where trades don't go in our favor. This happens to prevent us from being confronted with the cold, hard reality that it was our decision that got us the negative result.

Take this example, you've been monitoring RUT for the past week, and you see implied volatility has increased to a point where you're now happy to enter a trade. You wake up in the morning and get set to enter your strike prices, but before you do, you open up TradingView.com and go straight to the ideas section. You see that another user has a chart with an iron condor setup on AAPL. Somehow as if by magic, you find yourself back in your trading software entering the AAPL iron condor instead of the RUT iron condor you had planned to.

The logic behind this is simple. Your subconscious mind, in an attempt to avoid the pain of being wrong, allowed you to enter the AAPL trade, because the AAPL trade shifted the responsibility from you to the person who put up the chart on the internet. If that trade doesn't work out, it's not your fault, instead, it's the idiot who put the chart up.

See how we can easily rationalize away mistakes now? This is how so many traders fall victim to unstructured trading habits because these habits absolve them of responsibility.

So if your goal isn't to be right all the time, how is the second goal of developing an ever improving process any different?

The second goal involves developing a process in which you are continually refining and iterating to the point where your statistical edge grows larger.

The most important element of this goal is that it accepts that there will be losses, which as we mentioned in chapter 2, are simply a cost of being in the trading business. The best traders go beyond merely accepting losses; they actively encourage them as part of the bigger picture.

This is because they have removed their ego from the equation. They don't need to win every time. Just like they don't need for there to be a 100 year bull market. It's simply all part of the process.

By accepting risk as a built-in part of trading, your mind will be completely free to function without fear of these losses. This allows you to be systematic in your trading. Which means you take profits when your system tells you to and cut losses when it tells you to. You can do this because your motivation isn't being right, it's developing a process which gets better over time. Which then allows you to operate outside of the fear and rationalization paradigm suffered by those who are only motivated by being right.

Mutual Exclusivity

Trades themselves are mutually exclusive. The market does not care if you're on a winning streak or you've lost your last 100 trades.

2 traders with the same experience can look at the same chart, with access to all the same information. One trader will enter the trade, and the other trader won't. Why? Because the first trader was on a 5 trade winning streak, and the second was on a 5 trade losing streak.

Our minds are wired to seek patterns, and then associate these patterns with feelings. For the trader on the winning streak, the chart could have given them a positive feeling associated with a previous winner. For the trader on the losing streak, the opposite could be true.

Neither of these traders is necessarily right or wrong here, but it goes to show the fallibility of the human mind, which is why it's so vital to judge trade setups independent of previous ones. The best traders look at each potential trade as its own entity, not as the sum of something larger. They understand that each trade is unique, just like we know that the probability of a single roulette spin landing on red is still about 50/50, even if the last 10 spins have been red.

We have to look at each trade as its own entity because even though at certain moments, the market may look one way, there is no guarantee that the future results will play out like this same setup did in the past. Remember, for each setup, the market is made up of millions of traders and institutions, and unless the participants are the exact same as before, and their actions the same as before, then there is no way the outcome can be the exact same as before.

Now the point here is not to have you second guess all your chart setups, quite the opposite. It's to truly understand and internalize the fact that every single trade has the potential to go against you. With this understanding, you will no longer be focused on being right every time, but instead on developing your process so that it keeps getting better and better over time.

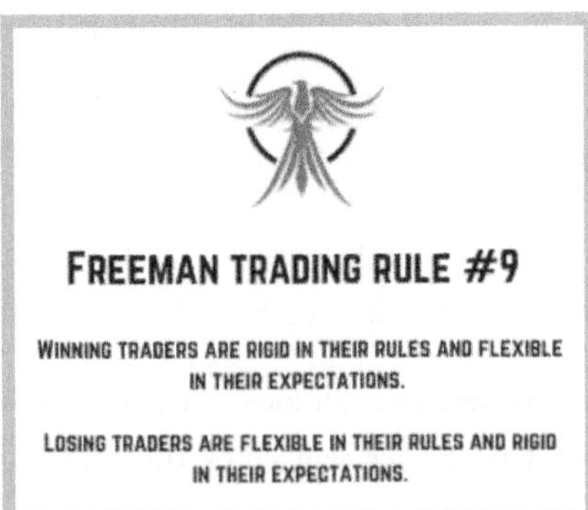

~

You Never Know What Will Happen Next

Imagine this scenario, Facebook has been trending sideways for 4 months straight now, their last earnings call was 2 weeks ago, and met analyst expectations on the dot. The greeks are set up nicely, and all indicators point to this being a perfect iron condor opportunity. You enter one 34 days out from expiry, and for the first week everything is rosy. Then you get a news alert on your phone, *"Entire Facebook board accused of being Chinese spies. Website banned in America effective immediately."* The share price plummets 50% in 30 minutes and the SEC halts trading. It doesn't take a genius to figure that this iron condor trade will be a loser. This is an extreme (and to be clear, purely hypothetical) example, but anything and everything *can* happen. After all, who could have predicted 9/11, or the COVID pandemic, and the subsequent effect these events had on the markets?

This means another key belief you need to internalize is that you don't *need* to know what will happen next. You can be right 100% of the time, but you just can't expect to be right 100% of the time. So if you are right on a trade, you can't expect the next time to give you the same outcome on a similar setup. By operating a rules-based setup, you can simply get out at the appropriate time, and then move on to the next trade. Most importantly, you can be ok with this because it's merely a cost of doing business as a trader.

Mistakes Are Not Something to Be Avoided

Did you know that Kobe Bryant holds the record for the most missed shots in NBA history? Or that Brett Favre, once the all-time leader in NFL touchdowns thrown, also holds the record for throwing the most interceptions. These 2 Hall of Famers have something in common. They weren't afraid to make mistakes.

Every person who has ever achieved greatness, did so with a huge number of mistakes along the way. It's often these mistakes that separate them from the rest of us, because it's in our nature to want to avoid mistakes, not seek them out. Like rationalizing our pain away, avoiding mistakes is another quirk of human behavior. Think back to when you were young, and you tried to grab something off the kitchen counter, which caused it to spill everywhere. A typical parent's reaction would be to shout at the child who, in turn, then begins crying. This negative reaction conditions the child to believe that they are bad, because of the inability to separate themselves from the mistake. The mindset shifts from "I am a person who makes mistakes" to "I made a mistake, which means I am a bad person"

Bryant and Brees never saw themselves as bad, they saw themselves as humans who were on a mission to be the best, and fully embraced that mistakes were part of that mission. The same goes for the best traders out there. They are fully able to separate themselves from bad trades. It goes back to internalizing the idea that you can't get every outcome right, and all you can do is learn from when it goes against you. Meditation is a tremendous tool for this because, at its core, it allows you to separate yourself from your actions, and not blame yourself when things don't go your way.

Everyone's background and childhood is different, but if you have a particularly tough time with separating yourself from your mistakes, then we suggest this visualization exercise.

Begin with a quiet room, and sit down in a chair, or on the floor against the wall – anywhere where you can keep your back straight. Close your eyes and take a few deep breaths and slowly count down from 10 in your head. Once you reach zero, imagine yourself walking into another room. In this room is a desk with a similar setup to yours. Go and take a seat at this desk.

Take a moment to get settled and focus on the sights and smells around you. Use as much detail as possible. Once you're comfortable, imagine your trading screen pops up, with a setup which looks profitable to you. Imagine entering the strike prices, stops, and number of contracts – then complete the order.

We then fast forward to the trade going against you. Now imagine exiting the trade for a small loss. Focus on your emotions at this time. Understand that the market simply went against you this time, and there was nothing you could do to control this. If your setup was right, and similar trades have gone in your favor in the past, then you did all you could. Now lock in this feeling by entering this losing trade in your journal, remember to fill in the notes section. Keep focusing on your emotions during this exercise; remember that this is all part of your goal, which is developing a trading process which continually gets better and better over time.

Once that's complete, slowly count back up to 10 and open your eyes.

It may seem strange to visualize a losing trade, but whether the trade goes in your favor isn't the point of the exercise. The exercise is designed to help you separate yourself from your results, and to understand that you are not your trades. In the early stages, it might help you to do this exercise every day as part of your trading routine.

The other reason why this kind of visualization works so well is that it is *process focused* rather than *outcome focused.* Many visualization techniques are outcome focused. These are the ones where they tell you to sit in a room and imagine the giant house, and sports car. These techniques do not work, because they do nothing to develop the process which *gets* you to this outcome.

Process based visualization can be as powerful as real, in-person practice. An interesting study was done in the 1960s by a high school basketball coach, and then included in Maxwell Multz's book *Psycho-Cybernetics.*

"Junior high basketball players are separated into three teams and asked to shoot free throws, with each individual's accuracy recorded. One of the teams practiced shooting free throws every day, while another didn't practice shooting at all. The players on the third team sat on a bench and imagined themselves shooting free throws. When the teams were tested in free throw shooting at the end of the experiment, the team that practiced every day showed the most improvement while the team that never practiced didn't improve at all. The third team, which never touched a basketball, improved by nearly as much as the team that practiced every day"

So the team who visualized the process improved almost as much as the team who practiced with real basketballs. This just goes to show the power of process-based visualization.

Learn To Take Losses & Imperfect Setups

As we've already mentioned, losses are a cost of doing business in trading. There is no strategy that will work 100% of the time and make you money as well. This thinking is excusable in newer traders, especially those who come from a background of directional trading and the need to be right. We can excuse such traders since their mistake emanates from ignorance.

Far less excusable is the approach of a trader who has been trading for a while and still expects to unearth some magic strategy that gives them a 100% success rate. Despite having been exposed to the markets, they're still stuck on the hamster wheel of trying to find the elusive perfect strategy.

The underlying problem is that these traders cannot accept or deal with the prospect of losing. Studying the risk management chapter from earlier in this book is a good way to install the correct mindset that you ought to approach the markets with. Remember, options trading isn't an exam where you get X number of questions correct and then earn money.

A loss is simply the cost of finding out whether the market will move in your desired manner or not. That's what your risk per trade really is. It isn't a substitute for how much money you'll make or how much you could earn per year etc. It's just the cost of finding out how right you are.

Look at it this way, and you'll realize that it doesn't matter what happens on a particular trade. Win or lose, the odds of your system are all that matter, and you'll make money no matter what over the long run.

Remove Your Negativity Bias with A Short Memory

Our minds have a built-in negativity bias, and this can cause us to overvalue certain events in our minds. We might replay certain losses over and over and not remind ourselves of the wins we've earned in the past. Each loss brings the idea of failure closer, and as a result, we start believing that we're bad traders or that we're destined for failure.

On top of this, there are certain cultural phenomena, most notably outside the United States, which actively discourages people from thinking highly of themselves. If you're from Australia or New Zealand, you may be familiar with the Tallest Poppy Syndrome. Dutch readers may have heard of *maaiveldcultuur*. Our readers from Scandinavia may know it as the "*Law of Jante*". In Ireland, or Irish communities, it's plain old Catholic guilt.

It all boils down to the same core idea, that it's not good to have an overly positive view of yourself or to feel good about your success. In a study of 1,501 participants by Thompson-Reuters, 81% said they had experienced hostility because of their success or achievements, and 64.7% of respondents reported lower self-esteem and self-confidence because of this hostility (Billan, 2019).

Now when you combine this with the general public's view of trading or the financial markets, it's very easy to get caught in the trap of negative bias.

The best way to deal with this is to have a short memory. Saying this is easier than doing it, of course. The place to start is to remind yourself of your negativity bias. This is just how human beings are designed, and you'll never change it. What you can do is bring awareness to it and remind yourself of its power to distort.

This way you can choose to act on those impulses and drown yourself in negativity or you can choose to remain separate from it. Another technique to adopt is to screenshot your winning trades and positive thoughts from your journal. When you're overwhelmed with thoughts about how you're not successful, then review these to give yourself the true picture.

Adopting successful routines is another important thing for you to do. Many traders take the time to journal their trades but don't spend time mentally strengthening themselves. Even if you take a loss, remind yourself of all the things you did well on that trade. For some, it may be beneficial to join a trading community, so that you are surrounded by people with the same worldview and goals as yourself.

Remember, a profit or loss is just the result of a trade. It isn't an indicator of how good a trader you are. It's a bit like looking at an athlete and thinking they're great because so many people venerate them. The truth is that they're great because they put the work into developing their skills and building competence. Losing a single game or race doesn't eliminate all of the skills they've built up over time.

Similarly, you have trading skills that you've worked on and are good at. A loss doesn't mean every single skill is poor. Review the things you did well right after a trade result, whether it's a win or a loss. Remind yourself of how well you did these things. Don't ignore the things you did poorly. Those can wait for the review session.

On the flip side to this, don't allow success to go to your head. It's good to have a positive self image, but when that turns into delusions of grandeur, problems can arise. In his seminal work on human psychology, *The Laws of Human Nature*, Robert Greene tells the story of how Michael Eisner let his personal problems affect his performance as the CEO of Disney. Eisner let his early successes go to his head, which ultimately led to the delusions of grandeur which cost him his job.

Similar stories are commonplace in the trading world. A trader experiences a good run of results, which then leads to increased risk taking, which leads to greater losses in the long run.

Let Trades Run

This is the opposite of most conventional trading advice. The reason is that the iron condor takes time to work, and for this reason, you'll need to exercise patience with regards to giving your trades time to work out. Traders often exit ahead of time due to fear of the position turning into a loss. This is a pretty typical emotional reaction that most traders have, and it causes them to miss out on the rewards that their systems provide them with.

As we mentioned earlier, the only time you should exit your trades prematurely is if you've committed an obvious error that goes against your system.

In such cases, undoing the mistake is appropriate, and if you cannot fix it by adjusting your trade, then exit it completely. For all other scenarios, remain in the trade no matter what. When it comes to iron condors, traders receive the maximum profit upfront, and this might tempt them to quickly close the trade and take whatever they can.

This is a mistake. The strategy has a high probability of working out, and one of the reasons it has such a high probability is because it takes time. The markets move in a certain direction for a week or two, but in a month, they usually revert to the mean. This means the overall price action remains sideways with perhaps a slight directional bias to it.

Thus the only way to take advantage of such price action is to remain in your trade. Do not let emotions or the fear of missing out cloud your judgment and overrule the right course of action.

One Trade Doesn't Define You

You've already learned that the success of your system is based on probabilities and on the relationship between your win rate and the average win-to-loss ratio. These two form a band of profitability that will make you money as long as you keep executing your strategy as defined in your trading plan.

In order for the odds to play out, you need to take a large number of trades. Think of it as a coin toss. If you were to toss a coin just four times (odds of a result is 50%), you could receive four heads in a row or four tails in a row or the distribution could be a perfect 50 percent between heads and tails.

If someone asked you to bet over the course of just these four tosses your odds of success will be low. However, if the same person asked you to bet over the course of a million coin flips, you can reasonably predict that roughly half will land heads, and the other results will be tails. Your odds of success became much higher.

When you proceed to flip the coin in this scenario, does it really matter which way the coin lands on an individual flip? It could land heads 10 times in a row, or it could land tails 20 times in a row. It doesn't matter. Over the course of the million flips, the distribution between heads and tails will be 50/50.

Following this line of reasoning, we can conclude that there is no reason to care about an individual flip's result. It could be heads, it could be tails, you could call it correctly, or you could call it incorrectly. In the long run, the odds will play themselves out.

Your trading system is pretty much the same. The results of an individual trade don't matter as long as your focus is on executing your plan over the course of a large number of trades. Winning or losing streaks won't matter because you'll end up receiving the results of those odds no matter what happens.

So why should you care about an individual trade's result? If you're correct about a trade's result, why is this a big deal? So what if you lost money on it? As long as your risk numbers were correct, then you're going to make money no matter what. It's mathematics. There's no guesswork involved here.

Paper Trade

Paper trading is both overrated and underrated at the same time. It's overrated because it's not fully possible to practice managing your emotions when your gains and losses are on paper. Some traders struggle to execute their plans as if they're trading live, so this defeats the purpose.

The positive of paper trading is that you can test new strategies and see if they fit you. The key is not to remain stuck in paper trading mode forever. With this in mind, it's important for you to paper trade for at least three months so that you have a chance to build skills and gather feedback on your strategy. A good balance when you begin live trading is to keep paper trading on the side to build up your skills alongside your live trades. This is especially important with iron condors because there will be many days when you will just be letting your trades play out, and therefore have more time to paper trade.

A Final Word on Avoiding Being Shamed by Society at Large

Most people view wealth as a zero-sum game. They believe people can only get rich at the expense of others.

Think about phrases which are part and parcel of our everyday lexicon like "Money doesn't grow on trees" and "Only take your fair share". Both of these confirm the idea that money is finite and limited. This idea is reinforced everywhere from major political parties to world religions. This is an apolitical and all-inclusive book, so we won't discuss specifics, but it's important to understand the root of many of these ideas.

Since 2008, there has been extra vitriol towards anyone involved in the financial world. Unfortunately, this trickles down, and the anger aimed at mismanaged hedge funds and investment banks ends up being directed at individual traders as well.

If you're unsure whether this is true, next time you tell someone that you trade options, just notice what kind of reaction you get. Because there are really only two you'll see regularly. The first is the eyes light up "how do I get in on this" type reaction. And the second, more popular reaction is what we call 'mild disgust", it's characterized by a short, curt response, which is then followed by complete disinterest.

As a trader, you will permanently be up against this negativity towards what you do. People will rationalize that you're a bad person, and you may hear phrases about your work such as "you don't create anything of value," "you don't create any jobs," or "you're making money at the expense of others." There is a degree of truth to all of these, which makes it hard for us to hear them. But it's vital that you do not let these words alter your beliefs.

To reinforce positive beliefs, you must always be engaging in activities which promote abundance. Things like being generous to those you love, supporting charitable causes dear to your heart, and even things as small as being a good tipper. These will go a long way to reinforce your belief in abundance and help you become immune to the constant chastising that comes with being an options trader.

For more in-depth explanations of the philosophy behind the subconscious building of wealth, we recommend Dan Kennedy's fantastic book *"No BS Wealth Attraction in the New Economy."* Don't let the woo-woo title dissuade you. The book is filled with practical advice that will benefit traders of all experience levels.

13

A CAUTIONARY WORD ABOUT "MAGIC" OPTIONS TRADING SERVICES

As part of your continuing education in iron condors you're going to read a lot more literature and will probably encounter a number of self-appointed gurus and trading alert services.

We're not one of those "all gurus are bad" organizations. There are some truly great subscription services and courses out there. There are also a large number of charlatans who will do nothing but cost you money. The nature of internet marketing these days has normalized tall claims. A lot of legitimate actors are forced to claim absurd numbers due to the large number of fake claims floating around. There's simply no other way to attract attention.

In this chapter, our aim is to help you understand some of the qualities of genuine online courses/teachers and subscription services. A lot of these courses and services cost upwards of four figures, so it's worth taking the time to review them thoroughly.

RECORDS

The most obvious thing to look for is the existence of actual trade records or credentials. Surprisingly, almost every single trade educator fails this basic test.

By trade records, we mean fully detailed, line-by-line records of trade history. If this history has been audited, then even better.

Truth be told, most trading educators don't bother to have their trade results audited. They claim to show you screenshots of trades, but most of these can be manipulated. There's just no way of determining whether these trades were genuine or not.

For example, when speaking of trade screenshots, the guru will show you the instrument name, the entry price and the exit price. They won't show you the position size or the profit and loss amount. They might color-code their trades to indicate which ones went for a profit or which ones went for a loss, so there is some information provided.

However, the most important thing to ask is whether these trades were placed on a demo platform or as live money trades. This question is never answered by them. Their position sizes don't necessarily reflect their levels of success, but they do show that they know how to handle large positions and are capable of practicing good risk management.

So don't believe simple screenshots showing purported profits or losses. Closely tied to this sort of "evidence" is the yearly return number. This is especially true when it comes to options trading and applies to trade signal subscription services as well. The ROI that these people display is usually not genuine.

We've already shown you how ROI ought to be calculated. The way these services calculate it is different. They multiply the individual ROI from every trade they've placed and present that as the total portfolio growth. For example, if they placed three trades successfully and earned 10% ROI on each trade, they present their system as having a 30% ROI.

Some people boost returns to 200% or 300% in this manner. This leads many prospective students or subscribers to believe that if they start with $1,000, they'll end up with $4,000 at the end of the year. In reality, their true ROI is somewhere around 10-12%, which is also very good. It's just not anywhere near what they claim.

"I USED TO RUN/WORK AT A FUND"

This claim is becoming increasingly common. The guru or subscription service seller claims to have worked at a financial institution. Technically speaking, the receptionist at Goldman Sachs can claim to be an employee just as much as the CEO. This doesn't mean the former knows everything about what happens inside the firm.

There's a simple way to check such claims. Every financial industry professional needs to possess a license that allows them to operate in the securities market. This is true even with the smallest of hedge funds. The person making this claim needs to present their FINRA-issued license. Even an expired one is fine.

In order to trade for an institution, a person needs to be licensed to deal securities in the markets. If they do not possess this or make excuses saying they don't have it for whatever reason, they're lying to you. You can check whether they're registered to deal in securities on FINRA's website. You'll be able to view the firms they have worked for, the licenses they hold and whether there are any outstanding regulatory issues being processed in relation to their conduct.

These people will typically turn around and accuse you of having a limited mindset and that this is the reason you're not able to be successful with your trading. Like with every con artist out there, this is misdirection. As if asking them to backup their claims is evidence of a limited mindset!

Watch out for trading systems or methods that are overly complicated or completely subjective. Every trading system is subjective to a large extent, but there are some that rely entirely on discretionary methods of figuring the markets out. This isn't the case with an iron condor since it's pretty straightforward.

If you plan to trade in a directional manner, this is something to watch out for. What usually happens is that the guru puts together two different trading systems, such as Elliot wave models and price action patterns, and claims it's a completely new trading system that no one else has figured out.

It might be a great trading system for them, but it does nothing for you. If it relies on discretionary judgment, then only the person that designed it can make it work.

REFUNDS

The sad truth is that it's close to impossible to get a refund from these trading gurus. Their conditions are so absurd that there's no way you can ever get your money back. They'll ask for documented evidence of having carried the system out to a "T." You can bet that there will be some clause that you will have missed.

Perhaps you risked 5% instead of 4.99% or something of that ilk. Some gurus flat-out refuse refunds due to the system being intellectual property. There's no arguing with such people.

When it comes to subscription services, the return and refund regulations are even more nebulous. These services usually state that returns are not guaranteed, therefore there's no way you can claim to get your money back. The only way to verify their claims is to take a look at reviews and follow their signals over time.

Usually these signal services tweet or post social media updates about their calls. Naturally, they'll only highlight the successful calls, but it's worth taking a look at these to figure out whether they're sticking to certain principles or not.

Don't get carried away by the ROI claims as we mentioned earlier. Most of these are made-up.

SALES-LIKE LANGUAGE

One of the hallmarks of a scammer is their ability to use lengthy sales letters that are full of outsized claims that focus solely on the returns. They'll never talk about the amount of capital it takes to make that much money or how much of their account they're risking. In fact, the term "risk-adjusted" will never be a part of their vocabulary.

Risk-adjusted returns refer to the amount of money they make relative to how much they're risking per trade. If trade A risks 10% of their account and makes 40% and trader B risks 5% to make 35%, it's clear who the better trader is. The scammer will always highlight the overall return and will never disclose any statistics of their trading system.

They might even constantly highlight how much money their students are making and there's no independent way to verify this. If the person claims to make that much money themselves, it's easy to ask them for screenshots or some kind of an audit trail. Claiming that a third person made that much allows them to blame someone else for not disclosing everything related to the trade.

A telltale sign of a scammer is when they make more money off their courses and newsletters than their actual trading. Trading successfully is a very profitable venture, and a successful trader would only ever teach other people if there's more money to be made by doing this or if they're exhausted from tracking the markets all the time. This is the case with many top traders like Victor Sperandeo who went into the education business once they retired from trading full time.

The latter is a good reason, and such people do exist. They usually start their own seeding firm or proprietary trading firm that allows them to educate new traders and invest through them. The former reason, of making more money selling courses, is an indicator that the person wasn't a very good trader to begin with.

A trader that can make between 10-20% returns every year and has audited their results can attract millions in institutional funding. Successful traders are hard to come by and institutional demand for them is high. Once they're trading millions of dollars, these people will collect half a million in income just in fees.

Compare that to some guru selling $500 courses to 1,000 people every year. Why would someone not use their trading knowledge to continue doing what they already know to make that much money? Why would they start an entirely new business and spend time building it up and marketing it when an easier path exists? It doesn't make much sense.

Most people selling courses tend to be great marketers and this is their real skill. They aren't selling you anything unique or profitable. They're simply packaging it correctly and making you think it's unique.

TYING IT ALL TOGETHER

Trading iron condors is a great way to boost your monthly income and earn cash flow from the markets. It's important that you understand this is a speculative strategy and isn't to be treated as an investment. Speculation typically involves short-term perspective.

As you've seen in this book, the iron condor is to be held for a period of 30 to 45 days, at most. The market moves differently in this time when compared to the usual investment horizon of 10 years or more. Buy and hold investment requires you to be patient and to hold on even when the market moves against you.

Speculative strategies call for a different approach. Due to your time horizon being short, you need to be very sensitive to where your capital is currently deployed. This is because while it's stuck in one position, there could be another instrument that is moving in a profitable manner.

This makes it very important for you to quickly evaluate whether your money is being deployed correctly. Unfortunately, this also leads to many traders making the mistake of expecting their trades to work out immediately. How can you draw the line between an unprofitable trade and one that just needs more time to work out?

The easiest way is to return to your entry criteria. The iron condor has some pretty simple ones. First, look for a range-bound market. While it's tough to find a market that is perfectly horizontal, they do exist. Indices are far less volatile than common stocks, so starting with them is a good idea.

Most ranges will have some degree of directional bias to them, and this is perfectly fine. Compare the range-bound movement to the prior trend to get an idea of the relative degree of sideways movement. Examining the choppiness indicator is a good way to get a quick view of how the market is behaving.

Next, you need to look at the relevant support and resistance levels and determine where you'd like to place your strike prices. There are different approaches you can take here as mentioned in this book. One way is to look at placing strikes B and C at least one standard deviation away from the underlying price.

Of course, all of this depends on volatility decreasing, and this is where evaluating the position of the VIX comes into play. Look to implement the iron condor only when the value of the VIX or the equivalent volatility index is greater than 20. Look to use this strategy when the VIX is declining from a value of greater than 20. This way you'll be able to receive the higher premium prices as a result of increased volatility.

Once your trade is up and running, it takes very little maintenance. You'll receive the maximum profit upfront and you'll simply need to wait for the remaining period to see whether you can hold onto it completely or not. The waiting period is the toughest, when it can be difficult for most traders to simply stand still and do nothing.

This highlights how important mindset is when it comes to trading.

A FINAL WORD ON MINDSET

We've given you a number of tools and methods you can employ to make sure you're thinking about the market correctly. Over and above this we would also like to point out something about positions and the market that most traders miss. Often, doing nothing is the right thing to do.

Jesse Livermore famously quipped that there were three things a trader could always do (Lefvre, 2019). They could go long, short or remain neutral. Remaining neutral or hanging onto your cash as a position is something that most unsuccessful traders don't do. They seek to take advantage of every single tick or move in the market.

It's impossible to always be right. Instead of trying to be right all the time, look to be patient and unearth those opportunities that will make you the most amount of money. An iron condor that fully satisfies all of your entry criteria is a far better bet than one that only satisfies it 90%.

A lot of traders convince themselves that they aren't spotting enough opportunities and this causes them to take positions that aren't well thought-out. The result is that they make less than they normally would or end up losing money in trades they have no business being around.

Protect your mindset like you would your life. In the markets, your mind is the only thing you have control over. You need to take time away from the markets and only trade when you're close to your best. Doing it any other way is simply preparing to lose money.

Remember to review and internalize the lessons you learned in the earlier part of this book that dealt with the true nature of the markets. We often approach every situation in life as if we need to get questions right on an exam. Trading and the markets don't work this way.

The markets and trading strategies depend on the probabilities inherent in your system. This means there are two pillars that support its success. The first is the win rate. This is the one we're most familiar with and all of us try to maximize by default. The second is the ratio between your average win and average loss. This metric is something almost no one looks at.

Traders might pay it lip service, but they don't fully understand what conclusions can be drawn from them. For starters, it means that profitability isn't a binary thing. It isn't as simple as winning or losing. The amount of money you make is an indicator of success in trading, but there are many ways to make money.

A trader who is correct just 30% of the time can be far more successful than someone who is right 95% of the time. Remember that the odds play themselves out over the long run and that to be truly successful you need to be patient and allow them to play themselves out. We highlighted the example of a coin toss and this is a very apt example.

Make sure to review the content of those chapters repeatedly if you ever find yourself thinking incorrectly of what trading is. If you're stuck in a losing streak and are desperately seeking a win, go back to the information in there and then evaluate whether you're experiencing a normal losing streak or whether you're executing your strategy incorrectly.

Trading options might sound complicated, but as we've shown you in this book, reality is far different. It will take you some time to come to terms with the way volatility works in the market. Repetition is the key to success in the market, so take your time paper-trading and getting to know your instruments.

Follow the trading plan we suggested to ensure you're trying your strategy out in a risk-free environment. Don't linger there for too long or else you'll never have the nerve to work up to live trading.

We're positive that the iron condor will be a profitable trading strategy for you to implement. Remember to keep your speculative and investment holdings separate. We wish you all the luck and profits in your trading!

One final word from us. If this book has helped you in any way, we'd appreciate it if you left a review on Amazon. Reviews are the lifeblood of our business. We read every single one, and incorporate your feedback into future book projects.

To leave an Amazon review go to https://freemanpublications.com/leaveareview

"THE MOST SUCCESSFUL PEOPLE IN LIFE ARE THE ONES
WHO ASK QUESTIONS. THEY'RE ALWAYS LEARNING.
THEY'RE ALWAYS GROWING. THEY'RE ALWAYS PUSHING."
- Robert Kiyosaki

CONTINUING YOUR JOURNEY

Like Robert Kiyosaki said on the previous page, "The most successful people in life are always learning, growing, and asking questions."

Which is why we created our investing community, aptly named ***How To NOT Lose Money in the Stock Market.***

So that like-minded individuals could get together to share ideas and learn from each other.

We regularly run giveaways, share wins from our readers, and you'll be the first to know when our new books are released.

It's 100% free, and there are no requirements to join, except for the willingness to learn.

You can join us on Facebook by going to

http://freemanpublications.com/facebook

OTHER BOOKS BY FREEMAN PUBLICATIONS (AVAILABLE ON AMAZON & AUDIBLE)

The 8-Step Beginner's Guide to Value Investing: Featuring 20 for 20 - The 20 Best Stocks & ETFs to Buy and Hold for The Next 20 Years

Bear Market Investing Strategies: 37 Recession-Proof Ideas to Grow Your Wealth - Including Inverse ETFs, Put Options, Gold & Cryptocurrency

REFERENCES

Billan, R. (2019, May 31). Tall Poppy Syndrome: The office trend killing morale. Retrieved from https://www.hcamag.com/au/news/general/tall-poppy-syndrome-the-office-trend-killing-morale

Connington, J. (2017, June 23). If we are spending less cash, why are we printing more banknotes? *The Telegraph.* https://www.telegraph.co.uk/personal-banking/current-accounts/spending-less-cash-printing-banknotes/

Cox, J. (2018, May 4). *The value of what Buffett called "financial weapons of mass destruction" is plunging.* CNBC. https://www.cnbc.com/2018/05/04/the-value-of-financial-weapons-of-mass-destruction-is-plunging.html

Eske, J. (2019, March 26). *How long can you go without sleep?: Effects of sleep deprivation.* Www.Medicalnewstoday.Com. https://www.medicalnewstoday.com/articles/324799#48-hours-without-sleep

Goleman, D. (2005). *Vital lies, simple truths: The psychology of self-deception.* New York: Simon & Schuster Paperbacks.

Greene, R. (2018). *The Laws of Human Nature. Penguin USA.*

Hanson, R., & Mendius, R. (2009). *Buddha's brain: the practical neuroscience of happiness, love & wisdom.* New Harbinger Publications.

Lefvre, E. (2019). *Reminiscences Of A Stock Operator.* Bantam.

Maltz, M. (1967). *Psycho-cybernetics: A new technique for using your subconscious power.* Hollywood (Calif.): Wilshire Book.

Projectoption. (2017, April 17). *Iron Condor Management Results from 71,417 [STUDY].* [VIDEO]. YouTube. https://www.youtube.com/watch?v=cu1FXt4JEs8

Made in the USA
Las Vegas, NV
24 October 2024

10452947R00249